S0-GQF-165

THE ETHICS IN LITERATURE

Also by Andrew Hadfield

LITERATURE, POLITICS AND NATIONAL IDENTITY
Reformation to Renaissance

WILDE FRUIT AND SALVAGE SOYL: Spenser's Irish Experience

EDMUND SPENSER (*editor*)

REPRESENTING IRELAND: Literature and the Origins of Conflict, 1534–1660 (*editor with Brendan Bradshaw and Willy Maley*)

STRANGERS TO THAT LAND: British Perceptions of Ireland from the Reformation to the Famine (*editor with John McVeagh*)

EDMUND SPENSER: A View of the State of Ireland (*editor with Willy Maley*)

Also by Dominic Rainsford

AUTHORSHIP, ETHICS AND THE READER: Blake, Dickens, Joyce

CRITICAL ETHICS: Text, Theory and Responsibility (*editor with Tim Woods*)

Also by Tim Woods

CRITICAL ETHICS: Text, Theory and Responsibility (*editor with Dominic Rainsford*)

'I'M TELLING YOU STORIES': Jeanette Winterson and the Politics of Reading (*editor with Helena Grice*)

The Ethics in Literature

Edited by

Andrew Hadfield
Professor of English
Department of English and American Studies
University of Wales
Aberystwyth

Dominic Rainsford
Lecturer
Department of English
University of Aarhus
Denmark

and

Tim Woods
Lecturer
Department of English and American Studies
University of Wales
Aberystwyth

First published in Great Britain 1999 by
MACMILLAN PRESS LTD
Houndmills, Basingstoke, Hampshire RG21 6XS and London
Companies and representatives throughout the world

A catalogue record for this book is available from the British Library.

ISBN 0–333–71886–0

First published in the United States of America 1999 by
ST. MARTIN'S PRESS, INC.,
Scholarly and Reference Division,
175 Fifth Avenue, New York, N.Y. 10010

ISBN 0–312–21653–X

Library of Congress Cataloging-in-Publication Data
The ethics in literature / edited by Andrew Hadfield, Dominic Rainsford and Tim Woods.
p. cm.
Includes bibliographical references (p.) and index.
ISBN 0–312–21653–X (cloth)
1. Didactic literature, English—History and criticism.
2. Didactic literature, American—History and criticism.
3. American literature—History and criticism. 4. Ethics in literature. I. Rainsford, Dominic, 1965– . II. Hadfield, Andrew. III. Woods, Tim.
PR408.D49E84 1998
820.9'384—dc21 98–24314
CIP

This book is printed on paper suitable for recycling and made from fully managed and sustained forest sources.

10 9 8 7 6 5 4 3 2 1
08 07 06 05 04 03 02 01 00 99

Printed and bound in Great Britain by
Antony Rowe Ltd, Chippenham, Wiltshire

Contents

Acknowledgements

The chapters in this volume are all adapted from papers given at the 'Literature and Ethics' conference at the University of Wales, Aberystwyth, in July 1996. We would like to thank all of the speakers and other participants at the conference for helping to make it such an enjoyable and intellectually challenging event. We are also grateful for the financial support which the conference received from the Humanities Research Board of the British Academy, from the University of Wales, Aberystwyth Research Fund, and the Department of English of UWA. We would also like to thank Joan Crawford and June Baxter for their secretarial help in the preparation of the conference and this volume.

Notes on the Contributors

Janis McLarren Caldwell is Assistant Professor of English at Wake Forest University, where she teaches Literature and Science. She has an MD from Northwestern University Medical School (1984) and a PhD from the University of Washington (1996).

Ortwin de Graef gained his PhD in Literature and Philosophy in 1990 at the Katholiecke Universiteit Leuven, where he is now Lecturer in English and Literary Theory. He also lectures in the Belgian Inter-University Postgraduate Programme in Literary Theory, and is a Research Associate of the Belgian National Fund for Scientific Research. He is the author of two volumes on Paul de Man, *Serenity in Crisis* (1993) and *Titanic Light* (1995), and has published on Poe, Ernst Jünger, Wordsworth, Tennyson, Browning, Jon Elster, Arnold, Charles Taylor, Derrida and Henry Rollins.

Richard Freadman is Professor of English and Director of the Unit for Studies in Biography and Autobiography at La Trobe University. He is the author of *Eliot, James and the Fictional Self: A Study in Character and Narration* (1986), co-editor (with Lloyd Reinhardt) of *On Literary Theory and Philosophy: A Cross-Disciplinary Encounter* (1991), and (with Seumas Miller) author of *Rethinking Theory: A Critique of Contemporary Literary Theory and an Alternative Account* (1992). He is co-editor (with Jane Adamson and David Parker) of a forthcoming book on recent developments in ethics, and is working on a study of ethics and autobiography.

Andrew Gibson is Reader in English at Royal Holloway, University of London, where he is Course Director of the MA in Postmodernism, Literature and Contemporary Culture. He is the author of *Reading Narrative Discourse: Studies in the Novel from Cervantes to Beckett* (1990) and *Towards a Postmodern Theory of Narrative* (1996), and editor of *Pound in Multiple Perspective* (1993), *Reading Joyce's 'Circe'* (1994) and *Joyce's 'Ithaca'* (1996). He co-edited *Beyond the Book: Theory, Culture and the Politics of Cyberspace* (1996) and *Conrad and Theory* (forthcoming, 1998). He is currently writing *Redemptions: Postmodernity, Ethics and the Novel.*

Andrew Hadfield, co-organiser of 'Literature and Ethics', gained his BA at the University of Leeds, and a DPhil at the University of Ulster. He is Professor of English at the University of Wales, Aberystwyth. His main research interests are in Anglo-Irish literary relations; literature and politics; and Renaissance poetry and prose. His publications include *Literature, Politics and National Identity: Reformation to Renaissance* (1994) and *'Wilde Fruit and Salvage Soyl': Spenser's Irish Experience* (1997). He is a regular reviewer for the *Times Literary Supplement*.

David P. Haney received his PhD from the State University of New York at Buffalo in 1980. He has taught at Swarthmore College, and is currently the Hargis Associate Professor of English at Auburn University, Alabama, where he has taught since 1989. He is the author of *William Wordsworth and the Hermeneutics of Incarnation* (1993) and has published articles, mostly on Wordsworth, in *Studies in Romanticism, Style, Clio, the European Romantic Review*, and other journals.

Rebecca Hughes has a BA in English and a DPhil in Linguistics from the University of Oxford. She is currently Deputy Director of the Centre for English Language Education at the University of Nottingham. Aside from her academic work, she is a past winner of the Greenwich Poetry Festival Prize, and of the Bridport Arts Centre Short Story Prize. She is the author of *English in Speech and Writing: Investigating Language and Literature* (1996).

Terry Keefe studied at the Universities of Leicester and London. He was Head of French and Dean of the Faculty of Arts at Leicester until 1988. Since then, he has been Professor of French Studies and Head of Modern Languages at Lancaster University. He has published two books on Simone de Beauvoir, and one on moral perspectives in the existentialist fiction of Sartre, Camus and Beauvoir, and has co-edited books on Zola and existentialist autobiography. He is currently working on the early ethics of Sartre.

Ruth Kolani is a graduate of the High School of Music and Art and of the City College of New York, and received her MA at Hunter College, CUNY. She recently received her doctorate for a thesis entitled '*The Secret Agent*: An Ethical-Stylistic Study of Agency and the Rhetoric of Dissociation in Narrative' from the University of

Texas at Dallas. She was Affiliate to the Beatrice M. Bain Women's Research Group and Research Associate in the Department of Linguistics at the University of California, Berkeley in 1989–90, has taught at Georgia State University, and has been teaching for several years in the Department of English at the Hebrew University of Jerusalem.

Ian MacKillop is Reader in English Literature at the University of Sheffield. He is the author of *The British Ethical Societies* (1986) and *F.R. Leavis: A Life in Criticism* (1995), and is co-editor, with Richard Storer, of *F.R. Leavis: Essays and Documents* (1995).

Chris McNab is a PhD student in the Department of English at the University of Wales, Aberystwyth, researching contemporary fiction and theories of poststructuralism.

Cristina Mejía obtained her BA in Art History from McGill University, and is currently working towards an MA in English, also at McGill. Her thesis is on literature and the moral sentiments.

Kieron O'Hara has an MA in Philosophy and an MPhil in Logic and Metaphysics from the University of St Andrews, and an MSc in Software Engineering and a DPhil in Philosophy from Oxford. He is currently a researcher in the Artificial Intelligence Group at the Department of Psychology, Nottingham University. He has published papers in the areas of literature, film, philosophy, logic, psychology, artificial intelligence and education, and is the co-editor of *Advances in Knowledge Acquisition* (1996).

Dominic Rainsford read English at University College London, where he gained his PhD in 1994. Before taking up his present post in Denmark, as Visiting Lecturer at the University of Aarhus, he taught at University College London, Imperial College of Science, Technology and Medicine, the University of Warsaw, Loyola University of Chicago and the University of Wales, Aberystwyth. At Aberystwyth, he was principal organiser of the international conference 'Literature and Ethics' (1996). His publications include *Authorship, Ethics and the Reader: Blake, Dickens, Joyce* (1997) and he is currently writing a book on literature, identity and the English Channel.

Norman Ravvin works as a critic, novelist, and teacher. His degrees are from the University of British Columbia (BA and MA) and the University of Toronto (PhD). He has published essays on Edgar Allan Poe, Philip Roth, Leonard Cohen, Eli Mandel and Bruno Schulz, and, with McGill-Queen's University Press, *A House of Words: Jewish Writing, Identity and Memory*. His novel, *Café des Westens*, was published in 1991, and his short fiction has appeared in Canadian magazines and on CBC Radio. He teaches at the University of New Brunswick.

Susan Rowland is a Lecturer in English in the School of Humanities at the University of Greenwich. Her research is into Jungian ideas in relation to literary theory and contemporary writing. She has published in areas such as romance and sacrifice, alchemy and writing, feminist theory, spiritualism and detective fiction as well as on works by Doris Lessing, Lindsay Clarke and Michèle Roberts. She is currently working on *C.G. Jung and Literary Theory: The Challenge from Fiction* (forthcoming in 1999).

Valeria Wagner gained her PhD from the University of Geneva, for a thesis entitled 'Bound to Act: An Analysis of Models of Action as Dramatized in Selected Literary and Philosophical Texts'. A version of this thesis will be published by Stanford University Press. She has also studied at the University of Montreal. Her publications include essays in *Feminism Beside Itself*, ed. Elam and Wiegman (1995), and *New Essays on Hamlet*, ed. Burnett and Manning (1994). She has recently pursued research in Argentina entitled 'Making History: Action and Narration' funded by the Fonds National Suisse pour la Recherche Scientifique.

Tim Woods is Lecturer in English and American Studies in the Department of English at the University of Wales, Aberystwyth. His publications include articles on the work of Louis Zukofsky, several articles on contemporary poetry in Britain, the theories of Emmanuel Levinas and Theodor Adorno, and on Paul Auster in Dennis Barone (ed.), *Beyond the Red Notebook* (1995). He is currently writing a monograph on modern American poetics and ethics; a book entitled *Beginning Postmodernism*; preparing several collections of essays and co-authoring with Peter Middleton a book on the representation of histories in post-war literatures.

Introduction: Literature and the Return to Ethics

Andrew Hadfield, Dominic Rainsford and Tim Woods

Steven Connor has recently commented on the current ubiquity of ethical debates in literary studies: 'The word "ethics" seems to have replaced "textuality" as the most charged term in the vocabulary of contemporary literary and cultural theory.'[1] A careful search through the catalogues of academic publishers, along the shelves of contemporary journals in humanities' libraries, or through the review pages of broadsheet newspapers and supplements will reveal the force of Connor's observation. What is the reason for the obsessive attention paid to the question of morality? Is it just another passing intellectual fad?

One reason which might be put forward is the general discontent with what some have perceived to be the arid formalism which came to dominate the humanities throughout Europe and America in the late 1970s and early 1980s. Structuralism, Poststructuralism and then Postmodernism were intellectual movements with which everyone with any intellectual pretensions at all was often compelled to grapple. Battle lines were drawn up early in Britain between those who demanded a rigorous linguistically-based analysis of the text, often involving a vocabulary which non-initiates found bemusing, and more traditional humanists who insisted that literature should be about real life (whatever that might be). There were a number of significant flashpoints. A minor tremor occurred when a young English lecturer at the University of Cambridge, Dr Colin McCabe, did not have his temporary contract renewed, a decision, so his supporters alleged, motivated by the arrogant contempt of a conservative institution for an adherent of intellectual approaches the significance of which they refused to countenance. A much more significant event took place when the researches of an even younger Belgian postgraduate, Ortwin de Graef (one of the contributors to this volume), unearthed the wartime journalism of Paul de Man, one of the most high-profile champions of poststructuralist theory in North America, and exposed the recently deceased professor as a sympathiser with Nazi doctrines in his early years. A colossal amount of ink was spilt immediately afterwards as academics and journalists lined up on opposite sides.[2] Some suggested that de Man's early writings expressed the logical conclusion of what they claimed was, in essence, a right-wing ideology; others, that de Man's later writings were a powerful renunciation and correction of his youthful excesses and errors.

This crude caricature of complex debates is important in assessing the current significance of ethical thought in the humanities and literary criticism in particular. Some might argue that ethics has resurfaced because to deny the need for making value judgements when dealing with human interaction is a naive mistake, one which the purveyors of abstract ideas were too arrogant to recognise. Indeed, many in Britain and America would point to the strange coincidence that the rise of 'theory' in the academy took place at the same time as national politics moved sharply to the right under the governments of Margaret Thatcher and Ronald Reagan. For such commentators, Marxists and liberal humanists alike, we are now returning to a period of (relative) sanity, after a methodological and political disaster epitomised by outrageous statements such as Michel Foucault's famous assertion that the epoch of 'man' was about to come to a close.[3]

However, this brief history hides as much as it reveals. Although ethical debate may have been somewhat unfashionable and underrepresented, it never actually disappeared from poststructuralist discourse; at least, not from the writings of its most subtle and brilliant exponents. A watershed occurred in 1985, when Henry Louis Gates, Jr, printed a translation of Jacques Derrida's *Le dernier mot du racisme* ('Racism's Last Word'), as part of a special issue of the journal *Critical Inquiry*, later reprinted as the influential volume, *'Race', Writing, and Difference*.[4] Derrida's essay had originally been published for the catalogue which accompanied the exhibition collected together by the association of Artists of the World against Apartheid, opening in Paris in November 1983.

The essay drew a rather sharp critical response from two postgraduate students at Columbia University, Anne McClintock and Rob Nixon (now both established and prominent academics). While not doubting 'his commitment to change in South Africa', both questioned 'the strength of Derrida's method' to unravel the historical and political factors which constituted the notion of 'apartheid'.[5] Derrida responded with an excoriating attack, a complete departure from his established, urbane style of argument, which made it clear that the question of his philosophy's ability to deal with the problem of apartheid was as much an ethical as an historical one. Derrida's response demands to be read in full by anyone wishing to intervene in the debate about the political and ethical efficacy of deconstruction, but a sample of his writing gives some idea of the issues he felt were at stake in the exchange:

> Your [McClintock and Nixon's] 'response' is typical. It reflects an incomprehension or 'misreading' that is widespread, and spread about, moreover, for very determined ends, on the 'Left' and the 'Right' among those who think they represent militantism and a progressivist commitment .... On one side and the other, people get impatient when they see that deconstructive practices are also and first of all political and institutional practices. They get impatient when they see that these practices are perhaps more radical and certainly less stereotyped than others, less easy to decipher, less in keeping with well-used models whose wear and tear ends up letting one see the abstraction, the conventionalism, the academicism, and everything that separates ... words and history.[6]

Derrida's irate letter, in which he makes it clear that McClintock and Nixon's attack is not the first he has had to suffer, defends deconstruction and its attempt to undermine the certainties of Western metaphysics, as an ethical and political practice, one which may question the validity of 'man' and 'humanism', but ultimately seeks to re-enfranchise a larger public by giving individuals the power to cast off the chains of intellectual oppression.[7] His defence of deconstruction, as an ethically and politically sensitive 'method', centres upon the concept of 'patience'. Derrida argues that the easy assumption of commitment and apparently laudable attitudes is, all too often, unethical behaviour because such identity politics serve only to obscure the real issues – in this case Derrida's nuanced exploration of the ways in which strong stances against apartheid served to disguise and obscure racism nearer home, a biting irony given apartheid's European origins. Derrida's plea is for what might be termed 'an ethics of reading', a 'method' which refuses easy solutions in order to tease out the significance and implications of the text. Similarly, when Roland Barthes's later essays on reading and writing practices (especially of comprehending the visible and audible) were published, it was under the title *The Responsibility of Forms*. In this case, 'responsibility' appears to be closely linked to scrupulous attention to the formal inscription of structures and signs in the textual work of writers, musicians, painters and designers.[8]

It has not been our desire in compiling the chapters for this book to participate directly in any such debate, merely to point out the central relevance of ethical concerns in literary criticism and philosophy and to illustrate that the current upsurge of interest in ethics is not a phenomenon which has appeared from nowhere. Clearly, a hostile critic of Derrida could respond with the logic of the 'yes, but ...'. Scrupulous reading is something to be valued as Derrida argues, but careful weighting of all possibilities can serve as a substitute rather than a call for action, enabling the would-be ethical subject to hide behind convenient intellectual barriers (a charge Marxist critics have often levelled against Derrida and what they saw as his refusal to nail his colours to the mast).[9] Instead, the purpose of *The Ethics in Literature* is to interrogate and juxtapose precisely such divergent approaches to ethical questions in order to give the reader the means to participate in current debates and take a stand themselves should they so wish.

The chapters which follow reveal a variety of approaches to ethical questions: from ones that are based on careful reading of texts, notably Ruth Kolani's plea for the use of stylistics as a means of decoding behaviour and determining its moral significance, to more directly focused political approaches, as in the essays of Andrew Hadfield and Ortwin de Graef. Some draw attention to the problems of certain ethical approaches; for example, Rebecca Hughes and Kieron O'Hara suggest that Kant's perception of individuals as responsible moral agents is challenged by a short story such as John Cheever's *The Swimmer*, which shows how human beings are all too often trapped by their personalities and histories, preventing them from acting autonomously. A similar case is made by Cristina Mejía, who reads E. M. Forster's novel, *Howards End*, in order to challenge Richard Rorty's assumption that in attributing specifically human capacities to individuals one is committing a form of critical and interpretative violence. On the contrary, Mejía argues, using Margaret Schlegel's agonised rejection of the sensitive

Leonard Bast as an illustration, human beings act from a complex panoply of emotions and social constraints which can be described if one adopts a 'thicker' conception of ethics and moral agency than is allowed for in Rorty's philosophy.

Other chapters suggest that specific ethical terms have been neglected by philosophers, and that they deserve serious reconsideration. A case in point is Andrew Gibson's attempt to reclaim an understanding of 'sensibility' as central to our moral concerns through the reading of Jean Rhys and Anaïs Nin. Gibson argues that the ethical principles which these authors explore are similar to Emmanuel Levinas's conception of sensibility. Levinas construes sensibility as akin to vulnerability, an equation which disrupts the patriarchal hierarchy inscribed by the 'tyranny of an established reality', and points the way towards a feminist ethics. A related case is made in Janis Caldwell's argument that Mary Shelley's *Frankenstein* points out the need for nineteenth-century science to accommodate principles of sympathy within its analytic rigour, and in Susan Rowland's 'hysterical' reading of Michèle Roberts's novel *In the Red Kitchen*, whereby the reader refuses to privilege the (masculine) voice of reason and sanity and responds to the otherness of the individual female voice.

Feminism has arguably held the ethical high ground during all these often vitriolic arguments between Marxists and poststructuralists. Attempting to reorientate society towards a politics of everyday life, breaking down one of the most virulent hierarchies in our society, and fostering a *societas* based upon equality, feminists have sought to inculcate a new ethical consciousness of social justice. The notion that women are more moral than men has been around for decades, based upon such patriarchal narratives of moral fantasy as an 'Angel in the House', or the 'Earth-Mother'. Nevertheless, much feminist argument continues to present the willingness to nurture and a ready capacity for emotional involvement as being essential to a humane moral stance in a world of injustice and alienation. Indeed, an 'ethics of care' forms one of the central planks of feminist debates about alternative social practices, founded upon receptivity, relatedness and responsiveness as opposed to 'masculine' ethical preoccupations with property-rights, equality and duty. Eve Browning Cole and Susan Coultrap-McQuin have argued that while feminist ethics is not blind to the necessity of reinterpreting the moral significance of women as 'care-givers', it has maintained a commitment to the alternative ethical perspective provided by non-masculine experience. According to their book *Explorations in Feminist Ethics: Theory and Practice*, the debate over the past ten years has hinged on three principal issues:

(1) whether an ethic that stresses the centrality of *care* can be developed into a coherent, persuasive and politically defensible feminist ethic;
(2) whether *justice* as defined within classical liberal political frameworks can maintain its hitherto orthodox hegemonic role when one is working within a feminist ethical context; and
(3) whether a relational ethic which attaches such importance to personal intimate bonds between people, can be utilised within larger, more impersonal situations.[10]

Based upon the politicisation of the personal, feminist ethics attempts to break down the long held boundaries between public and private morality which have reinforced the power of those privileged few. Together with Habermasian notions of ethical goodness in public debate and argumentation, and postcolonial critiques of the racial constituency of capitalist western societies, this reconfiguration of the public sphere has led to new discussions about what constitutes an ethics within the context of debates about individuals' relations to the state and national identity. Ortwin de Graef's contribution is relevant here, insofar as it attempts to consider the relationship of the individual to the state in *Coriolanus*, and how this may suggest an ethical repositioning of Kant's ideas of freedom and independence. In focusing on the metaphor of the 'body politic', de Graef suggests that it is constituted by catachresis: 'Coriolanus must be *declared* – not just recognised but quite literally *made* – a representative of the people *because* he already is just that .... Thus, the impact of the people's voice is precisely nothing, yet unless this nothing is performed, the body politic is revealed as a monstrosity'. Acknowledging that political debate is a vital public ritual and a significant symbolic procedure in 'democratic' states, de Graef questions whether it is not monstrous that such political rhetoric can constitute a state, lacking any material constitution.

Andrew Hadfield's focus on the complex politics of Israel and of Jewish national identity in Saul Bellow's writing draws attention to the ethical debate concerning ethnic and racial identities. Any discussion of ethnicity and national identity is always also by implication a discussion of ethics. Hadfield argues that Bellow's sophisticated conception of the individual victim is ultimately vitiated by his myopic and simplistic treatment of nationhood: 'The Saul Bellow of *To Jerusalem and Back* appears to want to pose as a victim by dint of his race, without actually having borne the marks of experience, a position he carefully refused to validate in the earlier novel [*The Victim*].' The Jewish right to self-determination has often been obscured by theological and cultural arguments about racial differences. Indeed, as has been widely discussed, even Emmanuel Levinas appears to have based much of his ethical phenomenology on a correction of Graeco-Romanic Christian metaphysics by a more Semitic metaphysics.[11] This reorientation of Christian thought was designed to establish an ethics which countered the Protestant Christianity of Heidegger's national socialist sympathies and his ontological existentialism, the indiscriminate 'ethics' which resulted in Auschwitz and the Nazi atrocities.

The racial struggles to determine distinct national identities which have marked the second half of the twentieth century (in Israel, South Africa, West and East Africa, Ireland, Bosnia, Central Asia, North Africa, Central America, and elsewhere) have posed some of the century's most difficult ethical questions. Postcolonial criticism and the burgeoning influence of ethnic studies has directed new attention to the situation of oppressed and marginalised elements of our society and culture; attempting to foster some interracial dialogue without the imposition of a uni-racial perspective, postcolonial criticism strives for a new ethical consciousness of race and ethnicity. One might call this the 'ethics of the exile', the ethical outlook offered by the perspective of the exiled consciousness. Many postcolonial theorists of ethnicity take firm ethical stands with their central concepts: Spivak's 'subaltern theory', Bhabha's 'hybridity', Said's 'orientalism' to name but a few. Public space can no longer (if it ever was) be construed as an 'ethics free zone'.

Indeed, a major concern which the contributors to this volume share is to open out debates on the subject of ethics so that it does not remain as a compartmentalised branch of the discipline of philosophy. Hence there are a number of chapters included which argue the importance of literary texts and literary methods in establishing the importance of bridging the gap between philosophy and representations of ethical behaviour. In addition to Gibson, Rowland, Mejía and Hughes and O'Hara, one can point to important interventions by Ian MacKillop and Chris McNab. MacKillop follows up an observation by Alasdair MacIntyre to argue for the importance of 'conversation' as a central principle of ethics, arguing the case – via a wide range of examples – that conversation is important as a means of opening oneself out to the other. MacKillop's argument owes much to a notion of art as important because it is not restrained by the contingencies of the real world. Equally, however, one might suggest that MacKillop's essay bears more than a passing resemblance to the concerns of Derrida and, especially, Levinas. McNab's reading of Derrida and Salman Rushdie interrogates the problem of postmodernity, arguing that Rushdie's magic realism creates a space in which an ethics of possibility and mutability is made possible. McNab further suggests that Derrida's recent work, *The Gift of Death*, imagines an ethics of 'irresponsibilization', where the ethical reaches beyond its own framework (even challenging that framework), a project which has much in common with Rushdie's fictional explorations. The same can be said of Norman Ravvin's essay on a variety of responses to the Holocaust in film, criticism and fiction. Ravvin concentrates on the representation of the face as a visible sign of our responsibility towards the other. As in McKillop's and McNab's chapters, the need to face the other suggests that dialogical interaction should form the basis for ethical behaviour.

In similar vein is Terry Keefe's discussion of Simone de Beauvoir's 'ethical period', when she sought to explore the implications of existentialist ethics in both fictional and non-fictional works. Keefe points out how de Beauvoir's admirable commitment to the importance of exploring ethics leads her to radically different conclusions in different works. Moreover, her intellectual engagement with the possibilities of fictional forms means that she often goes beyond the ostensible doctrinal focus of the work in question. Keefe argues that two novels, *All Men are Mortal* and *The Blood of Others*, exhaust their initial premises: the former in expressing a sympathy for fatherhood and portraying the relations between men at length; the latter in exploring moral problems much more weighty than the simple 'lesson in the importance of freedom'.

A significant question raised by the chapters contained in this volume, and by the variety of approaches to ethical questions which they represent, is how can we talk to one another and determine a common ground which we all share in order to be able to establish workable and usefully related moral criteria? Perhaps this might be asking too much; after all, ethical thought contained within the rigorous boundaries of philosophy was always characterised by conflicts concerning the fundamental ground on which to base ethical behaviour. One might point to the fact that there seems to be little agreement between utilitarians who argued the case for various forms of consequentialism in moral behaviour, claiming that the end justifies the means – more subtly, that the end would justify the means in an ideal world – and moral absolutists or proponents of a deontological ethics.[12] There is still no clear solution to the dilemma of the fat man stuck in the cave, a problem posed by philosophy tutors who ask students what they would do were they and a number of others trapped behind him with the water level rising.[13] As Peter Singer, a prominent professor of philosophy and writer on ethics, has admitted, the question '"Why act morally" cannot be given an answer that will provide everyone with overwhelming reasons for acting morally'.[14] Singer suggests that in the absence of good reasons for accepting moral absolutes we should accept some form of utilitarian ethical principles: that is, it is not morally imperative that we refuse to kill the fat man in the cave providing we can justify his death in terms of saving more lives than will be lost by his death.[15] Not all would agree.[16]

Nevertheless, a case can be made that the contributors to this volume do share at least one fundamental principle of ethical thought. The famous question on which Aristotle based his ethical philosophy, how shall we live life, has been transformed into the question, how can we respect the other? What responsibilities do we owe to our fellows? This concern can be seen in David Haney's essay on the epistemological concerns of Coleridge's ethics. Haney sees Coleridge as negotiating between two conceptions of otherness; on the one hand, Coleridge seeks to define a 'Christian' sense of self-conscious humanity which contains otherness within it as part of the ethical self; on the other, according to Haney, Coleridge felt obliged to acknowledge a more radical Otherness against which the self had to be defined. Haney relates Coleridge's ideas to debates in contemporary philosophy: Hans Gadamer's perception that prejudices must be put at risk in true dialogue (a point which relates to MacKillop's stress on the importance of conversation), and, perhaps inevitably, Levinas's insistence on the ethical value of the other's power to disrupt subjective categories. We write 'inevitably' because if one figure stands behind this epistemological shift in the focus of ethical concerns, it is surely Emmanuel Levinas, the heir to a long tradition of phenomenological philosophy concerned to define the relation between self and other.

A more negative refiguring of the same problem is the central issue of Valeria Wagner's chapter on *Hamlet*. Wagner's focus is René Girard's often-cited essay on the play, 'Hamlet's Dull Revenge', which reversed a whole tradition of nineteenth-century criticism by asking why does Hamlet act rather than why does he not act, through the witty but horrific manoeuvre of imagining Hamlet with his finger on a nuclear button. Wagner suggests that in refusing to act and in contrasting his own failure with Fortinbras's ability to act precisely because he has no reason to do so, Hamlet's dilemma anticipates Bakhtin's commentary on the 'crisis of contemporary action'. Wagner concludes that only when we can assume responsibility for our untheorised acts can a proper discussion of ethics take place.

An exception to our generalisation is Richard Freadman's exploration of Stephen Spender's autobiographical account of his behaviour and discovery of his complex sexual identity, which directly confronts Aristotle's question. Freadman argues that Aristotle's concern demands that we include autobiography as a centrally important genre within the range of ethically focused texts: 'Virtually all autobiographers ... are ethicists in some degree'. Freadman charts Spender's account of his rake's progress in the 1930s and 1940s, and his harsh self-criticism – notably when he deserts various lovers. Spender's search, according to Freadman, is to discover another being with whom he can live in reciprocal subjectivity, a means also of escaping the blame which haunts him on account of his former actions. For Spender, the 'affective will' must obtain a balance with another human being. Freadman's essay points to the difficulty of separating notions of the care of the self and the care of the other because, implicitly, the two are intertwined.

Ultimately, perhaps we ought to ask whether literature is able to explore ethical questions in a manner which goes beyond formal philosophical reasoning. Many of the contributors – Keefe, MacKillop, Hughes and O'Hara and Gibson, for example – show how literary works either call into question the terms of specific philosophical doctrines, or else provide the basis for concepts which would provide new stimuli for philosophical debate, overlooked by professional philosophers. It would, of course, be arrogant and potentially dangerous to cast aside the contributions of philosophy as if they amounted to little more than an adjunct to the explorations carried out in works of literature and literary criticism. It might also unfairly privilege a style of argument which assumes that moral questions can only be dealt with in terms of contingent examples and is therefore better addressed in novels and other fictional forms, without making the attempt to deduce logical rules in formal philosophical debate.

Nevertheless, the point should be made that many ethical codes and practices are intimately related to literary examples and depend on a reading of literature for their intellectual substance. One pertinent example is Marxism, many prominent exponents of which have neglected the ethical dimension of Marx's writings in a fruitless search for scientific detachment.[17] The ethical force of the famous eleventh thesis on Feuerbach, 'Philosophers have only *interpreted* the world, in various ways; the point is to *change* it' [emphasis added], is obvious.[18] At such points in his writings Marx seeks to appeal to a higher ethical reality to go beyond mere hermeneutics (the similarity of such clarion calls to Derrida's treatment of apartheid is clear). Moreover, it is noticeable that Marx often appeals to literary examples at key points in his writings in order to emphasise the power of his moral critique. One famous example is his use of both Goethe's *Faust* and Shakespeare's *Timon of Athens* to point out the alienating effects of money. Marx quotes copious extracts from Timon's railings against the corrupting power of money, including the lines:

> O thou sweet king-killer, and dear divorce
> 'Twixt natural son and sire! Thou bright defiler
> Of Hymen's purest bed! Thou valiant Mars!...
> Thou speak'st with every tongue,
> To every purpose! O thou touch of hearts!
> Think, thy slave man rebels; and by thy virtue
> Set them into confounding odds, that beasts
> May have the world in empire!

According to Marx, Shakespeare's words brilliantly express the ways in which 'the *divine* power of money lies in its *nature* as the estranged and alienating *species-essence* of man which alienates itself by selling itself. It is the alienated *capacity* of *mankind*' [Marx's emphasis].[19] Not, perhaps, the young Marx's most eloquent formulation, but certainly among his most passionate outbursts at the evils of capitalist society.

Equally, one might argue the case that psychoanalysis, with its origins in medical practice, is a discipline which owes as much to ethical as to scientific discourse through the desire to cure patients and return them to ordinary society. As has been exhaustively catalogued, not only did the literary-minded and well-read Sigmund Freud borrow the names for many of his discoveries from literary sources (most famously, the Oedipus complex from Sophocles' play), but his methods of analysis bear a striking resemblance to the detective fiction he so avidly consumed in his spare time.

Indeed, literary representations have significantly influenced and altered ethical perspectives concerning the historical and political activities of nations for centuries. Many literary works have played a vital role in raising ethical consciousness. To take one recent example, the US Commission on Wartime Relocation and Internment of Civilians, established in July 1980 to investigate the social, political and ethical treatment of various ethnic minorities during the Second World War, made significant use of Miné Okubo's novel, *Citizen 13660*. Okubo states in her preface to the book: 'I testified at the hearing in New York City. As *Citizen 13660* had been widely reviewed and was considered an important reference book on the Japanese American evacuation and internment, I presented the Commission with a copy of the book in addition to my oral testimony.'[20] It is clear that the Commission felt that this literary work bore witness to an ethical consciousness that the public could not escape. Similar examples of literary works having profound effects by raising ethical consciousnesses retrospectively about political, social and cultural actions abound: one might consider *Uncle Tom's Cabin* by Harriet Beecher Stowe, to whom Lincoln is alleged to have said 'So you're the little woman who wrote the book that made this great war!'; Toni Morrison's *Beloved* (1987); and Marilyn French's *The Women's Room* (1978), all of which have had pathbreaking roles in altering social perceptions of ethical responsibility for the (mis)treatment of various groups of people.

The aim in assembling this collection has been to present the reader with a number of stimulating and provocative pieces which are not only worth grappling with in their own right, but also present a range and diversity of approaches to the problems outlined in this introduction. Some of the chapters show how fictional forms pose questions which are often ignored in non-fictional writings, pointing out the dangers of ignoring fiction as a site or form of social knowledge (Rowland, Mejía, Gibson,

Hadfield, Hughes and O'Hara). Some read literary texts as explorations of ethical problems which can be related to similar debates in formal philosophy (de Graef, Kolani, McNab, Wagner, Keefe). Some suggest that literary texts provide new forms for debating ethical questions, pointing to the question of the link between generic form and content when establishing the message that a text conveys (Caldwell, Freadman, Haney, MacKillop, Ravvin). The recent upsurge of interest in ethical questions is to be welcomed. We would suggest, though, that literary and ethical questions have always been related, whether through the ethical nature of literary criticism, or through the use of literary texts to provide the basis for ethical thinking.

Notes

1. Steven Connor, 'Honour Bound', *Times Literary Supplement*, 5 January 1996, 24–6; 24.
2. On the debate concerning Paul de Man's wartime writings, see Werner Hamacher, Neil Hertz and Thomas Keenan, eds, *Responses: On Paul de Man's Wartime Journalism* (Lincoln, NE: University of Nebraska Press, 1989). For a useful overview of the debate, see Patrick Parrinder, 'The Fall of Paul de Man', *Literature and History*, 2nd series, 1, 2 (Autumn 1990) 68–76.
3. 'As the archaeology of our thought easily shows, man is an invention of recent date. And one perhaps nearing its end.' Michel Foucault, *The Order of Things* (London: Tavistock, 1970) 387.
4. Henry Louis Gates, Jr, ed., *'Race', Writing, and Difference* (University of Chicago Press, 1986) 329–38.
5. Anne McClintock and Rob Nixon, 'No Names Apart: The Separation of Word and History in Derrida's "Le dernier mot du racisme"', in Gates, ed., *'Race', Writing, and Difference*, 339–53; 352.
6. Jacques Derrida, 'But, beyond ... (Open Letter to Anne McClintock and Rob Nixon)', in Gates, ed., *'Race', Writing, and Difference*, 354–69; 367.
7. Christopher Norris points out Derrida's commitment to the teaching of philosophy in French schools as an aspect of this overall aim in *Derrida* (London: Fontana, 1987) 13–14.
8. Roland Barthes, *The Responsibility of Forms* (Oxford: Blackwell, 1986).
9. Derrida was frequently taunted with his neglect of the study of Karl Marx (see his interview with Jean-Louis Houdebine and Guy Scarpetta, in *Positions* translated by Alan Bass [University of Chicago Press, 1981]), until the publication of *Specters of Marx: The State of the Debt, the Work of Mourning, and the New International* (New York and London: Routledge, 1994). However, even this has not allayed all

criticism from the Left. See Terry Eagleton's excoriating critique, 'Marxism Without Marxism', *Radical Philosophy*, 73 (1995) 35–7.

10. Eve Browning Cole and Susan Coultrap-McQuin, eds, *Explorations in Feminist Ethics: Theory and Practice* (Bloomington and Indianapolis: Indiana University Press, 1992) 1–2.
11. For arguments about this, see Susan A. Handelman, *Fragments of Redemption: Jewish Thought and Literary Theory in Benjamin, Scholem and Levinas* (Bloomington and Indianapolis: Indiana University Press, 1991), and Robert Gibbs, *Correlations in Rosenzweig and Levinas* (Princeton University Press, 1992).
12. See the relevant entries in *The Oxford Companion to Philosophy*, ed. Ted Honderich (Oxford University Press, 1995).
13. Ethical problems of this sort are discussed in Jonathan Glover, *Causing Death and Saving Lives* (Harmondsworth: Penguin, 1977).
14. Peter Singer, *Practical Ethics* (Cambridge University Press, 1979) 220.
15. Ibid., 13.
16. Compare Philippa Foot, *Virtues and Vices* (Berkeley: University of California Press, 1978).
17. Steven Lukes, *Marxism and Morality* (Oxford: Clarendon Press, 1985).
18. Karl Marx, 'Theses on Feuerbach', in *Early Writings*, trans. Rodney Livingstone and Gregor Benton (Harmondsworth: Penguin, 1975) 421–3; 23.
19. Karl Marx, *Economic and Philosophical Manuscripts* in *Early Writings*, 279–400; 376–7. See also *Grundrisse*, trans. Martin Nicolaus (Harmondsworth: Penguin, 1973) 163.
20. Miné Okubo, *Citizen 13660* (1946; Seattle and London: University of Washington Press, 1983) xi. Our thanks to Helena Grice for this observation.

Part I
Self and History

1
Ethics, Autobiography and the Will: Stephen Spender's *World Within World*

Richard Freadman

> Politics without ideology and with a strong tendency towards autobiography equals liberalism.
>
> Stephen Spender, *The Thirties and After*

> Transcendence is the constitutive structure of consciousness.
>
> Jean-Paul Sartre, *Being and Nothingness*

1.1 POSTMODERNISM AND ETHICS

During the period of what has come to be known as Contemporary Literary Theory ethical criticism of what I would call a substantive kind has had to struggle for survival. By substantive I mean the kind that proceeds on the assumption that ethics is a quasi-autonomous discipline possessing its own conceptual and applied challenges, a conceptual vocabulary, a 'thick'[1] sense of how moral beings function or might function in social environments, and a belief in the centrality of ethical discourse to all forms of social description. This isn't of course to say that many of the political strains of recent Theory and criticism – feminism, cultural materialism, postcolonial discourses – aren't fundamentally ethical projects. Rather that postmodern theory and criticism have tended to adopt either a taken-for-granted attitude to the ethical which says that it will take care of itself if we demolish existing structures of power, or a hostile posture which reposes in the belief that 'traditional' ethical discourses and attitudes are complicit with, and have served to prop up, those structures of power. On this view ethics so conceived must also be demolished, deconstructed.[2]

The term 'postmodern' above is intended to highlight a further feature of the situation I have been describing: namely, the equation of forms of criticism and theory which eschew substantive ethical discourse with postmodernism. Indeed on some definitions this disposition towards the ethical is seen as a constitutive feature of the postmodern. But not all definitions of the postmodern see it this way, and not all postmodern practitioners proceed this way. The last decade or so has seen a so-called 'turn to the ethical' in literary studies in the work of writers like Stanley Cavell, Iris Murdoch, S.L. Goldberg, Martha Nussbaum, Richard Rorty, Cora Diamond;[3] that is, a turn (in part a re-turn) to substantive ethical discourse as I have characterised it. Work of this kind values the 'thick' descriptions of the ethical that literature can provide; it is centrally concerned with moral issues in literature; and it has a liking for the literature of personality. It picks out topics that hitherto would have been more likely to announce a philosophical book or essay: topics like the nature of the virtues, of the will, love, and so on, and it forges new links between literary theory/criticism and philosophical ethics. Thus Martha Nussbaum, a philosopher and a classicist, believes that literature and so literary theory can enrich ethical discourse in ways not possible through conventional philosophical inquiry: 'literary theory can improve the self-understanding of ethical theory by confronting it with a distinctive conception or conceptions of various aspects of human life, realized in a form that is the most appropriate one for their expression.'[4]

I want to insist that these developments too are a part, indeed an increasingly important part, of postmodernism, and that when it comes to the ethical we should now speak of two postmodernisms: a substantive and an antihumanist. I have also suggested elsewhere that some forms of rapprochement between the two streams of the postmodern are possible.[5]

1.2 ETHICS, AUTOBIOGRAPHY, STEPHEN SPENDER

If we take ethics in its broad, Aristotelian sense to be about how a life should be lived, then surely autobiography can lay claim to an important place in ethical-literary discussion. This applies not only to those autobiographies from Augustine on which present the first person life as moral exemplum, but also to life-narratives that eschew, or even denounce, such exemplary aspirations. Genet in *The Thief's Journal*[6] reports but does not overtly seek to recommend a life of crime and sensuality, yet sensuality and the transgressive emerge from the narrative as intrinsic features of a certain vision of life's possibilities. *Roland Barthes by Roland Barthes*[7] too eschews the exemplary function; it also refuses the unitary aspirations of temporally structured individual self. Yet here a certain ethical vision rises from among the fragments: a vision of love, of loyalty to others, to the self, of connectedness to the past.

Virtually all autobiographers, then, are ethicists in some degree. Most are not just concerned but preoccupied with questions about will and circumstance, self and the social code, virtues and vices. One such autobiographer is Stephen Spender, poet, novelist, essayist, critic, political commentator, diarist and author of one of the finest post-war life narratives in English: *World Within World*.[8]

In the Introduction to *World Within World* Spender is explicit, if modest, about his ethical preoccupations. He foreshadows discussion of 'certain moral problems' (p. vii) and says that he has 'tried to write of experiences from which I feel I have learned how to live' (p. viii). The unassuming tone of this belies the complexity and indeed the momentousness of the 'I' in the narrative, for this is a work in which the self is constructed as central, and indeed centred, in a variety of important ways. Some of these are temporal. The moment of writing, or more precisely, the state of the self at the time of writing, is central in the author's personal history: *World Within World* is of that Dantean tradition of autobiographies written in the middle of the journey. Spender writes it at age forty-two, the mid-point between an often unhappy and restrictive Edwardian childhood and the future that awaits the man who has partially emerged from that childhood and from resultant confusions that beset him as a young adult. The moment of writing is also central because the very activity of writing autobiography is, or can be, central to a life: it epitomises a kind of agential self-fashioning that Spender values very highly. The time of writing – 1947–50 – is also central in the sense that the now of the writing is an historical watershed. *World Within World* is written 'through this frame of European Ruins' (p. 151), in the wake of two world wars and the catastrophes of totalitarianism. I want to suggest that here *World Within World* takes its place in another tradition, or perhaps sub-genre, of autobiographical writing: one in which post-war intellectuals used autobiography as a means of reflecting upon the nature and impact of totalitarianism and of affirming the culture of the self in the wake of Hitler and the appalled awareness of the realities of Stalinism. Arthur Koestler, perhaps the greatest practitioner of this kind of autobiography, sets the context unforgettably in his first major autobiographical volume, *Arrow in the Blue*:

> At a conservative estimate, three out of every four people whom I knew before I was thirty were subsequently killed in Spain, or hounded to death in Dachau, or gassed in Belsen, or deported to Russia; some jumped from windows in Vienna or Budapest, others were wrecked by the misery and aimlessness of permanent exile.[9]

I propose to term this kind of autobiographical writing post-totalitarian autobiography. Spender's importance as an autobiographical ethicist stems in part from the way he fuses elements of an intensely self-conscious Rousseauvian tradition of self writing with this more public, politically engaged post-totalitarian form. A recanted Marxist, he uses autobiography to announce his 'revolt against the concept of myself as "social man"' (p. 310), and to call for a new political culture of the individual. He seeks the searing honesty about self of Rousseau or of the Rembrandt who discloses an 'ultimate self' in self-portraiture;[10] yet at the same time he knows that the deepest forms of interiority have a public trajectory, that even the romantic isolate yearns for, can only confess to, a community. In an important essay, 'Confessions and Autobiography', he argues that 'all confessions are from subject to object, from the individual to the community or creed. Even the most shamelessly revealed inner life pleads its case before the moral system of an outer, objective life'.[11]

Each autobiographer must strike a balance between the subjective and more communal impulses. There may be times when the former can or should take priority over the latter, but Spender believes that 1947 is not such a time. He notes that 'a pastoral poem in 1936 was not just a pastoral poem. It was also a non-political poem' (pp. 251–2). Just so, what is called for now, in the late 1940s, is not solipsistic self-contemplation, for this too would be a non-political act, but a form of self-writing which focuses upon the self-societal relation, and which aims even to reconfigure that relation. Such an effort is, he believes, fundamental to the processes of post-war reconstruction. The culture of the self must be reconstructed after Hitler and Stalin. To write autobiography in this way is to use it as what I call a respondent act. In the hands of Spender, Koestler or Malraux, the form becomes a mode of intervention, of reconceptualisation and of personal-political exemplification in response to political realities.[12] Anti-humanist postmodern views that see autobiographers and their form as mere conduits of cultural-ideological forces can have little so say about work of this kind. Criticism can only do an autobiography like *World Within World* justice from the standpoint of a (theoretically aware) postmodern humanism.

The self in *World Within World* is central also, then, in the sense that it lies at the point of intersection, or more precisely, that it is the point of intersection, between the 'private' and 'public' histories. Yet even the figure of intersection doesn't quite get Spender's full sense of the self's centrality, for his account of the self–societal relation is hierarchised in a way that makes the self generative of new forms of that relation. Louis MacNeice's comment that Spender wants to 'redeem the world through introspection'[13] is barbed but apt. This is in a sense what Spender as poet, autobiographer, diarist, seeks to do: Spenderian introspection is a search not only for an authentic self but for the internal resources that will shape and enable humane political transformation. And this leads to a complex set of figurations of the self and its social world, in particular to the dominant figural motif of his autobiography: that of concentricity, of worlds within worlds. Beyond and in connection with this lies the ethical theme that more than any other impels *World Within World*: the issue of the individual will; more specifically, the problem of weakness of the will.

Spender foregrounds the issues of will and concentricity, and prefigures his spatial geometry of the self, in the poem (one stanza of which is given below) which prefaces the volume, 'Darkness and Light':[14]

> To break out of the chaos of my darkness
> Into lucid day, is all my will.
> My words, like eyes in night, stare to reach:
> A centre for their light: and my acts thrown
> To distant places by impatient violence

Yet lock together to mould a path
Out of my darkness, into a lucid day.

It's no great poem. Like many of Spender's lesser pieces it uneasily combines ponderous self-reflection with the more detached play of Audenesque wit. But it says a lot about Spender's ethical pre-occupations. If some of its details are obscure the general import of the poem seems (on first reading at least) to dramatise existential binaries, or what I shall call modalities of the will. One modality it depicts involves asserting the will in a way that might deliver the self from the 'dark' 'chaos' of paralysing confusion; another modality involves not quite the suppression, but rather a kind of reclusive re-direction of the will such that it thwarts its own drive towards enlightened deliverance, deliberately consigning the self to the very darkness that at another level it seeks to transcend. The imagery of darkness and light intersects in sometimes opaque ways with a motif that runs throughout Spender's work: that of centre and circumference. In the first modality, the self is figured as on the circumference, seeking through path-forging 'acts' a light at the centre which will in turn centre, existentially ground, the self. In the second modality, the self is again on the circumference but now its energies, its acts, chart an 'avoiding' journey away from the 'light'. In each case the will functions, but in the second the will might be said to be weak, albeit in a highly specific way. Whether failing in its quest for the light at the centre, or through refusing the light and embracing the darkness of the periphery, the self's benighted exertions forge a paradoxical link between weakness, centre and circumference: 'Centre and circumference are both my weakness.' The memorable line in the 4th stanza which follows – 'O strange identity of my will and weakness!' – sets the emotional and indeed conceptual terms for much of the moral action and reflection in *World Within World*. But what of the last stanza? 'I grow towards the acceptance of that sun' suggests a process of maturation in which the will gravitates towards the light. The 'black and white total emptiness' then referred to seems obscure (and quite possibly inept), but the concluding three lines seem again to suggest that a process of at least partial resolution between opposing tendencies – light, dark, chaos, lucidity – can occur. The nature of this relationship is far from clear; but it seems to involve a rhythm of synthesis and separation out of which comes an empowering differentiation, or capacity to differentiate, between darkness and light, lucidity and confusion; in other words, some degree of emancipation of the will. This rhythm is echoed in the larger structure of the autobiography.

To call this a spatial metaphor is apt but, I would argue, not adequate. At one level what Spender is giving us is an ontological map of the self-in-the world according to which things are arranged in concentric circles. The innermost sphere comprises the unconscious, primordial parts of the self;[15] this is encircled by ego-like dimensions that are 'private' but available to consciousness and susceptible of social connection. In these first two circles resides that which makes the individual self eccentric. Beyond these lie aspects of self that are more the products of social construction and so less marked by differentiation from other selves; then, circling these, are the regions of not-self: the 'external' world in which the self must operate and in which it may seek to intervene. Yet Spender is trying to figure not just a map but a process. Concentricity so conceived is about movement among psychological, spiritual and political coordinates. But movement doesn't just mean the journey of a given self through a given world. Like autobiography itself, the motif tries to capture the sense of the self's unfolding, including the sort of unfolding that the self brings about through its own choices, its activities of self-fashioning; in other words, through the process of self-transformation. Movement here also entails the way the self acts upon and transforms the world as it travels: in *The Struggle of the Modern* he writes of the 'modern "I"' which through 'receptiveness, suffering, passivity, transforms the world to which it is exposed',[16] and Spender's great claim as an autobiographical-political ethicist is that the self cannot act appropriately upon the world until the process of self-transformation – also those of self-understanding – have rendered it fit to do so:

> For our individualistic civilisation to be reborn within the order of a new world, people must be complex as individuals, simple as social forces. They must recognize their public duties, accept sacrifices, recognize necessity: but at the same time they must insist on their individuality, their difficulties, their privacy, their irrationality. (p. 191)

Autobiography fits the bill because it is par excellence an act which at once exemplifies the self as individual and records its attempts to re-fashion itself and its world from the wellsprings of conscience and creativity. *World Within World* is structured in just this way: it begins with childhood, proceeds through the psychological complexities of adolescence and early adulthood, and charts the evolving self in relation to its political attitudes: from apolitical self-indulgence, to an engagement with Marxism (this is one of those autobiographical accounts – I term them narratives of affiliation – by a recanted communist made famous by Crossman's anthology, *The God that Failed*),[17] to a reconstructive post-war liberalism. Interestingly, it ends where it begins – with childhood – as if to say, *pace* Wordsworth, that we cannot grow if the sparks are not there from the outset.

What then are we to call such a metaphor? James Olney's notion of 'metaphors of self' is very helpful here, especially given his emphasis on the way metaphors of self are implicated in the processes of change.[18] I propose to use a term adapted from the sociologist Anthony Giddens and to call such motifs metaphors of self-constitution.[19] This I think captures the two senses we need here: that the self exists, is already in some sense constituted, in and as a part of a sort of provisional ontological landscape, but also that it re-makes, or re-constitutes that self, that landscape, that self–societal relation, in the act of autobiographical narration. Indeed I suggest that this term is applicable for most autobiographies of any real complexity and ethical aspiration. In Spender's case the metaphor has profound significance as a respondent act because it is, *inter alia*, a calculated affront to the god that failed, to three of the defining aspects of totalitarian ideology: the belief that the individual self is infinitely malleable by forces from without; the control and usurpation of private morality by the state or party; and the essentialising of self in terms of cultural or racial stereotypes.[20] Spender's metaphor of self-constitution repudiates each of these dogmas. It insists that self-transformation, though never total, must be effected from within, by the individual; that morality, though a consensual aspect of culture, can only be held and appropriately internalised by particular individuals; and, as I shall argue presently, that the emancipation of the will is intimately bound up with the emancipation of selves and relations between selves from cultural stereotypes and stereotyping. The very title of the book, then, is counter-totalitarian.

I suspect that it comes (at least in part) from a D. H. Lawrence poem, 'Red Moon-Rise', which contains the following lines:

for now I know
The world within worlds is a womb, whence issues all
The shapeliness that decks us here below

One of several admiring comments about Lawrence in *World Within World* lends credence to this suggestion: 'He [Lawrence] had the sense that distinctions between outer and inner are sacred: that whilst the inner world should meet the outer, the outer should not become the inner world of the writer' (p. 97). Since the writer, not least the autobiographical writer, is for Spender something of an exemplary post-totalitarian individual, this sense of distinctness-within-relatedness applies, ideally at least, to all people. But, as I've argued, this sense of the self–societal relation is not for Spender a given. It is something that must be brought about by the activities of the will. However, as 'Darkness and Light' shows, the will for him is no simple thing. His whole sense of engagement with the world is predicated upon it, yet his writings, not least the autobiography, dwell continually on a fear that his will, and perhaps that of many others, may be weak, incapable of the rigours that this moment in history demands. This from the sequence 'Spiritual explorations':

Beneath our nakedness, we are naked still.
Within the mind, history and stars expose
Our bodies' frailty and a new day blows
Away huts and papyri of the will.[21]

1.3 WEAKNESS OF WILL

Like 'Darkness and Light', the rather Eliotean account of the 'modern "I"' which I quoted above suggests that Spender's understanding of the relations between will, ethics and transformation needs some elaboration. How, after all, can it be that 'receptiveness, suffering and passivity, transforms the world to which it is exposed'? What meaning can such redemptive rhetoric have for a post-war political pragmatist who made his name as a 'thirties' engagé poet? One answer, as I've suggested, is that autobiography as an exemplary act is on his view supposed to promote forms of self-awareness that will in turn promote social transformation. But autobiography, too, is an exertion of the will. How can it come about if the will is weak? Can it in some way re-constitute the self that would write as strong through the act of writing? What do we, what does Spender, mean by weakness of will? Such questions can best be addressed, I believe, through the sort of twinning and twining of literary and philosophical discourses that we find in 'turn to the ethical' criticism.

There is of course a large philosophical and theological literature stretching back to the Greeks about the notion of weakness of the will. I shall use the Greek term *akrasia* (meaning incontinence, lack of control) for it, though such a usage begs many questions. For current purposes perhaps the most important of these questions asks whether *akrasia* should be seen in what Gosling calls 'rationalistic' terms,[22] or what I'll simply call broader terms. The 'rationalistic' view, which has very powerful support (Plato, Aristotle, Ayer, Davidson, O'Shaunessy, Gosling, Dunn, Charlton), sees weakness of will as arising because rational deliberation is overcome by passion, or impeded by ignorance, or because an agent doesn't actually believe that a chosen course of action is the best one. Thus for Aristotle, 'the good man obeys his reason',[23] and the *akrates* who succumbs to passion in selecting a lover acts from 'appetite', not from 'choice'.[24] A broader conception allows for a greater range of causal factors: it argues (*pace* depth psychology) that distinctions between 'rational' and emotive feelings and intentions are very difficult to draw and that complex psychological nuances enter into our ability or inability to exercise will 'appropriately'. This broader conception is closer to our customary colloquial understanding of weakness of will: it allows for such phenomena as lack of motivation, inability (for whatever reason) to initiate or pursue projects, indecisiveness, and so on. Spender is valuable as an autobiographical ethicist in part because he helps us to see that – and why – the broader conception is more powerful than the rationalistic one. This doesn't mean that he fully comprehends all of the issues pertaining to the weak will – sometimes he seems merely to understand the phenomenon as a sensation of will-lessness. However, his conception has important additional elements, among them a secularised form of the Judaic-Christian notion of the will as a specifically moral faculty; a power whose exercise will inevitably take morally significant forms. In this sense he is closer to Augustine and Aquinas than to Plato or Aristotle.

I think we need some further detail on these matters. We need a term, however provisionally, for the experience of complete absence of will (as in the case of severely depressed people who lose all desire to act or feel, even the desire to eat). I propose to call this radical passivity. We also need to accommodate the relatively unproblematic case in which the will is misdirected through ignorance of the relevant facts. Let's just call this ignorance. Then, in addition to the rationalistic/broad distinction between conceptions of weakness of will, I want to distinguish between variants – or, to use my earlier term, modalities – of the will in general which take observable forms such as action, and forms which are internal and not susceptible of external observation: for example, intentional states, like hoping that things turn out well for someone, that do not issue in action.[25] I'll call this a distinction between internal and observable modalities. Further I want a distinction between forms of the will in which it is directed at short term objectives (this particular purchase), and the longer term, more global orientations that characterise major life commitments (acts in pursuit of political or religious beliefs, for instance). I'll call these immediate and global modalities respectively. Along another axis lie differences between exertions of will which are genuinely in one's best interests, and those which are predicated on a mistaken, often conventional, understandings of what one's best interests are: to leave an abusive marriage is an instance of what might be termed (*pace* existentialism) an authentic exercise of the will; to stay in such a marriage for reasons of social expectation and protocol would on this view be an inauthentic exercise of the will. A further kind of case, interestingly discussed by Dunn,[26] is that of what might simply be termed self-destructive uses of the will where the agent acts in a way (suicide, for example) which is calculated to bring about some harmful outcome for the self.

Finally, and from a different angle again, I want to propose terms for certain cases in which the will is exercised without a clearly formulated outcome in mind. Gambling on a roulette wheel is a case in point because here the agent submits to the pure play of contingency: the will is involved in joining the game, but thereafter all capacity to predict and control outcomes is forfeited. I'll term such instances, common in existential literature, the modality of surrender. A related but ethically far more significant phenomenon is what I think of as heuristic exercises of the will. Here actions or inclinations issue less from a settled sense of self and intention than from a desire to find out more about self through the unforeseen consequences of certain choices. Like the surrender modality this one is reminiscent of certain existential conceptions in that it sees will as a synthesis of cause, motive and end, a synthesis which transforms a proto or potential self into one which assumes transitive self-definition through action. As Sartre puts it in *Being and Nothingness*: 'the cause, the motive, and the end are three indissoluble terms of the thrust of the free and living consciousness which projects itself towards its possibilities'.[27] And again: 'I can also find myself engaged in acts which reveal my possibilities to me at the very instant at which they are realized.'[28] Finally, I suggest a different kind of distinction again – between divers spheres of the will's activity: private and public, journalistic and autobiographical, and so on.

So how might we characterise Spender's 'strange identity of my will and weakness!' in terms of the above? It doesn't seem to be radical passivity because neither in the poem nor in the narrative more generally does he describe states of total enervation or entropy. Indeed in a journal entry he quotes from the twenties the complaint is not that he lacks will altogether, but that his will seems only to be active when he is writing:

> I have no character or will power outside my work. In the life of action, I do everything that friends tell me to do, have no opinions of my own. This is shameful, I know, but it is so. Therefore I must develop that side of me which is independent of other people. I must live and mature in my writing.
>
> My aim is to achieve maturity of soul ... After my work, all I live for is friends. (p. 105)

This then seems to have more to do with the spheres of the will's activity, and with its hiddenness from external observation, than with its capacity for activity *per se*. Yet the concern, the fear of a kind of will-lessness, is all-pervasive in the first half of the book, and it applies particularly to a sphere which is highlighted throughout: that of personal, and especially intimate, relations. It's a striking fact about *World Within World* that for all its self-preoccupation, and its insistence on the unbreachable integrity of the inner being of the individual, its conception of self is actually dialectical. The clear implication of its rich and frequent accounts of interpersonal relations is that the self can only 'mature' through relations with others. Spender is one of those autobiographers whose history of Self is also a history of the Other. Writing, which is addressed to the

Other, is a part of this – not least the powerfully maturational form of writing that is autobiography. In 'Confessions and Autobiography' he defines confessional autobiography as 'the record of a transformation of errors by values'.[29] In *World Within World* that 'transformation' goes on principally at the interpersonal level and – to return to the concentric metaphor – it operates first centripitally, as the inauthentic social self is centred, emancipated from the periphery to the centre. Its effects then radiate out centrifugally from the personal towards the socio-political ('the life of action'). In charting this progression Spender employs novel-like techniques of characterisation and analysis. Here especially, his autobiography takes its place in the literature of personality. His great theme here, as always, is that founding preoccupation of the classic novel, the centring of the self. I turn finally to Spender in relationships of love.

1.4 THE *AKRATES* AS LOVER

In what sense can a lover really be an *akratic*? Plato's and Aristotle's understanding of *akrasia* is premised on an 'homogeneous view of human motivation'[30] which presupposes a synthesis between goodness, motivation and action: in the good man understanding leads ineluctably to right action. So-called 'clear-eyed' *akrasia* – choosing to act against rational best interest – is therefore logically inconceivable in the case of the good agent. The Judaeo-Christian tradition, and perhaps the later Plato of the Laws, allow for intrapsychic conflict that entails conflicting desires accompanied by conflicting convictions about best interests and about the good life itself. For Kant, by contrast, romantic love is an inherently appetitive, will-less phenomenon; and since for Kant moral appraisal only obtains where conduct is deliberative and will-governed, romantic love cannot on his account be subject to moral assessment. In *The Critique of Practical Reason* (also in *The Metaphysics of Morals*) Kant in fact draws a distinction between will-less and will-governed love: pathological love is romantic, non-will-governed love; the contrasting form, practical love, is an attitude of concern for others which one can will oneself to have. The former sort lies outside of the realm of morality; the latter falls within its domain:

For love, as an affection, cannot be commanded, but beneficence

> for duty's sake may; even though we are not impelled to it by any inclination – nay, are even repelled by a natural and unconquerable aversion. This is practical love, and not pathological – a love which is seated in the will, and not in the propensions of sense …[31]

Spender, we might say, does believe in the possibility of weakness of will, but he does not conceive of the weakness of will as intrinsic to romantic love. Just as importantly, he does he not see such weakness as beyond moral appraisal, or as beyond educative moral development. On the contrary, the moral action of *World Within World* centres on a process whereby what I shall call the affective will is emancipated and educated in relationships of love. The narrative deals with a series of romantic relationships in which this development takes place: principally his early homosexual relationships, then in a series of heterosexual ones. In all but the last case much is made of the nature of the choice involved in entry into relationships of this kind.

Here is the description of Spender's first encounter with the Oxford undergraduate, Marston:

> I first noticed him – I remember – in the train to Oxford, at the beginning of my second term. He was with a crowd of other 'hearties', but there was something watchful, withdrawn, in his attitude which made him separate from them. Sometimes he smiled to himself with the secret jauntiness of a very modest person who does not realize that his modesty makes him different from the others.
>
> At that moment I made a decision to get to know him, when I quite well might not have done so. There was a moment of pure arbitrariness when I thought: 'I need not do this, but I will do it'. This decision remained like a core of emptiness at the very centre of everything I felt afterwards, however strong the feeling might be. (p. 64)

The designation of this movement of feeling as 'arbitrary' is interesting and typical. In Spender's novel *The Temple* the Spender surrogate, Paul, says to his friend Joachim of Joachim's latest infatuation: 'I don't really understand that you can fall in love with someone because you have said that you were going to fall in love.'[32] In the Marston passage the motivational state is offered as an instance of the weakness of will, yet it is a complex phenomenon. Clearly, will of a kind is exerted; a choice is made. What is missing is not volition but certain forms of deliberation and passional engagement which might ideally condition volition (though there is a hint of desire in the sense that Stephen may identify with and be attracted to Marston's apparent insularity). The choice in question precipitates the chooser into a situation which he seeks neither to know, to predict nor to control. He chooses to submit to sheer contingency. This is the will in the modality of surrender, and it is to have painful but mixed consequences. Psuedo-existential though it might in some ways be, the choice proves destructive in the sense that the lack of deliberative, and in particular of affective, motivation results in a 'core of emptiness' at the centre of the friendship. The choice lacks personal investment; only the will as abstract potentiality is engaged. The 'core' metaphor is of course highly significant: this is a relationship in which the self-as-innermost-centre is absent from the concentric configuration of commitment and action. It proceeds from an empty choice. Nevertheless, the relationship has important developmental implications: soon after, he begins to write poetry.

The next important 'phase of a search for the identification of my own aims with those of another man' (p. 67) is with Walter, an unemployed German youth. Here again, the initial moment of interested engagement is characterised as arbitrary: 'At one Lokal [in Hamburg] I met an unemployed young man called Walter, in whom I rather arbitrarily decided to take an interest' (p. 117). Walter exploits Stephen for money, but exploitation is to some extent mutual: Stephen repeats the pattern of identification with the outsider which had earlier been a feature of his rebellion against his family. Yet there is more to the relationship than mutual convenience:

> I cannot just dismiss Walter as part of my very gullible past when I allowed myself to be victimized by a tramp. For in this relationship there was a grain of real affection of a kind which I had not had before. It is as though I was in need of some precious ore and had been driven to seek it in the smallest quantities and the roughest places .... With him I escaped to some extent from the over-spiritualism, puritan, competitive atmosphere in which I had been brought up, to something denser, less pure, but out of which I could refine little granules of affection. From such

> experiences I gradually learned a feeling which I could later bring to the highest relationships.
>
> Through Walter, I imagined the helplessness, the moral weakness, the drift, of unemployment. I imagined, I suppose, that something which I was now beginning to call in my mind 'the revolution' would alter his lot, and I felt that as a member of a more fortunate social class I owed him a debt. (pp. 117–18)

Once again, there is a moment of choice, and though it is to some degree and in some respects arbitrary, there are clear psychological and sociological factors conditioning this choice. The situation here is morally complex. To the extent that the decision to get involved with Walter is exploitative and lacks developed emotional investment, it is morally suspect. It involves a kind of categorial love where one loves the other in part as Other, but also in part as the embodiment of a social stereotype. In so far as it exposes him to danger the act of will involved is also in a sense self-destructive. But there are also senses in which the choice seems authentic: it is part of the repudiation of the inauthentic account of self he receives in childhood and of an heuristic search for the 'real self' (p. 311) – a process which includes release from puritanic attitudes to the body, and the capacity to give and receive affection. It also has some positive moral–political content because it contains an element of genuine political sympathy. While Marston was roughly of Stephen's class, Walter is not. The will to love Walter is in part motivated by the desire to bring about a fairer world. In love the *akrates* is beginning to learn not only more authentic – affective – private modalities of the will, but the possibility of deep interconnections between will of this kind and the political will. If the will is weak here it is so in a special sense, and less so than in the case of Marston. Here the gaining of wisdom presages not only greater strength of will, but a greater range of its applications.

It is in his next important relationship, with Christopher Isherwood in Berlin, that he experiences what he calls a 'prolonged and deceptive docility' (p. 175), but also a growing awareness of the political as they witness the rise of Nazism. He takes up with Jimmy (Tony Hyndman) when he moves from Germany to London in January 1933. This relationship, which is accorded more detailed description and analysis than any other in the book, begins characteristically: Spender describes his decision to invite Jimmy to be a live-in secretary as 'this very arbitrary decision of mine to take him as a companion' (p. 177). Companionship develops into an intense and tortured bond which the narrative anatomises in emotional, moral, political and gender terms. The central moral problem is one to which Spender refers in his Journals: the threat of a loss of self, or 'absorption', in relationship. Unhealthily dependent relationships are

> a way of entering into a kind of dual subjectivity, a redoubled and reciprocal egotism; it is an alliance of two people who form a united front to deal with the problems of the objective world. The problem of married people is not to become absorbed in each other, but how not to become absorbed in each other; how, in a word, to trust one another in order to enter into a strong and satisfactory relationship with the outside world.[33]

Hitherto it has been Stephen who feels absorbed, selfless, with others; but the situation with the unemployed, working-class former soldier Jimmy is reversed: away from the Army Jimmy 'seemed lacking in will and purpose' (p. 176); he develops what Stephen sees as a 'hopeless dependence on me' (p. 183), and concludes that '[m]y character undermined his belief in himself; his dependence and lack of anything to do threatened my creativeness' (p. 183). Here again, however, the mode of surrender in which he initiated the relationship returns to haunt it. As with Walter, 'There was real affection, real happiness, real interest in our life together: but also a sterility which sometimes affected me so much that I would lie down on my bed with a sensation I have never known before or since, as though my mouth were full of ashes' (p. 176). The asymmetry of the two wills involved – Stephen dominant, Jimmy subordinated – leads to passionate struggles and conflicts during which Jimmy 'broke through the barrier of self-protection' that had for so long been 'surrounding' – encircling – Stephen (p. 182). This is crucial to Stephen's development, but this relationship can only develop so far. In part this is because of the way in which the externality of its political entailments shadows, in a sense usurps, its emotional centre. Again, on the initial decision: 'this very arbitrary decision of mine to take him as a companion, having once been made, became a social phenomenon, as though in him I had taken into my home the purposelessness of the life of the Depression outside' (p. 177). Jimmy is body and soul, but also social embodiment. This, too, is a categorial love: 'I was in love, as it were, with his background, his soldiering, his working-class home' (p. 184).

Spender now turns to heterosexual relationships, first with an American, 'Elizabeth' (in fact Muriel Gardiner, to whom he later dedicated his journals). In an important phrase he imputes to her a certainty he does not and cannot have: she was 'in possession of all of the threads of her life' (p. 200). He remains emotionally disorganised. His attraction is again partly categorial: the fact that she was American 'mystified and attracted me' (p. 194). He finds himself torn between the ill Jimmy (with whom he is still involved) and Elizabeth. There is 'a real inability on my part to choose .... Something which we called my "ambivalence" forever kept unsleeping watch between us, like a sword' (p. 197).

Marriage to Inez, a politically engaged student and would-be novelist, begins with another moment of sudden decision. He meets her at a function at which he speaks in Oxford in 1936; asks her to his house-warming party a few days later; thence, the next day, to lunch, when he proposes to her. They marry three weeks later. Of his impulse to propose he says:

> It is difficult at this distance of time to understand why I did this. I certainly felt strongly attracted and this made me feel that if I did not marry her quickly someone else would .... My lack [of previous impulse to marry] could be used as evidence that I was not acting on impulse. But, of course, beneath this fallacious and superficial ratiocination was my despairing knowledge that if I did not act on impulse I decided nothing. So that action for me consisted of seizing on to impulses without considering results, and letting me carry them whither I would. (p. 205)

In 1941 he marries Natasha Latvin. Nothing is said of the prior stages of the relationship, and very little of the relationship itself. The sequence of the *akrates* in love essentially concludes with this paragraph:

> When we were first married, I suffered from an exacerbated sense of guilt arising from the break-down of the relationships I have described in these pages. I was for ever attaching blame either to others or to myself for what I regarded as failures. One day, Natasha said to me: 'From now on there is no question of blame. There is only us,' and this was the faith, the research for a

unity which was ourselves belonging to one another, on which our marriage was founded. (pp. 279–80)

No longer immobilised in his own 'blame' he has found the 'faith' that the humanist seeks in 'the highest relationships'. He can now live with, not merely through, another. They have a unity with independence; subjectivity which is reciprocal rather than 'dual'; belonging without 'absorption' of one in the other. The progression of feeling involved in this transition is (disappointingly) not otherwise described; but the affective will, it seems, has found the place at the centre from which it can attain a balanced, a properly articulated, relatedness with inner and outer worlds. Such an exertion of will might be termed an integrative act.

We cannot know whether this was in fact the case for him – at least without detailed biographical inquiry – though his candour inspires a fair degree of trust from the reader. More to the point, however, is the way in which Spender uses autobiography as a means – at once retrospective and prospective – of trying to imagine what the affective will might look like: of how it forms, where it resides, how it is exercised, how it traverses personal and private worlds. It must be conceded that his account of the will is not always convincing or sufficiently precise: the insulation of the will from ideology seems too absolute; and the lack of detail about achieved states and acts of the emancipated will, either in marriage or in politics, is a limitation in this ethical vision. Nevertheless, *World Within World* is a powerful and nuanced call for renewal, a call which imagines some of the processes of renewal that ethical beings now need to undergo, and which works through a complexity of conceptual-imagistic organisation which is characteristic of fine literature. 'Politics', he writes, 'without ideology and with a strong tendency towards autobiography, equals liberalism'.[34] If the desire wholly to transcend ideology seems utopian, the attempt to imagine a new liberal order after totalitarianism is urgent, especially at a time when for many post-war liberals such an order seemed quite literally unimaginable.

Notes

1. I take this term from Clifford Geertz, *The Interpretation of Cultures* (New York: Basic, 1973). See especially, Ch. 1, 'Thick Description: Towards an Interpretive Theory of Culture'. Geertz gets the term from Gilbert Ryle.
2. These postures are discussed in more detail in Richard Freadman and Seumas Miller, *Rethinking Theory: A Critique of Contemporary Literary Theory and an Alternative Account* (Cambridge University Press, 1992).
3. For discussions of these developments, see David Parker, *Ethics, Theory and the Novel* (Cambridge University Press, 1994), especially Ch. 2. See also Parker's Introduction in Jane Adamson, Richard Freadman and David Parker, eds, *Renegotiating Ethics* (forthcoming, Cambridge University Press), and the Introduction to Leona Toker, ed., *Commitment in Reflection: Essays in Literature and Moral Philosophy* (New York: Garland, 1994).
4. Martha Nussbaum, *Love's Knowledge: Essays on Philosophy and Literature* (New York: Oxford University Press, 1990) 191.
5. Richard Freadman, 'Disciplinary Relations: Literary Studies and Philosophy' in John Barnes, ed., *Border Crossing: Studies in English and Other Disciplines* (Melbourne: La Trobe University Press), 1991.
6. Jean Genet, *The Thief's Journal*, trans. Bernard Frechtman (London: Faber, 1965).
7. Roland Barthes, *Roland Barthes by Roland Barthes*, trans. Richard Howard (New York: Hill & Wang, 1977).
8. Stephen Spender, *World Within World* (London: Hamish Hamilton, 1951). All subsequent page references to this text will be given in parentheses in the body of the article.
9. Arthur Koestler, *Arrow in the Blue: An Autobiography* (1953; New York: Stein and Day, 1984) 131–2. Others to have written post-totalitarian autobiography include Irving Howe, Simone de Beauvoir, Bertrand Russell, Primo Levi, Elie Wiesel and André Malraux.
10. Stephen Spender, *Journals 1939–1983*, ed. John Goldsmith (Oxford University Press), 179.
11. Ibid., 120.
12. On the 'double perspective' of 'self and history' in *World Within World* see Brian Finney, *The Inner I: British Autobiography of the Twentieth Century* (London: Faber, 1985), Ch. 10.
13. Louis MacNeice, *The Strings Are False* (London: Faber, 1965) 113–14.
14. The poem was originally published in 1935 and included with minor revision in Spender's *Collected Poems: 1928–1953*, but was omitted from the *Collected Poems: 1928–1985*, published in 1985.
15. Spender attempts, not altogether satisfactorily, to conceptualise this dimension of self in *The Struggle of the Modern* (1963; London: Methuen, 1965) 117.
16. Ibid., 72.
17. Richard Crossman, ed., *The God that Failed* (New York: Books for Libraries, 1949). Spender contributed an essay to this volume.

18. James Olney, *Metaphors of Self: The Meaning of Autobiography* (Princeton University Press, 1972). See especially his discussion of metaphor, 30–2.
19. Anthony Giddens, *The Constitution of Society* (Cambridge: Polity Press, 1984).
20. On totalitarianism see Hannah Arendt, *The Origins of Totalitarianism* (New York: Harcourt Brace Jovanovich, 1951), and Leonard Schapiro, *Totalitarianism* (London: Macmillan, 1972).
21. Stephen Spender, *Collected Poems* (London: Faber, 1985) 113.
22. Justin Gosling, *Weakness of Will* (London: Routledge, 1990) 163. See also Robert Dunn, *The Possibility of Weakness of Will* (Indianapolis: Hacket Publishing, 1987), William Charlton, *Weakness of Will* (Oxford: Blackwell, 1988) and G. Mortimore, ed., *Weakness of Will* (London: Macmillan, 1971).
23. Aristotle, *Nichomachean Ethics*, trans. W.D. Ross, in *Basic Works of Aristotle*, ed. Richard McKeon (New York: Random House, 1941) Bk. 10, Ch. 8, 1087.
24. Ibid., Bk. III, Ch. 2, 10015.
25. Iris Murdoch gives an example of this kind in *The Sovereignty of Good* (London: Routledge, 1970) 17–23.
26. Dunn, *The Possibility of Weakness of Will*, Ch. 5
27. Jean-Paul Sartre, *Being and Nothingness: An Essay on Phenomenological Ontology*, trans. Hazel E. Barnes (New York: Philosophical Library, 1958) 449.
28. Ibid., 36.
29. Stephen Spender, 'Confessions and Autobiography', in James Olney, ed., *Autobiography: Essays Theoretical and Critical* (Princeton University Press, 1980) 121. My colleague John Gatt-Rutter points out that John Sturrock argues a similar line in *The Language of Autobiography* (Cambridge University Press, 1993). My thanks to John, and to another colleague, John Gillies, for helpful comments on this paper.
30. Gosling, *Weakness of Will*, 31.
31. Immanuel Kant, quoted from *Kant: Selections*, ed. Theodore M. Greene (New York: Scribner's, 1957) 278.
32. Spender, *The Temple* (London: Faber, 1988) 122.
33. Spender, *Journals*, 33.
34. Stephen Spender, *The Thirties and After: Poetry, Politics, People 1930s–1970s* (New York: Vintage Books, 1979) 236.

2
'Ethics cannot afford to be nation-blind': Saul Bellow and the Problem of the Victim

Andrew Hadfield

In this short chapter I wish to point out a problem and pose a question rather than reach for a conclusion. In his credo, 'What I Believe', written in 1939, E. M. Forster made a characteristically blunt, neat and straightforward separation between the moral duties one owes to individuals and those one owes to wider communities and abstract ideas: 'I hate the idea of causes, and if I had to choose between betraying my country and betraying my friend, I hope I should have the guts to betray my country.... Love and loyalty can run counter to the claims of the State. When they do – down with the State, say I, which means that the State would down me.'[1] Strong words, especially in 1939, but they conflate and confuse a number of issues in order to create the illusion of a simple choice which casts the author as a courageous moral hero standing up to the encroaching tyranny of state power, not least, in equating the notion of a 'cause' with the bullying intrusion of the nation. Reviewing David Miller's recent book *On Nationality*, a defence of the need to preserve national identity from the Scylla and Charybdis of 'virulent ethno-nationalism' and 'sanitised globalism', Charles King pointed out the problems of Forster's position: 'Ethics ... cannot afford to be nation-blind, for national boundaries play a special role in structuring morality.'[2] According to Miller, an individual's identity is formed within the boundaries of the states and communities within which he or she exists, so that 'the duties one owes to one's fellow countrymen are of a special kind, different from, and more extensive than those duties one owes to human beings as such'.

Miller's is an arguable claim which can be set against the universalist ethical impetus based on personal relationships proposed by Forster. The problem of moral responsibility to others – as well as to oneself – has been a major theme of the novels of Saul Bellow, a writer who has always used his fictional narratives as means of exploring fundamental moral questions. In his acceptance speech for the Nobel Prize (1976), Bellow argued that the novel is a form which should 'promise us meaning, harmony, and even justice', thus placing an ethical weight upon his profession which looked back to the basic Aristotelian notions of literature's function.[3] For Michael Glenday, Bellow's novels are pessimistic sallies at the trivialising effects of contemporary American culture which militate against the establishment of a workable form of communitarian ethics, an opinion seemingly vindicated in Bellow's recent endorsement of Allan Bloom's *The Closing of the American Mind* (1987), as a book which exposes the harmful effects of the politicisation of the university. The 'heat of the dispute between Left and Right', according to Bellow, has scorched 'the habits of civilised discourse'.[4] For Daniel Fuchs, Bellow is a traditional moralist, arguing that ethical problems remain both constant and a pressing concern in all societies – hence the need for their constant reiteration through the power of fiction.[5]

Nevertheless, there has been one huge change in Bellow's lifetime relevant to the question in focus here, the creation of the state of Israel in 1948. Bellow would seem to be caught between a number of identities to which he can legitimately lay claim and has often chosen to explore in his work: Jewish, American, and that of Western liberal democrat, the assumption of which demand importantly different ethical responsibilities and demand different, often conflicting, moral responses. I want to compare and contrast Bellow's self-fashioning and ethical position in two works written 30 years apart: first, his second novel, *The Victim* (1947), written on the eve of the establishment of the modern state of Israel, and second, his account of his first visit to his racial homeland, *To Jerusalem and Back* (1976). If the former appears to manipulate the reader's responses one way, the later work is designed as a tart reminder in the opposite direction.

2.1 BELLOW'S *THE VICTIM*

The Victim tells the story of a few weeks in the life of Asa Leventhal, a moderately successful editor of a New York trade magazine. While his wife is away visiting her mother, Leventhal is forced to deal with two crises which have profound moral implications: his young nephew, Mickey, contracts a serious disease from which he eventually dies; and at the same time he is haunted by a drunken former acquaintance, Kirby Allbee, who claims that Leventhal's aggression towards his boss cost him his job. Allbee eventually moves into Leventhal's apartment, tries to force his unwilling host to find him a job, brings back a prostitute when he thinks that Leventhal is out of town, and attempts to commit suicide before he eventually disappears from his life, resurfacing at the theatre some years later, prosperous and accompanying a reasonably well-known actress whose star is on the wane.

The Victim deals directly with the question of responsibility for others, a common theme in Dostoevsky and Dreiser, two significant influences on Bellow's writing.[6] The novel opens with Leventhal having to excuse himself from work because of his nephew's illness when his sister-in-law, Elena – significantly, of Italian, not Jewish, descent – demands that he help as her husband is away. Leventhal is irritated, not least, because when he returns for his coat he overhears his boss, Mr Beard, complain, 'Takes unfair advantage … like the rest of his brethren'.[7] Later, Leventhal reflects that not only was Beard's remark 'disgusting', but that it was the sort of random prejudice that he, Leventhal, was fated to face: 'If a man disliked you, he would dislike you for all the reasons he could think of' (*The Victim*, p. 29). When the dishevelled Allbee accosts Leventhal in the park, thinking that he has received his note and come to stare at the misfortune of a gentile, the confused Leventhal tries to be aggressive and asks what he thinks is a rhetorical question: 'I haven't thought about you in years, frankly, and I don't know why you think I care whether you exist or not. What, are we related?' Allbee's response suggests that he sees a different bond: '"By blood? No, no … heavens!" Allbee laughed.' In fact, Allbee immediately denies any sort of racial bond between the two men by casting Leventhal as an outsider. When Leventhal attempts to walk away and is hauled back by Allbee, the latter opines, 'I didn't think there would be any physical violence. That's not how you people go about things' (*The Victim*, p. 34).

These opening pages would seem to cast Leventhal as a victim, forced to be his own brother's keeper, racially abused at work, and then confronted by another bigot who hauls him out of the crowd and claims that he also owes him a debt, although he is keen to preserve an exclusive racial distance. Needless to say, matters turn out to be more complex and Leventhal is forced to delve into his past in order to make sense of himself and the boundaries of his duties to others. Reconstructing the past in order to establish the extent of the debt – or lack of it – is similarly problematic. Although Leventhal tries to dismiss Allbee's charges as the product of his undoubted excessive drinking, a matter which leads to Allbee's countercharge that Leventhal is a Jew stereotyping drunken gentiles (*The Victim*, p. 38), both agree on the basic outline of events. Some years before, the unemployed Leventhal had asked Allbee to recommend him for a job with his notoriously tyrannical boss, Rudiger, despite the fact that the two men only knew each other through a mutual acquaintance, Harkavy, and clearly did not get on. After Leventhal's interview, Allbee lost his job, according to Allbee, as a direct result of Leventhal's performance. For Allbee, Leventhal's actions were a deliberate act of revenge for a casual anti-Semitic remark and he is incensed that Leventhal claims that he cannot remember what happened.

Leventhal relives the scene after Allbee has gone and it becomes clear to the reader that the interview has been of especial importance for the establishment of Leventhal's sense of identity as a victim standing up against the powerful forces which would exclude him at every turn because of his race. In many ways the confrontation is richly comic. When he realises that he has no chance of getting a job, Leventhal lights a cigarette without asking permission and tells Rudiger what he thinks of his trade paper:

> 'Anybody who can write English can write for it. If you gave a man a try and then thought he couldn't make the grade, I'd say you knew your business a lot better. That's a prejudice, Mr. Rudiger, about newspaper experience.'
>
> Rudiger shouted, 'Oh, is it?' Leventhal saw that he was not invulnerable ...
>
> 'Sure it is,' said Leventhal rather easily. 'It's a guild. Any outsider hasn't got a chance. But as a matter of fact you ought to think of your paper first and hire people because they can do the work. It wouldn't hurt'. (*The Victim*, p. 47)

The interview ends predictably enough, with the vindicated, morally self-righteous Leventhal taunting, 'I guess you can't take it when people stand up to you, Mr. Rudiger', and the apoplectic Rudiger 'pushing over his desk with both arms' and bellowing, 'Out, you nut case, you nut, you belong in the asylum! Out! You ought to be committed' (*The Victim*, p. 48), which would appear to prove Leventhal's case. However, Leventhal starts to feel more than a little guilty, shrinking from such recollections, recognising that 'even one tenth of the reality was calamitous', and realising that 'Under no circumstances could he imagine doing now what he did then' (*The Victim*, p. 47). His case is not helped by the fact that both the friends he consults, Harkavy and Williston, feel that his actions did result in Allbee's dismissal (*The Victim*, pp. 84, 105), although the extent of his responsibilities to Allbee are by no means clear.

Leventhal has to rethink the notion of victimisation: his sense of exclusion on the grounds of his race is mirrored by Allbee's racist belief in a Jewish conspiracy. When Allbee invites himself into Leventhal's flat, the two discuss the rights and wrongs of their particular case, but the issues range much wider. Allbee attempts to goad Leventhal into accepting that he is not to blame for his state by claiming that the latter's Jewishness prevents him from recognising their common humanity (a move which in itself mirrors Williston's argument that it is Allbee's WASP identity which causes him to behave obnoxiously [*The Victim*, p. 45]):

> You won't assume that it isn't entirely my fault. It's necessary for you to believe that I deserve what I get. It doesn't enter your mind, does it – that a man might not be able to help being hammered down? ... No, if a man is down, a man like me, it's his fault. If he suffers, he's being punished. There's no evil in life itself. And do you know what? It's a Jewish point of view. You'll find it all over the Bible. God doesn't make mistakes. He's the department of weights and measures .... That's what Job's friends said to him. Take it from me, I know what I'm talking about. To you the whole thing is that I must deserve what I get. That leaves your hands clean and it's unnecessary for you to bother yourself. (*The Victim*, p. 132)

Allbee is once again attempting to fashion himself as a victim of Jewish actions and logic, and in playing such identity politics, to force Leventhal to accept responsibility for him by providing him with food and shelter and finding him a job. Leventhal counters with the game of identity politics himself, playing the obvious card: 'I don't see how you can talk that way. That's just talk. Millions of us have been killed. What about that?' (*The Victim*, p. 133). This time the question does possess a rhetorical force because Leventhal wanders off and Allbee makes no effort to restrain him.

It is certainly unclear how we should respond to this exchange: is Leventhal right to take on the mantle of Jewish suffering, or is his identification 'just talk' exactly like Allbee's? At what point can one talk about suffering and be authentic? And, to bring such problems back to the central concern of this chapter, to whom does one owe responsibility? Mankind, one's family, anyone one has wronged, or, one's people (whoever they are)?

Whatever one's perspective on this problem, the point to be made is that the answer to this question of identification and, hence, the moral right to pontificate about suffering, is not clear. To a large extent Leventhal is made to come to terms with his Jewish identity in the course of the novel. Although he feels racial slights deeply, he does not construct his identity in terms of his race and this is the only time that he counters Allbee's taunts with a racial memory.[8] As Michael Glenday suggests, Bellow appears to undermine rather than advertise Leventhal's Jewishness and it is foolhardy to read him as the novel's spokesman.[9] Plagued by guilt and unable to shake off his worst nightmare, Leventhal behaves shamefully in trying to get Allbee a job with Shifcart, who works in the film industry, for which Allbee is patently unsuited. Although Leventhal has earlier mentally chastised Harkavy for brushing aside Allbee's racial slurs as part of Leventhal's sense of 'imaginary persecution' (*The Victim*, p. 49), he willingly goes even further than Allbee in his acceptance of a Jewish business conspiracy in order to make life easier for himself. Harkavy asks:

> 'And where does he get the idea that Shifcart can help him?'
>
> Though he knew he was making a mistake, Leventhal said, and to some extent it was involuntary, 'I think he believes it's all a Jewish setup and Shifcart can pull strings for him ... Jews have influence with other Jews.'
>
> 'No!' Harkavy cried. 'No!' His hands flew to his head. 'And you're trying to do something for him? You're willing, regardless? Boy, do you know what this does to my opinion of you? Are you in your right mind?' (*The Victim*, p. 229)

Although he admits to himself that what he said was 'a real mistake' and that Leventhal is 'not even sure that Allbee means that' (*The Victim*, p. 230), the damage is done. Leventhal cannot claim the moral highground through the use of his racial identity.

Indeed, *The Victim* might even be read as privileging Allbee's sense of a common human bond as such sentiments are echoed by the aged journalist Schlossberg, an undoubtedly more devout Jew than Leventhal and a man who is decent enough to support his large family even though they are quite grown up. To his assembled Jewish friends in the restaurant – Harkavy, Leventhal, Goldstone, and Shifcart – Schlossberg makes a good humoured speech:

> We only know what it is to die because some people die and, if we make ourselves different from them, maybe we don't have to? Less than human is the other side of it. I'll come to it. So here is the whole thing, then. Good acting is what is exactly human. And if you say that I am a tough critic, you mean I have a high opinion of what is human. This is my whole idea. More than human, can you have any use for life? Less than human, you don't either. (*The Victim*, p. 121)

The speech serves as a *memento mori* to Leventhal and the reader, uniting the two pressing problems which beset Leventhal and emphasising to both that Leventhal is guilty of spending more energy on the one than the other. On the other hand, such a reaction lures the reader into the same sort of moral one-upmanship which the novel would seem to condemn because Leventhal, after all, is simply another weak human being who acts as we all might in such circumstances. Nevertheless, it is in the next chapter that Leventhal tries to browbeat Allbee with his identification with Jewish suffering, a move which makes him less likeable – and, presumably, less Jewish – than Schlossberg.[10]

Although Allbee makes numerous resolutions that he wants to change and start life afresh, it is unclear what the encounter between the two men has achieved at the end of the novel.[11] There is a touching scene with homosexual overtones when Allbee ends up stroking Leventhal's hair before the latter jerks his chair away in – presumably – embarrassment (*The Victim*, pp. 197–8). Reflecting on Allbee after he has gone, Leventhal pities the other man's situation and reflects that he, unlike Allbee, has 'got away with it', in terms of not really paying for his actions and also because his life has been relatively secure. When the two meet by accident in the final scene, their opening words reflect those at the beginning. When Allbee asks if he still looks the same, Leventhal notes that he still drinks, leaving the door open for Allbee to respond: 'Ever since I saw you. I've been wondering whether you'd mention that. You're true to form' (*The Victim*, p. 254). This may seem harmless enough, but any criticism levelled at his drinking by Leventhal was dismissed as racially motivated so that the exchange has wider implications. As the conversation draws to a close, Leventhal tries to find out just how successful Allbee has been. Allbee explains that he has obtained a 'middle-sized job' in radio advertising because he is 'not the type who runs things' (*The Victim*, p. 255). The novel concludes with Allbee running away from Leventhal – a neat reversal of the opening scene – and the latter's question, 'Wait a minute, what's your idea of who runs things?' (*The Victim*, p. 256), left hanging, leaving us unsure, like Leventhal, whether this was yet another of Allbee's racial slurs.

The Victim can be read as an extremely pessimistic novel, even though the characters are left in a state of well-being (Mary, Leventhal's wife, is heavily pregnant when they visit the opera). Although a number of moral problems occur in the course of the narrative, it appears to be the case that they go away rather than get solved. One is left – as in *Herzog* – caught between a sense of a benign notion of human frailty which forgives people their sins (in *Herzog*, 'potato love') and a feeling that justice requires a sterner, more abstract moral code (in *Herzog*, 'crisis ethics').[12] One might conclude that *The Victim* performs the task of pointing out the need for moral action and judgement, while leaving open the question of its achievement. Life should be sorted out by concepts more profound than 'moral luck', but is it?[13]

2.2 BELLOW'S *TO JERUSALEM AND BACK*

One should also point to the problematic conception of racial identity and identification in the novel; being Jewish does not necessarily tell us a great deal about Leventhal's moral status, nor does being descended from governor Winthrop tell us a great deal about Allbee's. Clearly, the same cannot be said of *To Jerusalem and Back*, the very existence of which depends upon the author's own

Jewish identity. It is perhaps a sense of the embarrassment surrounding this work which makes critics reluctant to write about it. In an article which made a forceful claim for Bellow's adherence to Judaic philosophy in his novels, L.H. Goldman made no mention of the book, despite its being his most obviously Jewish work.[14] In her study of Bellow's use of history in his novels, Judie Newman referred to the work only in passing, even though the defence of Israel in *To Jerusalem and Back* clearly depends upon a sense of history which, as Newman herself argues, is not obviously present in most of Bellow's novels.[15] The few comments made on the work are not generally complimentary.[16]

What exactly is wrong with *To Jerusalem and Back*? The problem is that it would seem to endorse the sort of easy moral positions which are condemned elsewhere in Bellow's work, and specifically in *The Victim*, where Leventhal is not allowed to use his race as an excuse nor to leave his own sense of being a victim unexamined. In other words, the interrelationship of identity politics is again pushed to the forefront.

Bellow appears to fall into all the traps which Edward Said and Christopher Hitchens have outlined via their conception of 'blaming the victims'.[17] Bellow attacks George Steiner's argument that 'Zionism was created by Jewish nationalists who drew their inspiration from Bismarck', claiming instead that such a political force stemmed from the fact that 'they alone, amongst the peoples of the earth, had not established a natural right to exist unquestioned in the lands of their birth', adding the jibe, 'This right is still clearly not granted them, not even in the liberal West'.[18] This assertion opens up a whole host of problems regarding the connection between race, ethics and nation, and the right to a land of one's birth. After all, the establishment of Israel involved the expulsion of Palestinians from the lands of their birth. Bellow does not deal with the question directly, but provides a number of defences of Israel's existence throughout his travelogue. The basic defence is that you cannot make an omelette without breaking eggs. Telling the story of his late friend and colleague at Chicago, Marshall Hodgson, a scholar of Islam, Bellow sets up a supposedly telling opposition between the romantic and unworldly Arabist and himself. Bellow tells the story of their heated disagreements:

> He told me, and was probably right, that I didn't *understand*. Though he once wrote me a letter saying that he wanted to join

> the Mississippi civil-rights marchers, he had no sympathy whatever with Zionism. After the war of 1967 he cried out, 'You have no business in Arab lands, you Jews!' ... Of course few people do understand the complexities of Arab history, and it made Marshall frantic when he saw a pattern of Western political ideas being imposed ignorantly on the Middle East. But he knew as little about Jews as I did about Arabs. Nation-states have seldom if ever been created without violence and injustice. Hodgson believed that the Jews had behaved as though the Arabs were an inferior, colonial sort of people and not the heirs of a great civilisation. Of course the Arabs had themselves come as conquerors, many centuries ago. But one didn't present such arguments to Marshall. The Arabs were his people. *He* failed to understand what Israel meant to Jews. (*To Jerusalem and Back*, p. 109)

I have cited this passage at length because it serves as a key point in the narrative of Bellow's justification and relates many points to other arguments elsewhere. The central tenet is repeated almost verbatim later: 'Nation-states have never come into existence peacefully and without injustices' (*To Jerusalem and Back*, p. 160). This, in essence, is what damns Hodgson, in all other respects an admirable figure who cares for his two daughters, tragically dying of a congenital disease of the nervous system. Otherwise the passage sets out a straight fight between the two men and – very important to Bellow's stance as a narrator in this book – illustrates the fact that he is impartial enough to respect, if not accept, other viewpoints.

However, such logic enables Bellow to avoid the question of whose land it really is which the exchange points out (unless one accepts that the actions of the Arab conquerors many centuries ago returns the guilt upon their ancestors, enabling others to dispossess them, the sort of argument given short shrift in *The Victim*). More upsetting, and downright immoral one might argue, is the apparent sympathy for Hodgson's anger at the misrepresentation of the Arabs as 'an inferior, colonial sort of people' without a civilisation, because that is exactly – and very deliberately – how Bellow portrays them in *To Jerusalem and Back* as a means of asserting his case. Bellow feels able to speak darkly of the problems of 'the mental character of the Muslim world' (*To Jerusalem and Back*, p. 46), despite the admission elsewhere that he knows nothing of such people; suggests that 'rational judgement' goes beyond the mere contingencies of Arab history (*To Jerusalem and Back*, p. 92); dismisses all Arab intellectuals as wedded to 'traditional religious patriotism' and so irrational and impossible to deal with (*To Jerusalem and Back*, p. 144), exactly the sort of casual racism which is portrayed as immoral elsewhere in his work. One of Bellow's chief aims, and a key plank in the anti-French thrust of the work (the French are seen to be the most naive of Western nations, easily taken in by plausible terrorists in their search for intellectual chic), is to contrast Israel as an outpost of European liberal values with the backward and barbarous Middle East surrounding it. According to Bellow, the Zionists who founded Israel came to a country which was nothing but 'a desert, a land of wandering populations and small stony farms and villages' (*To Jerusalem and Back*, p. 37) and transformed it into one of the great success stories amongst the new states created after World War II (*To Jerusalem and Back*, p. 159), exactly the sort of comment which one imagines would have offended Bellow's late colleague so badly.

Bellow is concerned that Israel appears as the West's bad conscience – a mirror image of Allbee's claims upon Leventhal. He portrays a series of ordinary Jews in Israel who, perhaps quite understandably, given their losses in wars, do not want to hear the even handed scruples of the West. Bellow is sparing in his use of the Holocaust as an ultimate moral argument, as he was in *The Victim*. The one reference argues that Hitler's genocide serves 'as a deliberate lesson or project in philosophical redefinition', forcing the civilised world to rethink their conception of humanity: 'you think you know what a human being is. We will show you what he is, and what you are. Look at our camps and crematoria and see if you can bring your hearts to care about these millions' (*To Jerusalem and Back*, p. 58). Elsewhere Bellow refers to the Israeli-Palestinian problem as 'a moral resort area' for the West because easy stances can be adopted, an analysis which resembles Derrida's description of apartheid as 'racism's last word'.[19] The difficult, tough and morally challenging stance is the acceptance of Israel's right to exist.

In attempting to persuade the reader of his case, Bellow makes an identification which hinges upon the ethical status of the victim, equating America and Israel as two misunderstood and badly treated nations. Picking up a magazine on the floor of his hotel room in Jerusalem, Bellow turns to an interview with Gore Vidal, which he reads with pleasure. Vidal's words start Bellow meditating on the nature of contemporary American experience: 'We have become the most pleonastic, bombastic people in the world and furthermore, a nation of liars.' But what masquerades as self-criticism is, in fact, self-justification: 'I add to this that no people has ever had such a passion for self-criticism. We accuse ourselves of everything, are forever under horrible indictments, on trial, and raving out the most improbable confessions. And all for the world's consumption' (*To Jerusalem and Back*, p. 77). So that is what is wrong. This aspect of Bellow's account was too much for Irving Howe who failed to see how a country which bombed Vietnam to pieces could be cast as the innocent abroad in nasty world politics (*To Jerusalem and Back* has a bitterly comic moment when Bellow, without apparent irony, refers to Kissenger's 'Byzantine intrigue' [*To Jerusalem and Back*, p. 101] being beyond him). Howe was similarly unimpressed with Bellow's representation of the Arab world.[20]

2.3 CONCLUSION

To Jerusalem and Back attempts to establish a clear opposition between the true and false victims and their respective champions; on the one side stand the Arab world and France (who symbolise the pusillanimous West, afraid to delve into the limits of the liberties they enjoy), and against them Israel and the United States of America. What is difficult to accept about the book is not simply its shoddy scholarship and selective use of detail by one who should know better (it is, after all, a personal account), but that when confronted by the question of the nation, the complex ethical world Bellow establishes in his novels appears to crumble into simple choices. Bellow does not deal with his friend, Hodgson's, objections but rhetorically fashions himself as a hard-headed realist who can love the man, sympathise with the politics, but feel satisfied that his own case is far superior (so much for the innocent abroad). In this way he trumps Forster's symbolic move of opposing nations and individuals. Indeed, Bellow's stance as the enlightened liberal who is simultaneously a friend of Israel and so versed in the limits of the West's conceptions of tolerance, bears a striking resemblance to that of Solzhenitsin's narrator in *The Gulag Archipelago*. Solzhenitsin represents himself as someone who can tell us the truth about Russian communism because he once believed and so is able to share the anxiety of his addressee who is assumed to be gradually more horrified as he or she is persuaded by the case the author makes. But then again, part of Solzhenitsin's success depends upon the fact that he did suffer the horrors of the Gulag. The Saul Bellow of *To Jerusalem and Back* appears to want to pose as a victim by dint of his race, without actually having borne the marks of experience, a position he carefully refused to validate in the earlier novel.

To Jerusalem and Back, despite its lively depictions of a multitude of Jews, prominent and otherwise, is a myopic book which avoids the ethical complexities of *The Victim*. Whereas the earlier novel confronted the reader with the problem of identifying the victim before one could even determine how far moral responsibility travelled, the latter makes such choices as easy as possible, despite the attempts to disguise this simplification (which only makes matters worse). If one work gestures in the direction of inclusiveness, the other works in terms of exclusive categories. In *The Victim*, people can appear in two roles, metaphorically stand in two places at once; in *To Jerusalem and Back*, problems are solved by removing vast hordes of people from the map, literally and metaphorically. It seems that when confronted with the problem of the nation and the ethical demands it makes upon us, Bellow is as much in need of the sort of charity Schlossberg advocates in *The Victim* as the people he would appear to deny are part of a common humanity he shares in *To Jerusalem and Back*. It's never simply a question of my country right or wrong.

Notes

1. E. M. Forster, 'What I Believe', in *Two Cheers for Democracy* (London: Arnold, 1951) 77–85; 78. My thanks to Clive Meachen for advice on this essay.
2. Charles King, 'Fellow-feelings' (review of David Miller, *On Nationality* [Oxford: Clarendon Press, 1996]) *Times Literary Supplement*, 10 May 1996, 4–5.
3. Cited in Malcolm Bradbury, *Saul Bellow* (London: Methuen, 1982) 15.
4. Michael K. Glenday, *Saul Bellow and the Decline of Humanism* (New York: St Martin's Press, 1990) 2; Saul Bellow, 'Foreword', in Alan Bloom, *The Closing of the American Mind: How Higher Education Has Failed Democracy and Impoverished the Souls of Today's Students* (New York: Penguin, 1988, rpt. of 1987) 11–18; 18.
5. Daniel Fuchs, *Saul Bellow: Vision and Revision* (Durham, NC: Duke University Press, 1984) 25, 34–6.

6. Tony Tanner, *Saul Bellow* (Edinburgh: Oliver and Boyd, 1965) 27.
7. Saul Bellow, *The Victim* (New York: Signet, 1965, rpt. of 1947) 13. All subsequent references to this edition in parentheses.
8. As Maxwell Geismar argues, Allbee might be said to be more Jewish than Leventhal in terms of his knowledge of Judaism; 'Saul Bellow: Novelist of the Intellectuals', in Irving Malin, ed., *Saul Bellow and the Critics* (New York University Press, 1967) 10–24; 16.
9. Glenday, *Saul Bellow and the Decline of Humanism*, 30. See also Ralph Freedman, 'Saul Bellow: The Illusion of Environment', in Malin, ed., *Saul Bellow and the Critics*, 51–68; 57.
10. Glenday describes Leventhal as the least likeable of Bellow's heroes; *Saul Bellow and the Decline of Humanism*, 27. For the opposite case, see Fuchs, *Saul Bellow: Vision and Revision*, 46–8.
11. See Glenday, *Saul Bellow and the Decline of Humanism*, 34.
12. See Gabriel Josipovici, '*Herzog*: Freedom and Wit', in *The World and the Book: A Study of Modern Fiction* (London: Macmillan, 1971), Ch. 9.
13. Tanner, *Saul Bellow*, 31.
14. L. H. Goldman, 'Saul Bellow and the Philosophy of Judaism', *Studies in the Literary Imagination* 17, 2 (1984) 81–96.
15. Judie Newman, *Saul Bellow and History* (London: Macmillan, 1984).
16. See Bradbury, *Saul Bellow*, 102; Newman, *Saul Bellow and History*, 10; Irving Howe, 'Review of *To Jerusalem and Back*', *New York Times Book Review*, 17 October 1976, 1–2. An exception is Paul Johnson, 'The Issue of Israel', *Times Literary Supplement*, 3 December, 1976, 1509.
17. Edward W. Said and Christopher Hitchens, eds, *Blaming the Victims: Spurious Scholarship and the Palestinian Question* (London: Verso, 1988).
18. Saul Bellow, *To Jerusalem and Back* (Harmondsworth: Penguin, 1978, rpt. of 1976) 26. All subsequent references to this edition in parentheses.
19. Jacques Derrida, 'Racism's Last Word', in Henry Louis Gates, Jr, ed., *'Race', Writing and Difference* (University of Chicago Press, 1986) 329–38.
20. Howe, 'Review', 2.

3
Have You Reread Levinas Lately? Transformations of the Face in Post-Holocaust Fiction

Norman Ravvin

Not unlike handsome cities razed to rubble by war, our contemporary intellectual traditions undergo repeated attack and burial. Schools of thought spread their influence to a variety of fields and then are dismissed as outmoded; prophets are uncovered then deposed; even particularly charged words – once on everyone's lips and in book-title after book-title – are condemned to a long afterlife as journalistic clichés. In the context of this seemingly unflagging embrace of abandonment and change, consider the name, the work, the face of Emmanuel Levinas. As I write, and possibly still as you read, Levinas is a kind of prophet. Through his interrogation of the Western philosophical tradition he has become the source of one of the key paradigm shifts of postmodern culture: a return to ethics, a remaking of our tradition in the direction of the other. In his words, the 'being of animals is a struggle for life. A struggle for life without ethics. It is a question of might .... However, with the appearance of the human – and this is my entire philosophy – there is something more important than my life, and that is the life of the other.'[1]

But what of Levinas had we heard, was present though unnoticed even before we knew of him or read the work of his many interlocutors? What of Levinas will remain, taking its rightful place at the centre of contemporary thought? And what will be forgotten, evaded, buried for its very provocation and difficulty? The first of these questions may be the easiest to answer. French philosophers and the Parisian avant-garde of the 1960s were transfixed by

Levinasian ideas. We find, in the most unlikely places, a language of responsibility, of an ethical stance of submission before the other. In Jean-Luc Godard's 1966 political farce *Made in USA*, the film's Bogart-like female sleuth makes the following declaration as the camera presents her left and right profile, and then shows her, in the words of Godard's scenario, 'full-face': 'Whatever I do I can't escape my responsibility towards another person. My silence acts on him, just as my words do. My going away worries him as much as my presence. My indifference may be as fatal to him as my interference. My sometimes thoughtless concern is deadly to him.'[2]

It may be that the apparent echoes of Levinas in this speech are distilled through Godard's familiarity with Jean-Paul Sartre, who acknowledged that he 'was introduced to phenomenology by Levinas'.[3] Sartre's notion of a *littérature engagée* – though it does not make use of Levinas's key motif of the face – presents a dynamic of mutual responsibility and action that places writers and readers in an ethical relationship: 'You are perfectly free to leave that book on the table. But if you open it you assume responsibility for it.'[4] In Sartre's last words – in the 1980 interviews he gave on his legacy, influences, and his understanding of an irreducible 'primary kinship' between men and women – he speaks without acknowledging it in a Levinasian voice:

> [By] ethics I mean that every consciousness ... has a dimension ... the dimension of obligation. 'Obligation' is a poor word.... By obligation I mean that at every moment that I am conscious of anything or do anything, there exists a kind of requisition ... [that] results in the fact that the action I want to perform includes a kind of inner constraint.... [E]verything that takes place for a consciousness at any given moment is necessarily linked to, and often is even engendered by, the presence of another.[5]

Here Sartre echoes the language that Levinas himself used to explain his outlook on numerous occasions, including an interview he gave in 1981. Summing up the 'fundamental difference' between his own work and Martin Heidegger's philosophy, Levinas explains his view of 'ethical thought':

> I am defined as a subjectivity, as a singular person, as an 'I', precisely because I am exposed to the other. It is my inescapable and incontrovertible answerability to the other that makes me an

> individual 'I'.... I become a responsible or ethical 'I' to the extent that I agree to depose or dethrone myself – to abdicate my position of centrality – in favour of the vulnerable other.[6]

3.1 THE FORMATION OF THE ETHICAL BOND

In the interviews collected under the title *Hope Now*, Sartre, like Levinas, searches for what might be called an irreducible shared experience or aspect of human relationship, on which one might 'work toward society'. Sartre settles on birth as this irreducible experience, arguing that for 'every person birth is to such a degree the same phenomenon as it is for his neighbour'.[7] For Levinas, a similar ethical bond is formed through the act of facing another. Susan Handelman describes the implications of Levinas's conception of the face: 'In Levinas, facing is being confronted with, turned towards, facing up to, being judged and called to by the other. Facing is a disruption of that free autonomous self which through its reasoning and consciousness thinks it can construct the world out of itself, or know the world from itself.'[8] In the words of another commentator, 'the self's responsibility to the other who faces is immediate, originary, and irreducible'.[9]

So it may be that Levinas's language – if not an understanding of its unique context rooted in phenomenology and the Talmud – has been available to us much longer than we have thought. But still, we must answer a more difficult question: What of Levinas will remain, taking its rightful place at the centre of postwar thought? Although attention to Levinas's consideration of Jewish texts and history increases apace, it is the philosophical texts that have attained for him a central, canonical status. His re-reading of the philosophical tradition – against the grain – has changed the way philosophers, literary theorists and historians view the work of Hegel, Husserl, Heidegger, Bergson and Rosenzweig, among others. This influence is not limited to the content of Levinas's interpretations, but extends to his style as well. Jacques Derrida has characterised one of the most remarkable aspects of Levinas's oeuvre as its desire for a 'language ... purified of all rhetoric', a language which, rather than argue and conceptualise, moves 'with the infinite insistence of waves on a beach: return and repetition, always, of the same wave against the same shore, in which, however, as each return recapitulates itself, it also infinitely renews and enriches itself'. Such a style, according to Derrida, characterizes Levinas's *Totality and Infinity* as 'a work of art and not a treatise'.[10] As Levinas's influence on the form and aim of Derridean deconstruction has been recognised, he has come to be seen by some as a grandfatherly practitioner of postmodernity's more difficult and radical methods of reading. In the words of a reviewer in the *New York Review of Books*, he is a deconstructor who 'doesn't make you anxious about your children'.[11]

But it may be exactly such a comfortable assimilation of Levinas's work by a mainstream audience that should worry his dedicated readers and anyone committed to thinking in an age that Levinas described as being 'dominated by the presentiment and the memory of the Nazi horror'.[12] Would it not be a grave failure, an ironic and ultimately counter-ethical development, if Levinas's oeuvre simply led to *more of the same*: to a more thorough analysis of Heidegger's ontology; to a reassertion of 'Western philosophy's very decision, since Plato, to consider itself as science'; to a form of deconstruction deemed 'safe,' even suitable for children?[13] This would be a curious legacy for a thinker who was motivated to write against notions of God, morality, and the individual's place in society which sought solace in childish complacency, who, in a piece called 'Loving the Torah more than God' termed suffering and the absence of a beneficial interventionist God an appeal 'to the full maturity of an entirely responsible' individual. A God who hides his face is said to be neither 'a theological abstraction or a poetic image. It is the moment in which the just individual can find no help. No institution will protect him. The consolation of divine presence to be found in infantile religious feeling is equally denied him, and the individual can prevail only through his conscience, which necessarily involves suffering'.[14]

Using 'Loving the Torah more than God' as a starting point, we can begin to examine more directly what of Levinas's work may be evaded and forgotten due to its sheer originality and provocation. This short essay was composed in 1955 for radio broadcast but did not become widely known among English-speaking readers until 1979 when the journal *Judaism* published Richard Sugarman's translation and commentary on it; in 1990 a different translation was included in the collection entitled *Difficult Freedom: Essays on Judaism*. In 'Loving the Torah more than God' Levinas focuses on a text he has 'just read' entitled 'Yossel, son of Yossel Rakover from Tarnopol, speaks to God'. Though this 'text presents itself as a document written during the final hours of the Warsaw Ghetto resistance,' Levinas recognises that it is fiction – 'both beautiful and true, true as only fiction can be'.[15] His discussion focuses on the narrative's use of a notion central to both mystical and liturgical considerations of Jewish catastrophe – the idea of *histeres-ponim*, the veiling of God's face. 'What more, oh, what more must transpire', Yossel Rakover implores, 'in order for You to reveal Your face again to the world?'[16] We can assume that Levinas's fascination with this text derives not only from his respect for the power of its narrative voice, or from its expression of a key Kabbalistic belief in the withdrawal of the divine from creation, but also from the uncanny way it echoes his own attempts to thematise fundamental ethical issues.

In a 1991 review of *Difficult Freedom* Jill Robbins points to other important, though implicit concerns, which are inscribed in the collection that includes 'Loving the Torah more than God':

> The overall project of *Difficult Freedom*, and this would extend to all of the confessional writings, is to render explicit what Levinas calls 'the hidden resources' of the Judaic tradition. These resources are hidden, if you will, because they have been for the most part covered up by the negative and privative determinations of the Judaic within the dominant (Greco)-Christian conceptuality. Levinas is attentive to those aspects of Judaism that appear unintelligible or lacking within the dominant conceptuality of the West. The 'hiddenness' of Judaism has to do with the way in which its central achievements – the law and the talmud – become obscured when they are viewed through the Greco-Christian filter.[17]

Robbins points to the difficulty in uncovering the 'hidden' Judaic resources in Levinas's philosophical writings, and implicitly suggests that the richest reading of his ethics might come from a consideration of what links these two aspects of his work. The cry of Yossel Rakover to an empty heavens introduces the notion of a 'radical aloneness', the absence of the divine that places human responsibility at the centre of all existential considerations. In Robbins's words, which are in line with Levinas's view, the Nazis' 'violation of the ethical, exemplified by murder ... brings the ethical, the infinite alterity of the other, into view'.[18] A 'fully mature' theology then, is based on *histeres-ponim*, on the veiling of God's face, which forces us to view the individual's responsibility toward the other – a 'triumph ... in his own conscience' – as a source of world-preserving power.[19] It is in this idea, Robbins adds, of a person

> capable of responding, defined by response-ability, that Levinas's confessional writings and his philosophical works seem especially close. What does this proximity say about the relation between the philosophical and the non-philosophical works? Levinas keeps the two apart as the difference between phenomenological evidence and adhesion to an exegetical tradition.... Suffice it to remark that the distinction between the philosophical and the confessional works is not absolute, because of the important way in which Levinas mobilizes the nonphilosophical – empiricism, God, Judaic theology – *in* his philosophy, as a challenge to the dominance of the Same, and as a certain escape from the ontotheological tradition.[20]

Here I should sketch in the curious history of the narrative presented as the appeal of Yossel, son of Yossel, which had so powerful an effect on Levinas some ten years after he himself was released from a German prison camp following the liberation of France. Written in Yiddish in 1946 by Zvi Kolitz, 'Yossel, son of Yossel' first appeared in the Argentinean newspaper *Di Yiddishe Tsaytung* (*El Diario Israelita*); an English translation appeared in New York in 1947. Meanwhile, the Yiddish text found its way to Israel, where, in 1953, a prestigious Yiddish journal published it – not, however, as a story, but as a 'testament' said to have been found in a bottle.[21] In its Israeli appearance the authorship of the narrative was not attributed to Kolitz, but instead to a fantastic-historical figure by the name of Yossel Rakover who was brought to life through a bibliographical error.[22] The story's strange reception – as fact then fiction, as document as well as fabulation – seems to have been recognised by the time Levinas encountered it (he cites as his source *La terre retrouvée*, a Parisian Zionist journal).[23] But there are many ways in which the text itself, as well as its reception, helps us address the questions concerning the future of Levinas's work posed at the outset of my discussion.

Toward the end of Yossel Rakover's appeal, Kolitz depicts his fictional ghetto fighter as he takes account of what will most likely be his final resting place:

> I am lying on the floor as I write these lines, and around me – my dead comrades. I look into their faces, and it seems to me that a quiet but mocking irony animates them, as if they were saying to me, 'A little patience, you foolish man, another few minutes and everything will become clear to you, too.' This irony particularly cries out from the face of the small boy lying next to my right hand, as if he were asleep.[24]

Here, Kolitz employs a response destined to become central to Holocaust literature: the meditation upon the faces of the dead in order to conjure a form of dialogue and recovered intimacy in which the face acts as a guiding symbol for a reinvigorated bond. By focusing on the face of a haunting figure, writers develop a commitment toward the absent other that supports an ethic of humane community as a counter to the Nazi world view. We find in this development a dual urge: to both commemorate the victims of the Nazis and to point toward a relationship with the memory of the dead that will in some way reinvigorate the living. In texts that follow this model so much depends upon the 'odd configuration of lines that make up the human face'.[25]

In Holocaust writing, the first project motivated by the urge to meditate on the faces of the dead was the composition of *Yizkor Bicher*, or Memorial Books. These collections of survivors' descriptions of local customs and individuals included photographs of the inhabitants of the town or city to which a volume was dedicated. Appearing in the years after the war, in a combination of languages including Yiddish, Hebrew, and English, *Yizkor Bicher* were 'almost always printed in editions of less than a thousand; their audience is the community of survivors and emigrés from the town itself. Many readers would know the author of a piece personally. The connection, therefore, between the teller and the audience is immediate'.[26] In addition to this uncommon relation between reader and text, a remarkable inclusiveness is nurtured within the texts themselves:

> There is a generosity at work ... which is commensurate with the scope of the catastrophe. It seems that those people who worked together on the books recognized that every religious and political faction, every individual from the town rabbi to the assimilationist lawyer to the ragtag water carrier, had been an essential part of the town's genius. 'Every shtetl had its

madman,' reads one account. 'Our town was small, so our *meshugener* was only half-crazy.'[27]

Yizkor Bicher represent the first wave of Holocaust writing, and their tendency to juxtapose photographs of faces with memoir creates not only a commemorative text but a form of contact, of intimacy with vanished friends, family, or forebears, as well as with the everyday aspect of prewar European Jewish life. In *Jewish Mlave*, the Memorial Book dedicated to the Polish town where my mother's family lived, I have searched for faces of relatives in vain and must make do with a meditation on the variety of faces that appear – secular-seeming and religious, photographed for the yearbook of a workers' union, for a Zionist gathering or a school outing. Somehow, the presence of these unfamiliar faces offers a mysterious and melancholy connection with lost Mlave; a sentimental urge tells me that I 'know' these people, that in some of their faces I can see what I take to be a family resemblance, a point of intimacy.

As the energy (and numbers of living survivors) dedicated to composing *Yizkor Bicher* fell off, works that juxtaposed photographs and memoir fell out of fashion. With the exception of writing by survivors, it became increasingly common for commentators on the Holocaust to call for a prohibition against the representation of the victims of the Nazis in any form other than that using the language of religious commemoration or prayer. In spite of the difficulties raised by critics with regard to the limits of representing the Holocaust, many novelists of the postwar generation have applied a strategy like that used by Kolitz in his fictional narrative, meditating on the faces of the dead in order to build a structure of symbol and motif suggestive of the importance of ethical relationships. Among the writers who follow this tradition, Saul Bellow's work is particularly rich in situations and patterns in which the motif of the face, or the act of facing, appear as guiding symbols of an ethical bond. In the 1970 novel *Mr Sammler's Planet* Bellow's protagonist condemns any project that is based on a relationship between 'Me and the Universe'. In place of such reductive schemes Mr Sammler offers a relational view of human life evocative of Levinas's work. Sammler's 'personal idea was one of the human being conditioned by other human beings, and knowing that present arrangements were not *sub specie aeternitatis*, the truth, but that one should be satisfied with such truth as one could get by approximation. Trying to live with a civil heart. With disinterested charity. With a sense of the mystic potency of humankind'.[28]

It is the subordination of the self and an attention to the needs of others in Bellow's work that assure a humane culture. In an effort to explain his outlook Mr Sammler relies for his guiding image on a passage from *War and Peace*, which affirms the importance of the face and the power of the look in his view of an ethical relationship:

> 'There is a scene in *War and Peace* I sometimes think about', said Sammler. 'The French General Davoust, who was very cruel, who was said, I think, to have torn out a man's whiskers by the roots, was sending people to the firing squad in Moscow, but when Pierre Bezhukov came up to him they looked into each other's eyes. A human look was exchanged, and Pierre was spared. Tolstoy says you don't kill another human being with whom you have exchanged such a look.'[29]

In his biographical piece, 'Signature', Levinas refers to a similar passage in Tolstoy's novel: 'In a feeling of humanity stretched to the extreme, the crowd in *War and Peace* to which Count Rostopchin delivered up Vereshchagin hesitates to do violence before his face, which reddens and turns pale....'[30]

Though the work of Philip Roth differs in many ways from Bellow's, Roth shares a heightened interest in face-to-face encounters, and has made them central to his literary project. One of his earlier meditations on the 'odd configuration of lines that make up the human face' appears in an essay subtitled 'Looking at Kafka':

> I am looking, as I write of Kafka, at the photograph taken of him at the age of forty (my age) – it is 1924, as sweet and hopeful a year as he may ever have known as a man, and the year of his death. His face is sharp and skeletal, a burrower's face: pronounced cheekbones made even more conspicuous by the absence of sideburns; the ears shaped and angled on his head like angel wings; an intense, creaturely gaze of startled composure – enormous fears, enormous control; a black towel of Levantine hair pulled close around the skull the only sensuous feature; there is a familiar Jewish flare in the bridge of the nose, the nose itself is long and weighted slightly at the tip – the nose of half the Jewish boys who were my friends in high school. Skulls chiseled like this one were shoveled by the thousands

> from the ovens; had he lived, his would have been among them, along with the skulls of his three younger sisters.[31]

Here Roth creates an intimate connection with Kafka's face – with its expression and the prewar milieu that nurtured it. Engaging in what Michael André Bernstein has termed 'sideshadowing', he considers the historical possibilities that might have, but did not come to pass;[32] in this case, Franz Kafka's deportation along with his three sisters to Teresienstadt on the way to the death camps. Following this meditation Roth presents a fictional scenario in which a living Kafka – another sideshadowed possibility – is found after the war teaching Hebrew School in Newark. Similarly, in the novella *The Prague Orgy* and in *The Ghost Writer*, Roth imagines the fantastic reappearance of Bruno Schulz and Anne Frank, each in different ways 'alive' in postwar America. Such conjurings in Roth's oeuvre suggest a yearning not only to come face to face with the subjects of his fascination, but an urge to reinvest our world with the spirit of their writing, its particularity and outlook.

The face of Anne Frank may be the most recognisable, the most richly symbolic countenance among the victims of Nazi Germany. Since shortly after the war, her face has been traded as a kind of symbolic capital, fought over by commentators who hold different views of the Holocaust. Anne's father, who edited the first influential edition of the diary, insisted that it was 'not a Jewish book', and devoted much of his life to 'memorializing Anne by interpreting the "message" of her diary in affirmative, universalist terms'.[33] In editing the diary, Frank was inclined to remove almost all the revealing 'observations about Jews and Jewishness',[34] and through his labour, began the transformation of his daughter's face, which is an ongoing after-effect of the diary's success. The writers of the immensely successful Broadway play, *The Diary of Anne Frank*, followed Frank's lead, as did the makers of the Hollywood film based on the play. These two works – as celebrated in their time as *Schindler's List* has been in ours – helped create the image of Anne as an Americanised character who proved palatable and sympathetic to postwar US audiences. They contributed as well to Anne Frank's status as an icon of universal tolerance, a saintly martyr whose particular character was down-played in favour of an idealism designed to transcend the actuality of the camps. This transformation, of course, precludes any careful viewing of photographs of the victims of Belsen, where Anne and her sister died. When we do look, if we do, at such images, we no longer recognise faces, but an anonymous mass, literally a corpus of bodies stripped of their singularity. It is clear that the postwar fascination with the fictional Anne, with the reassuring, smiling face of an icon, has enabled us to bypass the 'demand' of her face, and defused any challenge to the 'happy spontaneity of the self'.[35] We proceed into the future, our world comfortingly intact. Possibly the most telling evidence of the transformation of Anne Frank's face from a troubling reminder of a vicious past into an icon of saintly and youthful stoicism is its recent appearance in an advertising montage for Microsoft.

It is Roth's attentiveness to what he calls 'the real Anne', to her voice conveyed through the diary, and to her face captured in childhood photographs, that motivates his 1979 novel *The Ghost Writer*. Interestingly, reviewers tended to minimise the importance of the novel's treatment of the Holocaust, concentrating instead on Roth's use of elements of the *Bildungsroman* and *roman à clef*. *The Ghost Writer* is set in 1956 – the year *The Diary of Anne Frank* played on Broadway. Roth's protagonist, Nathan Zuckerman, encounters, upon visiting a writer he admires, a woman whom he believes bears a striking resemblance to Anne Frank. During a sleepless night in his host's study, Zuckerman pens a fiction called 'Femme Fatale' whose premise is that Amy Bellette, the young woman compiling the famous writer's manuscripts, is actually Anne Frank. Having survived the war, she lives under an assumed name as one of the many 'displaced persons' building a new life in America. It is through Zuckerman's fiction that Roth draws our attention to the particularities of Anne's voice and face, to the manner in which they have been transformed as the diary has become one of the archetypal texts of Holocaust literature. Roth highlights these particularities by way of a detailed description of the face of the woman called Amy Bellette, her

> eyes pale – gray or green – and with a high prominent oval forehead that looked like Shakespeare's ... it was the drama of that face, combined with the softness and intelligence in her large pale eyes, that rendered all other physical attributes ... blurry and inconsequential. Admittedly, the rich calm of those eyes would have been enough to make me wilt with shyness, but that I couldn't return her gaze directly had also to do with this unharmonious relation between body and skull, and its implication, to

> me, of some early misfortune, of something vital lost or beaten down .... [36]

In his depiction of Zuckerman's encounter with what he believes may be the face of the most famous victim of the Nazis, Roth challenges influential responses that have transformed Anne Frank into an icon of universal suffering, the bearer of a visage devoid not only of Jewish character but of any singularity. He provokes, as well, a recognition of what there was in Anne Frank's gaze that distinguished it. The imperative of uncovering such distinguishing features is not unlike Levinas's demand that we confront, turn towards, face up to the other. Zuckerman is drawn to the face he encounters, yet he is unable to return its gaze. Here Roth depicts his protagonist in confrontation with what Levinas has called 'countenance':

> We meet this countenance in the look of the other, and it doesn't declare itself: but behind it there is the weakness .... I would even say it's naked. There is a nudity revealed ... there is the moment in the human face which is the most naked and exposed state of human experience ... together with this there is also the command, or the imperative: do not leave me in solitude.[37]

3.2 THE INFLUENCE OF LEVINASIAN IDEAS

Readings of literature in English that make use of Levinasian ideas are still somewhat rare, a fact that seems most strange in the context of Holocaust writing, considering Levinas's own committed response to the ethical demands of thinking through the repercussions of Nazi behaviour for postwar life. The inhibitions that have led to the rarity of such 'ethical' readings of literature may in part be caused by a number of difficult issues raised by our response to Levinas's oeuvre. By addressing these issues I hope to answer more directly the difficult question I raised at the outset of this chapter. What of Levinas's writing may be evaded and forgotten because of its very provocative nature?

Although Levinas studies have been influential in a broad range of disciplines, his philosophical handlers remain somewhat testy about the manner in which he is imported into literary and art criticism, psychology and biblical studies. The demand among interpreters of the phenomenological tradition is that *any* aspect of Levinas's thought – especially a motif as central as the face – must be applied with a healthy share of disciplinary rigour. Initial resistance among philosophers may be based, too, on Levinas's own statements about the care with which he separated his philosophical writings from what he called his 'confessional' writings: 'I always make a clear distinction, in what I write, between philosophical and confessional texts. I do not deny that they may ultimately have a common source of inspiration. I simply state that it is necessary to draw a line of demarcation between them as distinct methods of exegesis, as separate languages.'[38] The cultivation of what might be called The Two Levinases was supported until recently by the overwhelming volume (and difficulty for the non-specialist) of Levinas's philosophical work, contrasted with the rarity with which the 'confessional' writings were translated and collected. 'Loving the Torah More than God' proved to be a kind of breakthrough text in this regard; based on the attention it received, interested readers and potential translators followed its trail to the other 'confessional' writings, where they found that in spite of the author's insistence on a careful distinction between his philosophical and more essayistic works, there was in fact only one Levinas whose fundamental motivations, structures of thought, and even a characteristic tone and style, migrated between both types of texts. In her 1991 review of *Difficult Freedom* Jill Robbins points to the growing sense that a separation of the two aspects of Levinas's work was not tenable, or even desirable. Having pointed to the way *Difficult Freedom* renders 'explicit "the hidden resources"' of Judaism, those 'aspects of Judaism that appear unintelligible or lacking within the dominant conceptuality of the West', she goes on to outline how such concerns are inextricably bound to the problems of ethics raised in Levinas's philosophical studies.[39] Referring to an essay on Franz Rosenzweig included in *Difficult Freedom*, she argues that

> Levinas restores to religion its originary sense of ethics (and here one may recall the definition of religion proposed in *Totality and Infinity*, 'the bond that is established between the same and the other without constituting a totality'). In 'A Religion for Adults', we read: 'For Judaism, the world becomes intelligible before a human face .... My neighbour's face has an alterity which is not allergic but opens up the beyond.'[40]

Robbins's ability to shuttle between *Totality and Infinity* and the radio broadcasts Levinas made for the French programme *Écoute Israël* points to the gains that can be made in understanding his philosophy through an acknowledgment (rather than an evasion) of its relationship to Jewish sources.

A further resistance to making use of Levinas's ethical works to discuss literary texts is based on his own assertions in both the philosophical and 'confessional' writings that there can be no 'access to the ethical' in a work of art, since a mere representation of the face-to-face encounter can not reproduce the 'ethical language relation' found in a 'vocative or imperative discourse, face to face'.[41] Robbins points to Levinas's categorical assertions in *Totality and Infinity* and in the 1948 essay 'La réalité et son ombre' that 'to have an image of the face, to *image* a face, is to turn it into a caricature, frozen, petrified, a mask'.[42] Further, Levinas insists that in the effort to portray an interhuman relationship 'art constitutes, in a world of initiative and responsibility, a dimension of evasion'.[43] These remarks have been given great weight (somewhat naïvely, I would argue) and have helped preserve the splendid isolation of Levinas's philosophical works from a more interdisciplinary use. Philosophers, who rarely show interest in Mosaic law, point to the way Levinas's displeasure with artistic renderings of the face echoes the second commandment: 'Thou shalt not make unto thee a graven image, nor any manner of likeness, of any thing that is in the heaven above, or that is in the earth beneath' (Exodus 20.4). By pointing to these views, commentators focus on a Jewish aspect of Levinas's work in order to further contain the penetration of the philosophical by extra-disciplinary influences. One might point to this as an excellent example of the unintelligibility of Jewish thought when it is applied in the shadow of the 'dominant conceptuality of the West'; the biblical injunction against graven images is interpreted on a literal and normative level, without sensitivity to the ambiguities of the interpretive context that surrounds it.

Clearly we must think beyond the apparently literal, one might say orthodox use of such prohibitions by a writer whose thought is notable for its heterodoxy and radical provocation in the face of normative notions of morality. It may be that Levinas has contributed to a certain unintelligibility in his own work by echoing biblical injunctions (which require an attendant commentary for those of us unschooled in Talmud) as well as by taking, on certain occasions, such a hard line against the ethical possibilities of artistic works. As more of Levinas's 'confessional' pieces reappear in print and in translation, we recognise a more ambiguous and enabling attitude toward ethical readings of literary works. Included in a recent collection entitled *Proper Names* (1996) is a stunning portrait of the work of the nobel-winning novelist and story writer S.Y. Agnon (the French original appeared in 1973). Here Levinas rejects the notion – suggested by a literal reading of the second commandment – that literary language is ethically beyond the pale. Agnon, he argues, makes masterful use of *melitsah* – a biblical phrase whose literary flavour lends it an ambiguous and enigmatic power – to achieve a 'rhetorical effect' in his fiction.[44] In his reading of Agnon's story collection *The Fire and the Wood* Levinas points to the writer's use of faces and expressions to depict not only relationships among the living but the possibility of a reciprocity 'between the dead and the living'.[45] Most relevant for our discussion is Levinas's contention that in Agnon we find a writer venturing 'deliberately out beyond language' to create a 'writing as interrogation. Interrogation as relationship.'[46] Through such writing Agnon is said to develop not only a dialogue among the living but one with 'buried voices, dead forms', which, according to Levinas, supports a 'community of those human beings who are dedicated to the other'.[47]

In two further essays – 'Paul Celan: From Being to the Other' (1972) and 'Max Picard and the Face' (1966) – Levinas pursues the ethical possibilities inherent in literary work. In the Celan piece he admits that he must 'contend' with the poet's remark: 'I cannot see any basic difference between a handshake and a poem.' From this Levinas recognises that for Celan, a poem is an 'interjection, a form of expression ... a sign to one's neighbour'.[48] Here, of course, is language that parallels Levinas's notion of the ethical demand of the face as 'an irreducible means of access ... a demand ... a hand in search of recompense, an open hand'.[49] In a notably unguarded moment, Levinas confirms the attendant ethical demand of Celan's poetry: for Celan 'the poem is situated ... at the moment of pure touching, pure contact, grasping, squeezing – which is, perhaps, a way of giving, right up to and including the hand that gives. A language of proximity ... [of] responsibility for the neighbour.'[50] Contrary to the tone of prohibitive commandment found in other contexts, Levinas waxes rhapsodic about the way literature conveys such 'proximity,' such 'pure contact'. The poem, he adds, can be said to cause 'the interruption in the playful order of the beautiful and the play of concepts, and the *play of the world*; interrogation of the Other, a seeking for the Other. A seeking, dedicating itself to the other in the form of the poem.'[51]

There is one further passage in the essay on Max Picard – a writer of cultural philosophy and art criticism with a particularly idiosyncratic and poetic style – that helps us define a kind of codex for an ethical response to artistic work. Levinas cites Picard as an exemplary practitioner of work bent on '*deciphering the universe from these fundamental images and metaphors*, human faces; those we encounter in everyday life; those which, in their contact with eternity, we improperly call death masks; those which, having become portraits, observe us from the walls of museums'.[52]

A Levinasian criticism, then, with its fundamental images and metaphors, its dedication to a dialogue with the faces of both the living and the dead, as well as its complex sources drawn from continental philosophy and Jewish ethics, has yet to fully take shape. It may, however, prove best suited to deciphering the intractable questions asked by literature that strives to represent our post-Holocaust universe. How challenging this new form of reading, and how high the stakes in its discovery of a way to decipher the 'odd configuration of lines that make up the human face'.

Notes

1. Emmanuel Levinas, 'The Paradox of Morality', trans. T. Wright, in *The Provocation of Levinas*, ed. R. Bernasconi and D. Wood (London: Routledge, 1988) 169–80; 172.
2. Jean-Luc Godard, *Made in USA* (London: Lorrimer, 1967) 39–40.
3. Emmanuel Levinas, 'Ethics of the Infinite', Interview with Richard Kearney, in *Contemporary Continental Thinkers: The Phenomenological Heritage*, ed. Richard Kearney (Manchester University Press, 1984) 47–70; 52.
4. Jean-Paul Sartre, *What is Literature?*, trans. B. Frechtman (London: Methuen, 1983) 34.
5. Jean-Paul Sartre and B. Lévy, *Hope Now: The 1980 Interviews* (1991), trans. A. van den Hoven (University of Chicago Press, 1996) 69–71, 87.
6. Levinas, 'Ethics of the Infinite', 62–3.
7. Sartre and Lévy, *Hope Now*, 50, 59.
8. Susan Handelman, 'Facing the Other: Levinas, Perelman, Rosenzweig', *Religion & Literature*, 22, 2–3 (1990) 61–84; 64.

9. Jill Robbins, 'An Inscribed Responsibility: Levinas's *Difficult Freedom*', review of *Difficult Freedom: Essays on Judaism* by Emmanuel Levinas, *Modern Language Notes* 106 (1991) 1052–62; 1052.
10. Jacques Derrida, 'Violence and Metaphysics: An Essay on the Thought of Emmanuel Levinas', in *Writing and Difference*, trans. A. Bass (University of Chicago Press, 1978) 79–153; 312 n.
11. Denis Donoghue, 'The Philosopher of Selfless Love', *New York Review of Books*, 21 March 1996, 37–40; 37.
12. Emmanuel Levinas, 'Signature', in *Difficult Freedom: Essays on Judaism*, trans. S. Hand (London: Athlone, 1990) 291–5; 291.
13. Derrida, 'Violence and Metaphysics', 118.
14. Emmanuel Levinas, 'Loving the Torah More than God', in *Difficult Freedom*, 142–5; 143.
15. Ibid., 142.
16. Zvi Kolitz, 'Yossel Rakover's Appeal to God: A Story Written Especially for *Di Yiddishe Tsaytung*', trans. J. V. Mallow *et al.*, *Cross Currents* 44 (1994) 362–77; 370.
17. Robbins, 'Inscribed Responsibility', 1055.
18. Ibid., 1059, 1060.
19. Levinas, 'Loving the Torah More than God', 143.
20. Robbins, 'Inscribed Responsibility', 1061.
21. Zvi Kolitz, 'Yosl Rokover redt tsu got', *Di Goldene Keyt*, 18 (1954) 102–10; 102.
22. Kolitz, 'Yossel Rakover's Appeal to God', 373–5.
23. Levinas, 'Loving the Torah More than God', 142.
24. Kolitz, 'Yossel Rakover's Appeal to God', 368.
25. Emmanuel Levinas, 'Max Picard and the Face', 95.
26. Jack Kugelmass, ed. and trans., *From a Ruined Garden: The Memorial Books of Polish Jewry* (New York: Schocken, 1983) 14.
27. Ibid., 10.
28. Saul Bellow, *Mr Sammler's Planet* (1970; New York: Penguin, 1977) 140.
29. Ibid., 191.
30. Levinas, 'Signature', 293.
31. Philip Roth, '"I Always Wanted You to Admire My Fasting"; or, Looking at Kafka', in *Reading Myself and Others* (New York: Farrar, Straus Giroux). 247–70; 247–8.
32. Michael André Bernstein, *Foregone Conclusions: Against Apocalyptic History* (Berkeley: University of California Press, 1994) 7.
33. Lawrence Graver, *An Obsession with Anne Frank: Meyer Levin and the Diary* (Berkeley: University of California Press, 1995) 54, 56.
34. Ibid., 58.
35. Levinas, 'Signature', 293.
36. Philip Roth, *The Ghost Writer* (New York: Farrar, Straus and Giroux, 1979) 16, 24.
37. Emmanuel Levinas, interview with R. Mortley, in *French Philosophers in Conversation* (London: Routledge, 1991) 11–23; 15–16.
38. Levinas, 'Ethics of the Infinite', 54.
39. Robbins, 'Inscribed Responsibility', 1055.

40. Ibid., 1058.
41. Jill Robbins, 'Aesthetic Totality and Ethical Infinity: Levinas on Art', *L'esprit créateur*, 35, 3 (1995) 66–79; 66–7.
42. Ibid., 71.
43. Emmanuel Levinas, 'La réalité et son ombre', *Les temps modernes* 38 (1948) 771–89; qtd. in Robbins, 'Aesthetic Totality', 12.
44. Emmanuel Levinas, 'Poetry and Resurrection: Notes on Agnon', in *Proper Names*, trans. M. B. Smith (Stanford, CA: Stanford University Press, 1996) 7–16; 9.
45. Ibid., 13.
46. Ibid., 14, 8.
47. Ibid., 14–15.
48. Emmanuel Levinas, 'Paul Celan: From Being to the Other', in *Proper Names*, 40–6; 40.
49. Levinas, 'Paradox of Morality', 169.
50. Levinas, 'Paul Celan', 41.
51. Ibid., 46.
52. Levinas, 'Max Picard and the Face', in *Proper Names*, 94–8; 95.

Part II
Agency and Responsibility

4
The Unbearable Lightness of Acts

Valeria Wagner

Let me begin with a few words on the reference in the title of this paper to that of Milan Kundera's novel, *The Unbearable Lightness of Being*, a title which has become a rather current expression of existential *malaise*. The expression is certainly not unequivocal, but it is often used to formulate the discrepancy between the weight our culture gives to the fact of being alive, and the fundamental arbitrariness of its happening: being (alive) is unmotivated and hazardous.[1] In this sense its 'lightness' is an image for its ungroundedness: Being is not sustainable, it 'floats' in the air and cannot be borne – it is unbearable. This, I think, makes perfect sense insofar as Being is an abstraction: we cannot just BE, we must be something, somewhere, doing something. Unqualified Being is simply too abstract to be borne, and there should be, in principle, nothing unbearable about *that*: why should anyone want to just BE, anyway? The question, however, should be taken seriously, because it is only insofar as Being is asked to have weight that it may seem unbearably light. And Being is appealed to consistently, at least in Western tradition, whenever reasons and motivations fail to account for, unfold into, or 'control' actions. It is in this kind of situation that Being is asked to provide a ground and measure capable of justifying or sustaining acts, that it fails to do so, and that it appears, as a result, as unendurably inconsistent.

This is apparent in *Hamlet*, a play undeniably concerned with the relationship between Being and action. Hamlet himself formulates this relationship succinctly in IV, iv, as he is poignantly reminded of his inability to carry out his revenge by the news of Fortinbras's attack on Poland: 'I do not know / Why yet I live to say "This thing's to do" / Sith I have cause, and will, and strength, and means / To do't'.[2] Here the fact that Hamlet is inexplicably unable to do what he has motives and reasons to do raises the question of why he is still alive, as if the fact of being alive had to sustain his actions. It also suggests, significantly, that were Hamlet to do the 'thing', living would require no explanation. Similarly, although Hamlet's most famous soliloquy posits Being as the fundamental uncertainty from which all lack of resolution, including that necessary to act, would stem, the conclusion that Hamlet finally reaches implies that, if 'enterprises of great pitch and moment' did not 'lose the name of action' (III, i, 86–8), 'To be, or not be' would not be a question. In other words, whereas action seems capable of rendering the questioning of the fact of being alive irrelevant, the fact of being (alive) is not only incapable of containing the questioning of action, but is inevitably questioned *with* it. The lightness of being thus seems to be a secondary effect of – or at least not dissociable from – the unbearable lightness of acts.

Hamlet's dilemma – that 'this Thing's to do', and yet he does not do it – is paradigmatic of the 'unbearability of acts' that has particularly preoccupied Western tradition: how do acts 'descend', as it were, from abstraction to concretion? How are they *borne*, how do they take on weight? As M.M. Bakhtin argues in *Toward a Philosophy of The Act*,[3] one of his earliest writings, our conceptualisation of action suffers from two major and related flaws: there is, (1) on the one hand, 'a fundamental split between the content of a given act/activity and the historical actuality of its being'; (2) and on the other, 'an abyss ... between the motive of the actually performed act or deed and its product' (p. 54).[4] There is a missing link in the relationship between the performed act and its actual performance which, as Hamlet's inaction demonstrates, cannot be bridged by either Reason or the Will; and there is an inadequate conception of what it is that *makes us* act, of the relationship between reasons for acting and the fact that we do, eventually, act (or not). These rips in the fabric of action are, according to Bakhtin, at the heart of 'the contemporary crisis', which, he argues, is 'fundamentally a crisis of contemporary action': a crisis of actually performed acts, ongoing action, or action in process *in the first person*. In other words, what is missing from the conceptualisation of action is the performed act itself, whether abstracted from the product and unrooted in the motive, or devoid of the weight of its content, empty, transparent like a ghost.

But in what sense can the flaw in our conceptualisation of action be, in actual historical terms, a crisis? Indeed, the fact that acts appear at times as too light – abstract, inconsistent – to be enacted need not be a problem; it could even be argued that had there been more hesitant Hamlets in history, the world would be better off.[5] The problem I address in this essay is that the lightness whereby acts appear as too abstract to be enacted is intimately related to that whereby acts appear as too easily enacted with respect to their ethical import: pulling a trigger, for example, is an extremely easy and accessible act. In other words, the 'abyss' between motive and product, the 'split' between content and the historical actuality of the act, can take the form of a discrepancy between the sheer performance of the act and its ethical import. There are, thus, two distinct and related 'unbearabilities': that which pertains to the enactment of the act (and hence to Hamlet's inaction), and that which pertains to its ethical import (which I discuss below through the example of Fortinbras's war). The former, I contend, has tended to obscure the latter in Western tradition, obscuring in turn the nature of the relationship between the crisis of 'contemporary action', as Bakhtin puts it, and the crisis in ethics.

The pertinence of the following enquiry into the unbearability of acts can be suggested with an example in tune with this essay: consider *Hamlet* criticism and its persistent concern with why Hamlet does not act. Here the question of why Hamlet does not just DO IT has all too often obscured the particular nature of the unaccomplished deed, as if it went without saying that Hamlet should kill his uncle, and that he could do so easily. In an article entitled 'Hamlet's Dull Revenge',[6] René Girard parodies this critical position, inviting his readers to 'imagine a contemporary Hamlet, his finger on the nuclear button': would psychiatrists and professors of literature still wonder why he hesitates to press it? In other words, would his hesitancy be analysed in terms of the lightness of abstractions, or in terms of the weight of the act? We would like to think that the latter concern would overrule the former, but we have reasons to fear that it would not, for although wars on stage are not comparable to 'real' wars, the discourses on either can be compared. Consider for instance Jean Baudrillard's essay on the Gulf War, significantly entitled – in tune with his preoccupation with sheer, abstracted action – 'The Gulf War did not take place'. Apparently exasperated by the procrastination of the actual confrontation, Baudrillard argues that wars are in crisis, that the Gulf War is a 'degenerate war', a 'weak event',[7] and that it will not take place because the *passage à l'acte* has become impossible within the logic of virtual action (the media). As if forgetting the nature of the act that fails to be enacted, moreover, he criticises the 'bad' reputation of the *passage à l'acte* in itself and in general: according to him, it is assimilated to a 'psychotic process' (p. 16), and, as such, feared and avoided. Thus the postponement of concrete hostilities in the Gulf War would be an expression of the fear of the *passage à l'acte*, which would rule all our behaviour: 'fear of all that is real, of any real event ...'.[8] Following this analysis, it would have been 'saner' to launch the war immediately, to just DO IT and confront the event, overcome our neurotic relationship to action, and bomb and be bombed.[9]

But how are such 'ethical slippages' possible, and what do they say about how we tend to conceptualise action and ethical acts? The case of Hamlet is ideal for tracing one such slippage and considering its implications. As is well known, Hamlet has trouble giving weight to his projected revenge, which remains a painful abstraction throughout the play. As he attempts to elucidate the reasons for his inaction, he directs his attention to others' actions, and is struck by the 'abyss' he sees in them: they seem to be unmotivated, unreasoned, and ultimately, uncaused. Already in Act II, ii, Hamlet is appalled – 'is it not monstrous' (548) – at the player's ability to shed tears without 'real' reasons for it, while he 'can say nothing, no, not for a King' (566). Here the inverted symmetry of his and the player's situations contradicts Hamlet's assumption that the greater 'the motive and the cue for passion' (558), the more extreme the corresponding behaviour, suggesting in fact that, insofar as they surge independently from 'genuine' reasons, actions may well be independent from all reasons.

Intent on preserving a model of action capable of explaining (and eventually reversing) his inaction, however, Hamlet strives to save the formal continuity between motive and act. He thus speculates on the player's spectacular behaviour were he in his stead: he would 'drown the stage with tears' (559), in accordance with the law of proportionality Hamlet presupposes. By positing himself as 'unpregnant of [his] cause' (565), he further reaffirms the actual continuity between motive/reasons and acts. Here Hamlet's underlying belief is that his 'cause' *would* give effect to action, were he only impregnated with it – were he bearing it properly. Thus the final parallelism between Hamlet and the player is the following: the latter is not 'pregnant of his cause', because he is playing, but within the play the causal and proportional relationship between reasons and acts still holds; Hamlet's reasons *would* cause his revenge, but they do not do so because he is not properly imbued with them, a necessary condition in 'real' life actions. Hamlet can thus persist in his belief that reasons cause and ground actions, and concentrate his attention on how to appropriate his cause. Hence the ensuing mouse-trap, meant to enable Hamlet to see his uncle's guilt with his own eyes, to 'inseminate' himself with a proof of it.

But in the soliloquy following his encounter with Fortinbras's captain (IV, iv, 32–66), Hamlet is forced to revise his assumptions about the relationship between 'cause' and action. Upon hearing that the stakes of the war Fortinbras is launching are 'a little patch of ground', he first expresses incredulity: 'Why, then the Polack will never defend it'. Indeed, if actions were grounded and sustained by reasons to the extent of being caused by them, then such a war should simply not be. Instead, the sheer weight of Hamlet's reasons to revenge – 'a father killed, a mother stained' – should unfold effortlessly into the act Hamlet's 'blood' and 'reason' call on him to accomplish. The war, however, will be, while Hamlet's revenge is not yet; Fortinbras acts for 'an eggshell', while Hamlet, in spite of his load of reasons, 'lets all sleep'. It is not, then, a question of being 'pregnant' of one's 'cause', for Fortinbras, acting in 'real' life, does so without a proper cause, and hence without being impregnated with it. Thus, whereas Hamlet's failure to act according to his cause does not refute the role of reasons in action, Fortinbras's acting without cause demonstrates that reasons are neither compellent nor determinant, suggesting, moreover, that actions are fundamentally ungrounded in anything other than themselves. Hamlet can no longer sustain the hope that the justifiable nature of what he wants to do will suffice to make him do it , as if the moral obligation to revenge could result in the actual – almost physical – obligation to act.

Bakhtin addresses this issue through the concrete example of contractual obligations, arguing that

> [i]t is not the content of an obligation that obligates me, but my signature below it – the fact that at one time I acknowledged or undersigned the given acknowledgement. And what compelled me to sign at the moment of undersigning was not the content of the given performed act or deed. This content could not by itself, in isolation, have prompted me to perform the act or deed – to undersign-acknowledge it, but only in correlation with my

> decision to undertake an obligation – by performing the act of undersigning-acknowledging. And in this performed act the content-aspect was … but a constituent moment, and what decided the matter was the acknowledgement or affirmation … that had been actually performed at a previous time, etc. (pp. 38–9)

Bakhtin, then, locates what he calls the *ought* or the *compellentness* of acts, what ultimately *makes us act*, in the act of acknowledgement of the obligation *as* obligation. According to him, it is this act, figured in the signature, which then compels me to actually accomplish the obligation in question. The nature of the obligation itself is, as he puts it, 'but a constituent moment' of the undersigning, without which, of course, there would be no obligation (you do not sign undetermined contracts). The content of the obligation *does* play a role at the moment of its undertaking, insofar as one may refuse to undersign the document – but is not determinant when it comes to fulfilling it. In short, the *actual performance* of the act is not determined or decided by the content of the enacted act. Instead, what is compelling about action resides, Bakhtin argues, in the actually performed act itself: 'the *ought* is precisely a category of the individual act … it is a category of the individuality, of the uniqueness of a performed act, of its once-occurrent compellentness, of its historicity, of the impossibility to replace it with anything else or to provide a substitute for it' (p. 25).[10]

Hamlet is on the verge of concurring with Bakhtin halfway through his soliloquy as he considers Fortinbras's 'gross example'. First the incongruity of the situation is emphasised: a 'delicate and tender prince' leading an 'army of such mass and charge'; his spirit 'puffed' with 'divine ambition' as he confronts 'the invisible event'. But the ridiculous setting eventually foregrounds rather than diminishes the exemplarity of Fortinbras's act, which takes on a life of its own when Hamlet describes it as 'exposing what is mortal and unsure / To all that fortune, death, and danger dare / Even for an eggshell' (IV, iv, 51–3). What matters here is not why Fortinbras fights the Polacks, but *that* he fights them: the value of the act resides in what it exposes, regardless of whether Fortinbras does it for an eggshell or for a kingdom. The suggestion is in fact that Fortinbras fights the war because he fights the war, that the act motivates itself, and even that it is the decisive and singular nature of the act itself which ultimately determines (decides) Fortinbras's decision to undertake it. For the act in question is quite clearly paradigmatically decisive: it offers resolution to all uncertainties, it will settle life into life or into death. In Bakhtin's more moderate terms (to which we will return), the *ought* of Fortinbras's act resides in its irrevocability, its 'once-occurrent' compellentness.

Hamlet, however, radicalises this insight in the second half of his soliloquy, concluding that if actions are not determined by reasons, neither can they be judged by them. His initial assumption was that, because men were not given discourse and reason 'to fust (in them) unused', discourse and reason were given to them to result in action. But as his train of thought proceeds, Hamlet gives up the precedence of reason over action, and contemplates instead the possibility that it may well be action which puts reason to use. In which case, of course, acts constitute the measure of reason, and the measure of themselves (IV, iv, 53–6):

> Rightly to be great
> Is not to stir without great argument,
> But greatly to find quarrel in a straw
> When honour's at the stake.

Here argument – discourse and reason, as well as the construction of reasons and motives – is neither at the origin nor at the end of the quarrel, but at its service and even *produced by it*. As for the 'honour at stake' in the quarrel, it should not mislead us into thinking that Fortinbras's war is more motivated than it appears to be. Not only are there no indications that he is requiting himself of a wrong the Polacks might have done him, but the comparison structuring Hamlet's argumentation suggests that the honour in question is that upheld *in* action, and not that defended by it. Indeed, Hamlet's revenge cannot be compared to Fortinbras's war, because it has not been enacted; while Hamlet's reasons cannot be compared to Fortinbras's because the latter does not really have any: the only point of comparison left upon which honour could pivot is sheer action. Fortinbras's deed is thus abstracted from its content, to be measured against itself.

Before this turning point in Hamlet's reasoning, Fortinbras's deed was still implicitly considered in terms of reasons and motives or of concrete loss or gain, and consequently appeared as irrational and worthless – Fortinbras himself but a madman 'making mouths at the invisible event'. Once Hamlet considers the deed in terms of itself, however, it becomes a grand deed, the *grandeur* of which even constitutes the criterion for reason itself: Fortinbras is 'rightly great'. According to this logic, the fact that men will die like flies 'for a fantasy and trick of fame' increases the worth of the deed, which is to be measured by the incongruity between the size of the patch of land and the size of the army: the former is not 'tomb enough and continent / To hide the slain'. It is as if the greater the disparity between means and ends, and the more the act is severed from reasons, the greater the value of the act in itself. This incongruity awakens Hamlet's shame – not of Fortinbras, but of himself – leading him to conclude that he should follow Fortinbras's example, and rather than attempt to act according to righteous reasons and motivations, let himself be propelled into action by the thought of its *grandeur*: 'O, from this time forth, / My thoughts be bloody, or be nothing worth!' Fortinbras's irresponsible and condemnable war thus becomes, in Hamlet's argument, a commendable act.

In other words, as he discards the model of action that attributed to reasons and motivations the power to originate acts, Hamlet dissociates acts completely from their content and results – concretely, he neglects the import of Fortinbras's act, concentrating instead on its sheer enactment. This dissociation is *not* inevitable, for the acknowledgement of the lack of a causal link between reasons and acts need not entail the severance of all link between act and content/result. It is Hamlet's inordinate preoccupation with how to act in general which gradually distracts him from the particulars of action. This preoccupation, however, was itself produced by his reliance on an inadequate model of action, which failed to locate the compellentness of acts in the acts themselves. And it continues to haunt him once he confirms the inadequacy of his understanding of action – he then sets out to find other grounds to act, seeking, however, for the principle enabling *all* action, and thus shifting imperceptibly from the question of how (and whether) to accomplish *this*, to that of how to accomplish anything – how to act? As with Being, however, it is impossible to just act: one does something, behaves in a certain manner, runs or walks, and so on. Whether or not they are motivated and reasoned – that is, whether or not the question 'why am I / are you doing this' can be answered – actions cannot be unqualified, for abstract actions are definitely too light to be enacted. And sure enough, Hamlet's 'bloody thoughts' are to no immediate avail: he does not follow Fortinbras's example – a fact for which we would be thankful were Hamlet alive and unavenged.

Reformulated in Bakhtin's terms, Hamlet's dilemma is a consequence of his assumption that the relationships between the content and the historical actuality of an act and between its motive and its product must be somehow causal. More specifically, he assumes that in these relationships the content of an act must compel its historical actuality, and that motives are the compelling force of acts. This assumption reinforces, and even produces, the 'abyss' and 'split' at the origin of the 'crisis of contemporary action' from which Hamlet obviously suffers. Confronted with this abyss, Hamlet must conclude that there is no possible unity between content and enactment, motive and product, and hence that there is no relationship between the ethical import of an act and its actual enactment: the phenomenological and ethical dimensions of acts thus appear to be at best arbitrarily related, and, at worst, simply irrelevant to each other. But Hamlet's inaction suggests that a certain unity between these two dimensions is necessary for action, and that it is, consequently, also necessary to prevent the displacement of the abyss within 'contemporary action' to Being. Reconfiguring the relationships between the content of acts and their historical actuality, between motive and product, thus appears as an important task both for a philosophy of action and for reflections on ethics – a task which implied, for Bakhtin, a reconfiguration of the traditional hierarchy between Being and action.

Let us return to the moment Hamlet qualifies Fortinbras's deed for the first time: it exposed, recall, 'what is mortal and unsure / To all that fortune, death and danger dare ...'. At this point Hamlet has not yet abstracted acts from their content, shifting their lightness from their content to their enactment. Quite on the contrary, he is considering them in their full weight: they are decisive in that they are irrevocable and unique, they settle the present once and for all. In short, they play out the fact of being (alive) – to be or not to be; and what's more, to be this or that – and this inherent decisiveness is what compels their enactment. For a moment, then, Hamlet formulates the relationship between the categories of acts and of being (alive) as one of mutual concretion rather than hierarchical grounding. Acts determine the mode of being alive, being alive is the stake of acts; acts settle the fact of being alive, which in turn confers on acts their uniqueness with respect to other acts and to other moments in time: neither is an abstraction, both give weight to each other. This mutual concretion of action and being (alive) is important for two reasons: it re-introduces the actually performed act, as Bakhtin puts it, making actions bearable in the sense of feasible; and it introduces the decisiveness of the actually performed act as the criterion for ethical judgement and responsibility – or, to keep the initial conceit working, as the criterion for the ethical 'bearability' of acts.

Bakhtin's term for the 'bearability' of acts is translated as their 'answerability', a term evoking not only the interactive setting of all acts – they are responses to given situations – but also their *significance* as acts, their pertinence to the agent's life: 'for to *be* in life, to be *actually*, is to *act*, is to be unindifferent toward the once-occurrent whole' (p. 42).[11] In other words, our acts are our mode of being alive in the world, and acts always comprehend an attitude to, or evaluation of, at least the immediate world. To the extent that this is the case – we cannot not act – the beginning of any ethical responsibility for our acts would be in the active recognition of the 'unindifference' of acts, as acts and to ourselves. Bakhtin formulates this 'active recognition' as that of '*my non-alibi in being*': that whatever I do, and wherever I am, I cannot pretend I am not where I am or not doing what I am doing, for I am inescapably here and now in a unique and irreplaceable position and moment. The fact that my uniqueness is 'compellently obligatory', Bakhtin argues, is 'the point of origin of the answerable deed and of all the categories of the concrete, once-occurrent and compellent ought: I, too, *exist*, actually ...' (p. 40). Thus, for Bakhtin 'it is only my non-alibi in Being that transforms an empty possibility into an actual answerable act or deed' (p. 42): it is the irrevocable fact of my being here and now which entails the necessity to actually act in this or that way. The acknowledgement of the fact of my non-alibi in being is also what, according to Bakhtin, 'produces the ... actual heaviness, compellentness' of the answerably performed act; it *is* the basis for such answerability: 'an answerable act or deed is precisely that act which is performed on the basis of the acknowledgement of my obligative ... uniqueness' (p. 42). It would thus be in the 'unindifference' of those acts performed in the acknowledgement of one's 'obligative uniqueness', as Bakhtin puts it, that the ethical dimension of acts, their answerability with respect to other acts, and hence to people, is fully integrated.

Needless to say, Bakhtin's notion of what a properly ethical act is does not correspond to the understanding of ethics as providing a guide for judging what is right or wrong, and of acting 'right'. The kind of responsibility Bakhtin develops in his notion of answerability pertains to the manner of engaging oneself in action, and hence inevitably with others, but it does not say what one should do or should not do to others. It does not exclude the act of killing, for example, from the status of an answerably performed act. In this sense, his considerations are not a full-fledged ethics, or at least not a discussion of 'moral values'. It can be argued, however, that the main problem we encounter in discussions of ethics does not pertain to actual moral values: indeed, these are subject to historical change and must *remain* a problem, to be debated and argued. The main problem is that of *how* and *whether* one relates to those values – and we saw in the discussions of Hamlet's attitude to Fortinbras's 'example' and of Baudrillard's comments on the Gulf War that it is all too easy *not* to relate to them at all.

For Bakhtin this is due to the existing 'abyss' between the content of the act and its historical actuality and between its motive and its product, an abyss which, he argues throughout his essay, is opened by the movement of abstraction that dominates reflections on ethics. The ethical imperative of Kantian ethics, in particular – to which we appeal constantly – postulates the subject acting *as if* he were a universal subject, and hence as if he were himself abstracted from his acts. The abstraction of the 'I' implies the abstraction of the actually performed act itself, and hence the opening of the abyss within action. For Bakhtin, as we saw, this abyss is bridged in the performance of an answerable deed based on the fact of my 'non-alibi in being': that is, in the acknowledgement and affirmation of my 'obligatory uniqueness'. This affirmation cannot, as Bakhtin himself recognises, be *theorised* – 'it cannot be adequately expressed in the theoretical terms, but can only be described and participatively experienced' (p. 40). This, however, does not mean that ethics cannot be an object of discussion: it means, rather, that in order for it *to be* responsibly debated, we must assume responsibility for the untheorisable moment of our acts – and such a responsibility consists in weaving a relationship to our acts in our accounting for them.[12] And it is with this relationship to our acts that a properly ethical discussion of ethics can begin – and continue.

Notes

1. Even if we argue that being is motivated because it has origin – God created us, our parents gave birth to us – it remains an external motivation that cannot be borne in that it cannot be reciprocated: we can neither create God nor give birth to our parents.
2. William Shakespeare, *Hamlet*, ed. T. J. B. Spencer (Harmondsworth: Penguin, 1980) IV, iv, 43–6. Subsequent references to this text will be given in parentheses.
3. M. M. Bakhtin, *Toward a Philosophy of the Act*, trans. V. Liapunov, eds, V. Liapumov and M. Holquist (Austin: University of Texas Press, 1993). Subsequent references will be given in parentheses.
4. The terms Bakhtin uses to characterise this 'crisis of contemporary action' are determined by his critique of the two main trends in ethics, 'content-ethics' and 'formal ethics'. The former is articulated around the specification of the objective content of an action or of its ends, the latter around the motives of conduct (cf. the translator's comment in note 69). I do not insist on the distinction between these two 'splits', as I am concerned with their common 'abyss'.
5. I discuss the ways in which models of action interact with 'actual' action in my doctoral dissertation, 'Bound to Act: an analysis of models of action as dramatised in selected literary and philosophical texts' (University of Geneva, July 1995).
6. René Girard, 'Hamlet's Dull Revenge', in Patricia Parker and David Quint, eds., *Literary Theory/Renaissance Texts* (Baltimore: Johns Hopkins University Press, 1986) 280–302.
7. Jean Baudrillard, *La Guerre du Golfe n'a pas eu lieu* (Mayenne: Éditions Galilée, 1991) 11.
8. 'Le passage à l'acte est communément mal famé: il correspondrait à une levée brutale du refoulement, et donc à un processus psychotique. Il semble que cette hantise du passage à l'acte règle aujourd'hui tous nos comportements: hantise de tout réel, de tout événement réel, de toute violence réelle, de toute jouissance trop réelle. Contre cette hantise du réel nous avons créé un gigantesque appareil de simulation qui nous permet de passer à l'acte "in vitro" (c'est même vrai de la procréation). A la catastrophe du réel nous préférons l'exil du virtuel dont la télévision est le miroir universel ... La guerre n'échappe pas à cette virtualisation qui est comme une opération chirurgicale: offrir le visage lifté de la guerre, le spectre fardé de la mort, son subterfuge télévisuel plus déceptif encore ...' (p. 16).
9. I should stress that I am not suggesting that the actual 'delay' in the launching of the hostilities was motivated by ethical principles. The point is that Baudrillard's analysis of the situation overlooks the content of the act he 'wants' performed.
10. To locate the ethical *ought* in the act rather than in the subject obviously goes counter to Kant's famous and influential categorical imperative – 'Act only on that maxim through which you can at the same time will that it should become a universal law'. Kantian ethics, Bakhtin argues, articulates the ethical *ought* in the category of the

will, and postulates that 'the will itself prescribe the law to itself' (p. 26). But here, Bakhtin objects, 'the will-as-deed produces the law to which it submits, i.e. it dies as an individual will in its own product. The will describes a circle, shuts itself in, excluding the actual – individual and historical – self-activity of the performed act'. Thus what would be ignored in the Kantian staging of the self-willing will, is the *act* of willing – the will-as-deed – which introduces a discontinuity between the willing and what is willed. In other words, the will cannot will itself to will something: this is as impossible as to 'lift oneself up by pulling one's own hair', an example Bakhtin often gives to illustrate the tendency to forget the constitutive primacy of the performance of the act over its content.

11. The 'once-occurrent whole' is not a metaphysical concept in Bakhtin's philosophy: it denotes the fact that we only live a moment at a time, that each moment, as an experience, cannot be repeated, and that it is terribly singular.
12. I am here paraphrasing Michael Holquist, who argues in his *Foreword* to Bakhtin's text that for the latter 'responsibility ... is the ground of moral action': 'The act is a deed, and not a mere happening (as in "one damned thing after another"), only if the subject of such [an act], from within his own radical uniqueness, weaves a relation *to* it in his accounting *for* it' (p. xii).

5
Secret Agent, Absent Agent? Ethical-Stylistic Aspects of Anarchy in Conrad's *The Secret Agent*

Ruth Kolani

> Peut-être le poignard de l'anarchiste, qui croit réfuter en tuant, et la dague du garde de la police italienne qui, avec une logique à peu près semblable, prétend être l'arbitre de la pensée, s'apprêtent-ils alternativement à la réfuter d'un commun accord et d'une même manière: par la violence.
>
> Cesare Lombroso, *Les Anarchistes*

The ethical concerns of *The Secret Agent* and Conrad's treatment of the theme of moral anarchy have been subjected to considerable literary investigation; but there has been no critical consensus on the significance and scope of the anarchist theme in Conrad's narrative. Some critics have maintained that the author's portrayal of the anarchists does not do historical justice to the anarchist movement and that, unlike his other major works, this novel lacks 'a moral perspective to serve literary ends'.[1] Others have insisted that *The Secret Agent* is not about anarchism *per se* and that its anarchists are indeed not to be taken too seriously. For example, Leo Gurko argues that the anarchist theme provides mere 'political scaffolding' and that the author's overriding ethical concern is the dehumanising impact of London.[2]

To be sure, Conrad, like most of his critics, adopts the view accepted in popular usage that anarchy – whether political, philosophical, moral or social – is synonymous with disorder, chaos, violence, and nihilism (though such an interpretation would be seriously challenged by a number of professed anarchists and dispassionate theoreticians).[3]

However, there is an added dimension to the moral 'anarchy' that reigns in Conrad's atypical text: namely, that of unaccountability, of absent or deferred agency, the evasion of responsibility as a function of the dissociation between character and action. I wish to argue that an ethical rupture of this kind, which has been associated with modern bureaucratic institutions, manifests itself on several levels in *The Secret Agent*: on the private level of the domestic plot as it affects Verloc and his wife, who share 'indolent and secret habits of mind' and refrain 'from going to the bottom of facts and motives',[4] on the level of the public plot involving the lawless anarchists and the police, and on a more abstract, self-reflexive narratological level involving the authorial narrator's function.

As a moral-philosophical concept, agency – the capacity to act and to exert power and control – implies accountability on the part of the human agent. But, agency may also be defined as a fundamental aspect of linguistic structure whereby particular semantic (or 'participant') 'roles' are assigned to noun phrases in relation to verb phrases in clauses in answer to the question 'who does what to whom?' These 'participant roles' may be divided into two broad categories: *agent* (actor) and *affected* (acted upon). Such role assignments are essential to the stylistic analysis of literary texts proposed by systemic linguists such as M. A. K. Halliday and others.[5] The underlying assumption made is that semantic-syntactic choices in clause construction determine 'alternative representations of reality', and thus different world views.

To date, agency as a moral-philosophical issue and agency as a stylistic category have been treated as distinct phenomena. However, by analysing the language of agency in relation to fictional representation in *The Secret Agent*, I wish to demonstrate that the basic question of the stylistician (who does what to whom?) may also have ethical implications and that it becomes particularly relevant to a reading of the 'anarchic' vision in *The Secret Agent*.

Moral agency and personal responsibility are central to all of Conrad's major novels. But *The Secret Agent* focuses particularly on the evasion of agency. It does so through the portrayal of a series of 'agentless' acts – epitomised by Mrs Verloc's murder of her husband – and through the linguistic and rhetorical means of separating the doer from the deed which pervade the novel's episodes.

Conrad's *The Secret Agent* envisions the kind of world informed by Alasdair MacIntyre's conception of modern 'emotivist' society. In his study in moral theory, *After Virtue*, MacIntyre states: 'Our social order is in a very literal sense out of our control. No one is in charge.' Everywhere, says MacIntyre, 'arbitrary but disguised will and preference' are operative.[6] Similarly, the emphasis of anarchy in Conrad's novel is not on the etymological derivation of *anarchos*, 'without ruler', but rather on what Hannah Arendt referred to as 'the rule of Nobody' (with a capital N) by which she meant a chaotic political state of affairs wherein it is impossible to localise responsibility 'since there is no one left who could even be asked to answer for what is being done ...'.[7]

A stylistic approach to *The Secret Agent* might support the stated thematic interpretations of anarchy and the modernist vision of fragmentation and helps to account for the novel's rhetoric of dissociation and its dominant ironic mode.

Commenting on the actual bombing attempt on the Greenwich Observatory of February 1894, the incident that prompted him to write the novel, Conrad expresses his outrage regarding the gratuitousness of the violence perpetrated: 'one remained faced by the fact of a man blown to bits for nothing even most remotely resembling an idea, anarchistic or other' ('Author's Note', p. 9). The 'short passive' construction with its agent deletion is telling. The idea of 'a man blown to bits' through no fault of his own incenses the writer not only because of its sheer destructiveness but also because responsibility for the act resides in no single identifiable consciousness and is not claimed by any human agent. Elsewhere in the 'Author's Note', Conrad alludes to Winnie Verloc's 'anarchistic end'.

In the public sphere of the novel, the idea of the indecipherability of a gratuitous act of violence and the dissociation between doer and deed is also echoed in the words of Chief Inspector Heat, 'principal expert in anarchist procedure', as he manipulatively addresses his superior, the Assistant Commissioner:

> A given anarchist may be watched inch by inch and minute by minute, but a moment always comes when somehow all sight and touch of him are lost for a few hours, during which something (generally an explosion) more or less deplorable does happen. (p. 80)

Especially striking is the syntactic deletion of human actors. The implied distinction Heat makes is between an event as a 'doing' and an event as a 'happening' (a supervention process).[8] Explosions in Heat's view just happen: they are not the end of a process but rather 'sudden holes in space and time' (p. 80).

Significantly, the dissociation of doer from deed in *The Secret Agent* is most clearly demonstrated by the fact that the focal acts of violence in the novel – the Greenwich explosion; the death of the inarticulate Stevie, the retarded younger brother of Mrs Verloc, who is also the unsuspecting bearer of the bomb; the murder of Verloc; and Winnie's suicide – are portrayed as happenings. In effect, nobody does anything in the novel; things just happen. Almost every episode of *The Secret Agent* could serve to illustrate deferred agency and the concomitant rhetoric of dissociation, but I shall focus on a few illustrative instances.

The evasion of agency is further manifested on the level of the public plot in the fourth chapter of the novel. The chapter is set in the Silenus Restaurant with its 'walls without windows' and emblematic medieval frescoes of hunting scenes and revelry, a setting emphasising 'the romance of violence' so often associated with anarchism.[9] Against this claustral backdrop, the two anarchists meet: Comrade Ossipon and the nihilist Professor, 'the little man', who has single-mindedly engaged in scientific research to devise the 'perfect' detonator and who turns out to be the maker of the bomb that has killed Stevie. Suspense is created in this carefully structured chapter by means of fragmentary dialogue and various forms of textual lacunae. For example, Ossipon's opening remark to the Professor is fraught with mystery: 'Unless I am very much mistaken, you are the man who would know the inside of this confounded affair' (p. 61). An expectation that the information is immediately forthcoming is defeated by means of a delay caused partly by the intrusion of the highly charged image of a player piano: 'An upright semi-grand piano ... executed suddenly all by itself a valse tune of aggressive virtuosity' (p. 62).

The mechanical playerless piano serves as an objective correlative of absent human agency, a recurrent focal image of anarchy in the novel. The defeat of syntactic and semantic expectations is carried out by ironically casting the inanimate instrument in a human agentive role, as an *actor* in a *material-action-intention* process. Endowed with autonomous human qualities, the piano is reminiscent of the contingent objects introduced by the Dadaists some ten years after the appearance of *The Secret Agent*. Surely, the denizens of the Cabaret Voltaire in the staid Zurich of 1916 would have delighted in the comic absurdity of that object, which is only named as a 'mechanical piano' when it reappears at the end of the novel.

Notably, the image of the playerless piano is also linked in Ossipon's mind to a vision of a bombing:

> The piano at the foot of the staircase clanged through a mazurka with brazen impetuosity, as though a vulgar and impudent ghost were showing off: the keys sank and rose mysteriously. For a moment Ossipon imagined the overlighted place changed into a dreadful black hole belching horrible fumes choked with ghostly rubbish of smashed brickwork and mutilated corpses. He had such a distinct perception of ruin and death that he shuddered again. The other observed, with an air of calm sufficiency. (p. 66)

An association with the explosion at the observatory is implied. The passage above, with its emphasis on the gruesome effects of gratuitous violence, emphasises the disengagement of human agency and responsibility and thus encapsulates the moral vision and critique informing the entire novel.

The piano is then introduced with even greater comic pathos further on:

> The lonely piano, without as much as a music stool to help it, struck a few chords courageously, and beginning a selection of natural airs, played him out at last to the tune of 'The Blue-bells of Scotland.' The painfully detached notes grew faint ... (p. 75)

Earlier in the Silenus chapter, the reader remains entirely in the dark regarding Stevie's death until, finally, Ossipon announces the stark anonymous fact: 'there's a man blown up in Greenwich park this morning'. Ossipon pulls out a fragmentary news report whose truncated phrases do not refer to the death itself, the event itself, but only to its effect:

> Ah! Here it is. Bomb in Greenwich Park. Half-past eleven. Foggy morning. Effects of explosion felt as far as Romney Road and Park Place. Enormous hole in the ground under a tree filled with smashed roots and broken branches. All round fragments of a man's body blown to pieces ... (p. 69)

The ironic stylised description with its verbless syntactic fragments excludes a 'doing'. Inspector Heat too conceives of Stevie's death as an agentless murder as he beholds 'the shattering violence of destruction which has made of that body a heap of nameless fragments'.

The dissociation between character and action is repeatedly foregrounded in *The Secret Agent* through linguistic and rhetorical choices. By subverting the emphasis on human agency the author portrays the often passive, veiled and banal nature of violence and of evil. This is also evident in the depiction of the ghostlike characters of the novel. Verloc, for example, is a 'perfunctory' slothful being who periodically arrives in London 'like the influenza from the Continent' only to 'wallow' all day long in an unmade bed (p. 19). The self styled revolutionary anarchists include the effete Yundt, referred to as 'the old terrorist', 'a posturing shadow all his life', and of whom it is said that 'he was no man of action' (p. 51) and the Professor whose role is undermined by passive constructions. The Professor also conceives of violence in anonymous terms: 'Next time … a telling stroke would be delivered – something really startling – a blow fit to open the first crack in the imposing front of the great edifice of legal conceptions sheltering the atrocious injustice of society' (p. 76). Moreover, the Professor has denounced all human feeling in favour of devising the 'perfect detonator', paradoxically, in spite of his dedication and of his conviction of his own 'moral' agency. ('He was a moral agent – that was settled in his mind. By exercising his agency with ruthless defiance he procured for himself the appearances of power and personal prestige' [p. 77].)

Pseudo-agency and bureaucratic unaccountability in the exercise of power are most effectively dramatised in the Embassy episode in which Vladimir, the First Secretary of the Foreign (Russian) embassy, conducts a scathing interview with Verloc. Moreover, the episode demonstrates the kind of interrelationship between language and power established by sociolinguists like Roger Fowler and Deirdre Burton. Fowler defines power as 'a transitive concept entailing an asymmetrical relationship' and language as 'an instrument for manipulating concepts and relationships in the area of power'.[10] Such an asymmetry marks the Verloc-Vladimir interview.

As we accompany Verloc on his walk to the Embassy every detail contributes to the impression of unassertiveness, to the 'effect of unobtrusive deference',[11] to the fact that 'Mr Verloc … certainly knew his place' (p. 27). This effect is confirmed by a participant 'role' analysis of Verloc in the episode. Verloc's encounter with Privy Councillor Wurmt provides a macerating prelude to the actual meeting with Vladimir. The ensuing power-play becomes linguistically evident through an analysis of process options, participant roles, and particularly through the use of evasive linguistic features such as passivisation and nominalisation. Since nominalisations, as Fowler reminds us, 'permit deletion of both agency and modality' (p. 41), they help to 'make mysterious the participants' obligations and responsibilities spoken of in the discourse'. Wurmt's indirection, his avoidance of agency, expresses itself in a repeated nominalising process in the following pattern of ironic transformations addressed to Verloc:

> *what is desired* … is the occurrence of something definite which should stimulate their vigilance. That is within your province – is it not so? [the tag further mitigating Wurmt's pretending power] … *What is wished for* just now is the accentuation of the unrest ….
>
> *What is required* at present is not writing, but the bringing to light of a distinct, significant fact; I would almost say an alarming fact … (pp. 27–8 – my italics)

A hedging affect is created by these nominalisations ('*what is* …'); by the speaker's choice of vague *lexis*; the nominal 'accentuation of unrest'; the empty, redundant premodifiers.

Irony in the scene is intensified when Vladimir, the man plotting behind the scenes, distances himself from action through his use of passivisation. Vladimir resorts to an 'agentless' passive: 'A dynamite outrage must be provoked', he says to Verloc, an evasive intermediary in his own right. The statement is as close as Vladimir comes to issuing an order to his subordinate.

On the private, domestic level of the plot, the 'agentless' act of violence, devoid of human involvement and responsibility finds its paradigmatic expression in the murder of Verloc by his wife. The murder committed by Mrs Verloc constitutes a focal link in the chain of 'anarchic' occurences in the novel, marked rhetorically by a dissociation of the doer from the deed. The 'anarchic' character of the murder and its aftermath is confirmed both at the end of the

'Author's Note' when Conrad refers to Winnie's 'anarchistic end of utter desolation, madness and despair' (p. 13) and by the revisions Conrad made in the dramatisation of the murder in the subsequent versions of *The Secret Agent*. The fact that the author ultimately conceives of the novel as 'Mrs Verloc's story' (p. 11) may further tell us something of the unheroic nature of her husband and of another possible referent for the title of the book. From the outset Winnie is portrayed as a disengaged woman wearing an invisible veil. Verloc is first attracted to her by 'the provocation of her unfathomable reserve' (p. 19). Repeatedly, we are told that Winnie has the tendency to ignore the 'inwardness of things' (p. 132), so that her belief that 'things don't bear looking into very much' becomes her leitmotif. Winnie's body parts, her voice, and 'motionless eyes' are portrayed as if they had their own autonomous existence. This is made linguistically evident by the participant-roles assigned to them: 'Mrs Verloc's voice ceased, and the expression of her motionless eyes became more veiled' (p. 61), '... her sullen gaze moved along the walls' (p. 217). In her immobility she resembles the husband she kills. Ironically, Verloc's perception of his own predicament after the explosion foreshadows that of his wife: 'How ... could he tell her ... that a notion grows in the mind sometimes till it acquires an outward existence, an independent power of its own, and even a suggestive voice?' (p. 196).

What defeats the reader's expectations is not only the shock of the murder itself, the act of violence intruding suddenly into the superficial domesticity of the Verloc household, but primarily Winnie Verloc's total detachment from the act she commits. Here the lexical and syntactic, as well as the phonological, features of the text gradually communicate Mrs Verloc's dissociation from the act of murder itself, her self-effacement, and the shift away from the proleptic murder weapon, as illustrated by the following sentence: 'Her right hand skimmed slightly the end of the table, and when she had passed on towards the end of the sofa the carving knife had vanished without the slightest sound from the side of the dish' (p. 215). Mrs Verloc hardly makes contact with the surrounding reality. Her hand performs an agentive role in a highly transitive *action-intention* process: the verb 'skimmed' (barely touching) is reinforced by the adverb *slightly*. The actions 'had passed' and 'had vanished' are minimised by means of the perfective aspect, which serves a backgrounding function in the narration of events.

Stylisticians have offered meaningful analyses of the murder scene. Ann Cluysenaar (and other commentators)[12] demonstrate how Verloc's slow realization that he is about to be murdered is conveyed mimetically through syntactic delay, intransitive and mental verb processes and lexical repetition. Cluysenaar stresses how the actual strike catches both Verloc and the reader unaware. The narratological description climaxes in a passive sentence: 'The knife was already planted in his breast' (p. 216). This is how the veiled dance macabre is depicted in the text:

> He saw partly on the ceiling and partly on the wall the moving shadow of an arm with a clenched hand holding a carving knife. It flickered up and down. Its movements were leisurely. They were leisurely enough for Mr. Verloc to recognize the limb and the weapon. They were leisurely enough for him to take in the full meaning of the portent, and to taste the flavour of death rising in his gorge. His wife had gone raving mad – murdering mad. They were leisurely enough for the first paralyzing effect of this discovery to pass away before a resolute determination to come out victorious from the ghastly struggle with that armed lunatic. They were leisurely enough for Mr. Verloc to elaborate a plan of defence involving a dash behind the table .... But they were not leisurely enough to allow Mr. Verloc the time to move either hand or foot. The knife was already planted in his breast. (pp. 215–16)

All that the *experiencer* Verloc sees at first is 'the shadow of an arm' holding the knife. His cognition is delayed by means of the intervening, anticipatory adjunct 'partly on the ceiling and partly on the wall' and the repeated clause 'They were leisurely enough'. Leech and Short, citing Cluysenaar's analysis, comment on the stylistically subversive depiction of the murder and on how the lexical choices 'flicker' and 'leisurely' undermine the violence of the act. They query: 'How can a flicker be leisurely, and how can a death-blow be described with an adverb suggesting the absence of energy, tension and purpose?' ... But, they conclude, 'in this lies the point of the description' (p. 238).

The very subdued, and therefore, horrifying, tone of the murder scene is effected by the syntactic choices and stands in direct contrast to that of an earlier version. One of the revisions that *The Secret Agent* underwent from its original serial version to its final novel form pertains to the murder scene.[13] Interestingly, in the serial Winnie does assume an agentive role in the murder. Although the actual murder is described very briefly, a comparison of the serialised version with the revised account quoted above emphasises the fundamental difference in orientation: 'The last thing Mr Verloc saw in his life was the shadow of an arm on the wall. *She struck.* Accident has such accuracies. It was a most effective blow. Mr Verloc exhaled a deep sigh of death' (quoted in Davis, p. 251). In the revised novel, the murder scene, with its exclusion of the second sentence (*She struck*), is emblematic of the agentless event, which in turn, is central to the novel's theme of moral insulation and anarchy.

Evasion of agency is also manifested on a narratological level. The complex identity and function of the authorial narrator hinge on a question of pronominal reference. At a single point in the narrative, the third-person narrator refers to himself in the first-person. The following passage of narratological commentary occurs at the end of the embassy episode – the narrator is describing Verloc:

> But there was also about him an indescribable air which no mechanic could have acquired in the practice of his handicraft however dishonestly exercised: the air common to men who live on their vices, the follies of baser fears of mankind: the air of moral nihilism common to keepers of gambling halls … to drink sellers and, I should say, to the sellers of invigorating electric belts and to the inventors of patent medicines. But of that last I am not sure, not having carried my investigations so far into the depths. For all I know, the expression of these last may be perfectly diabolical …. What I want to affirm is that Mr. Verloc was by no means diabolical. (pp. 24–5)

This passage is marked by its fleeting, though powerful use of the first-person pronoun, followed later in the text by a return to the third-person authorial narrative that is sustained throughout the novel. The first-person is promptly depersonalised. The ambiguity created bears a curious resemblance to Conrad's own conception of the writer's role and the basic ethical paradox concerning artistic accountability as stated in 'A Familiar Preface' (1912):

> He stands there the only reality in an invented world among imaginary things, happenings and people. Writing about them,

> he is only writing about himself. But the disclosure is not complete. He remains, to a certain extent, a figure behind the veil; a suspected rather than a seen presence – a movement and a voice behind the draperies of fiction.[14]

Conrad could well be referring here not merely to the 'protective veil' of art, designed to shield the writer's privacy as Berman asserts, but rather to the personal evasiveness and indirection of the artist – another aspect of moral anarchy.

Only in the aftermath of the murder does Mrs Verloc assume personal responsibility for her deed. She engages in a gradual process of naming Verloc's death 'an extremely plain case of murder' (p. 219) with herself as its agent. For an instant Winnie still tries to distance herself from the act by the familiar means of blaming the victim: 'Her mental state was tinged by the sort of austere contempt for that man who had let himself be killed so easily' (p. 218). The passive construction underscores her contempt.

Earlier, just as she is about to commit the murder and in the delusional state that follows, the veiled Winnie is perceived and perceives herself as a 'free woman': 'She had become a free woman with a perfection of freedom which left her nothing to desire and absolutely nothing to do ...' (p. 216). The sense of autonomous freedom from all external constraints which characterises Winnie's deranged state violates Kant's notion that freedom implies that the individual must take responsibility for his actions. In this sense Winnie Verloc is not free until she recognises herself as murderer. Once she does so we are told that 'Mrs. Verloc was no longer a person of leisure and irresponsibility' (p. 219). Her fear transforms her as she confronts the punitive consequences of her deed. Again, as Leech and Short point out, her transformation is linguistically realised.[15] Winnie ironically directs her attention to the impersonal, agentless nature of her impending execution in the following succession of three structurally parallel simple sentences: 'She saw there an object. That object was the gallows. Mrs. Verloc was afraid of the gallows.' In her 'abstract terror', Winnie is engaged in *internal perception* process alone. She focuses solely on the goal object as she contemplates her 'verbless' execution: 'The drop was fourteen feet' – a finite assertion that leaves no room for the questions *who*? or *why*? or *how*? Her refrain of 'not looking into things' is replaced by the fragmented newspaper account of her suicide, the broken 'rhythm of journalistic phrases' in Ossipon's mind at the very end:

'An impenetrable mystery ... this act of madness or despair' (pp. 251–2). The portrayal of Winnie's disintegration – her 'anarchistic' end – is thus largely dependent on the force and iconicity of linguistic-stylistic textual features. The final passages of the text mirror her psychological and moral breakdown in syntactic and phonological detail. Winnie's 'act of madness and despair' takes us back to the public sphere of the novel, to Vladimir's lecture to Verloc on 'the philosophy of bomb throwing':

> But what is one to say to an act of destruction so absurd as to be incomprehensible, inexplicable, almost unthinkable, in fact mad? Madness alone is truly terrifying, inasmuch as you cannot placate it either by threats, persuasion or bribes. (p. 40)

Against this background the narrator quotes the late Baron Stott Wartenheim, Verloc's erstwhile employer. The Baron's grim warning is eerily prophetic in a historical context: 'Unhappy Europe thou shalt perish by the moral insanity of thy children.'

In the 'anarchic' world of *The Secret Agent*, a world of the *avant guerre*, a bureaucratic world (marked by the deferral of agency and 'the rule of Nobody' in the public and private spheres), identities are veiled and evasion of responsibility in the exercise of power culminates in purposeless violence, madness and devastation. Neither the law-abiding police hierarchy nor the lawless anarchists are exempt from this condition. In such a world human beings are considered means and not ends. In the bleak world of *The Secret Agent*, E.M. Forster's dictum 'only connect' is alien to the discrete emotivist lexicons of its somnambulist inhabitants.

In 1907, the world had not yet witnessed the impact of modern warfare and the atrocities of the 'death industry' devised by the Nazis. World-wide terrorism had not yet come into being. But what a sergeant writing about a bombed area in Europe had to say sums up the evasion of individual responsibility as conveyed in *The Secret Agent*: 'In modern war there are crimes not criminals .... Somewhere in the apparatus of bureaucracy, memoranda, and clean efficient directives, a crime has been committed.'[16] The rhetoric of dissociation and the deliberate distortion of the language of human action, which separate doer from deed in the novel, only serve to underscore the growing dangers of a moral malaise.

A stylistic approach to Conrad's 'atypical' text, with special emphasis on such linguistic techniques as participant-role analysis, confirms this vision. After all, by asking the ostensibly simple question 'who does what to whom?' the linguist is also posing the basic question of moral agency and one of the key moral questions of our time. As noted, the question of agency also affects narratological choices such as the writer's stance, the detachment and evasiveness of Conrad's authorial narrator (the aesthetic virtue of distancing) vis-à-vis the ethical call for personal accountability and sympathy – a paradoxical situation which suggests that aesthetic claims and moral claims may often be at odds. *The Secret Agent* suggests that the idea of irresponsible actions carried out by absent agents transcends the boundaries of clandestine anarchist activity in its narrowest political sense.

Notes

1. Irving Howe, 'Conrad: Order and Anarchy', *Politics and the Novel* (New York: Horizon Press, 1957) 96.
2. Various researchers have pointed out Conrad's familiarity with anarchist publications: see, for example, Norman Sherry, 'The Greenwich Bomb Outrage and *The Secret Agent*' (1967) and Ian Watt, 'The Political and Social Background of *The Secret Agent*' (1973) in Ian Watt, ed., *The Secret Agent, A Selection of Critical Essays* (New York: Macmillan, 1973) 202–29. J. E. Saveson argues that Conrad's characterisation of anarchists is closely based on Cesare Lombroso's account in *Les Anarchistes* and on editorials concerning anarchists appearing in *Blackwood's Magazine* between 1899 and 1907, the year the novel first appeared. Conrad himself denied an interest in the philosophy of anarchism (*Conrad, The Later Moralist* [Amsterdam: Rodopi, 1974]). Leo Gurko cites Conrad's letter to John Galsworthy dated September 12, 1906 in this regard: 'I had no idea to consider anarchism politically – or to treat it seriously in its philosophical aspect as a manifestation of human nature in its discontent and imbecility.' ('*The Secret Agent*: Conrad's Vision of Megalopolia', *Modern Fiction Studies*, 4, 4 [1958] 307–18.) See the *Collected Letters of Joseph Conrad*, ed. Frederick R. Karl and Laurence Davies, 3 vols (Cambridge University Press, 1990) III, 354–5, for the letter in its entirety.
3. The complexity and controversial nature of the multi-dimensional concept allows for no clear-cut definitions, as is made evident in the proceedings of the 1978 conference on anarchism held by the American Society for Legal and Political Philosophy. See J. R. Pennock and J. W. Chapman, eds, *Anarchism* (New York: New York University Press, 1978).
4. Joseph Conrad, *The Secret Agent* (New York: Doubleday–Anchor,

1953) 203. All subsequent references will be to this edition, a reprint of the original edition of 1907.

5. My analysis is based on the linguistic model of processes and participants in clause structure proposed by Elizabeth Closs Traugott and Mary Louise Pratt's semantic account of 'role relations' (Elizabeth Cross Traugot and Mary Louise Pratt, *Linguistics for Students of Literature* [New York: Harcourt Brace, 1980]) and Margaret Berry's detailed description of transitivity choices and exposition of process options (*An Introduction to Systematic Linguistics*, 2 vols [London: Batsford, 1975] 149 ff.). The following participant roles and process options are essential to the analysis: an Agent is responsible for the action performed; an Affected (or Patient) is the object acted upon; an Experiencer is emotionally or cognitively affected by an action and an Instrument signifies the means by which an action is performed. (For a more detailed discussion, see Traugott and Pratt, *Linguistics for Students of Literature*, 192–8 and Berry, *Introduction to Systemic Linguistics*, I, 150–3.) Regarding 'process options', Berry distinguishes between *material, mental* and *relational*; she further subdivides material processes into 'action' and 'event' processes, and 'action' processes into 'intention' and 'supervention' processes. Thus she differentiates between the voluntary participation of the agent (actor) and 'a process which just happens' (*Introduction to Systematic Linguistics*, 153). Both models are based on M.A.K. Halliday, 'Language Structure and Language Function', in *New Horizons in Linguistics*, ed. John Lyons (Harmondsworth: Penguin, 1970). Also see Deidre Burton, 'Through Glass Darkly: Through Dark Glasses', in Ronald Carter, ed., *Language and Literature* (London: Allen & Unwin, 1982) 195–214.

6. Alasdair MacIntyre, *After Virtue* (Notre Dame, IN: Notre Dame University Press, 1984) 107.

7. George Woodcock, *Anarchism: A History of Libertarian Ideas and Movements* (Harmondsworth: Penguin, 1963) 8.

8. The syntactic deletion of human actors (or what Roger Fowler terms 'pseudoagency' (*Linguistics and the Novel* [London: Methuen, 1977]) enables the distinction. As Julian and Zelda Boyd comment: 'What is crucial to a doing is human agency. Happenings are events without agency (this includes things like involuntary bodily movements) which happen to people.' See 'To Lose the Name of Action', *PTL: A Journal for Descriptive Poetics and Theory of Literature*, 2 (1977) 21–32; 23.

9. See April Carter, *The Political Theory of Anarchism* (London: Routledge, 1971) 338. Carter discusses the anarchist's attraction to violence and its Dionysian quality as well as his celebration of the sensual nature of man. The restaurant is thus aptly named for Silenus, the satyr and companion of Dionysus.

10. Roger Fowler, 'Power', in Teun van Dyck, ed., *Handbook of Discourse Analysis*, 4 vols (London: Academic Press, 1985) 65–80; 71.

11. A detailed 'role' analysis of eighty-eight clauses involving Verloc as participant (pp. 26–42; Ch. 2), from 'Mr. Verloc … was suddenly motioned' to 'he has armed himself with patience', confirms his state

of 'unobtrusive deference' in the embassy episode. In twenty-two clauses Verloc is assigned the role of Agent; however that agentive role is mitigated in various ways. In four of the clauses involving *material-action-intention* processes the action is negated, as in 'He did not take a seat' and 'Mr. Verloc made no answer' (p. 27). In three of the clauses the action process is qualified through modals, as in 'Mr. Verloc would have rubbed ...' or 'He would have winked at himself' (an interesting instance of self-reflexive transitivity). In one of the action clauses Verloc's agentive role is deflated by a passive Instrument: 'He had armed himself with patience.' Verloc fills the role of Experiencer of *mental-internalised-perception* processes in fourteen clauses and of Affected in six. His body parts or parts of his attire are assigned five agentive roles in *material-action-intention* processes; for example, 'The shoulders of Mr. Verloc, without actually moving, suggested a shrug' (p. 27) or 'his heavy-lidded eyes sent glances'. Five clauses also have Verloc's body parts in Experiencer and Affected roles.

12. Ann Cluysenaar, *Introduction to Literary Stylistics* (London: Batsford, 1976). See also Chris Kennedy, 'Systemic Grammar and Its Use in Literary Analysis', in Ronald Carter, ed., *Language and Literature*, 82–91.
13. See Harold Davis, 'Conrad's Revisions of *The Secret Agent*: A Study in Literary Impressionism', *Modern Language Quarterly*, 19 (1958) 244–54.
14. Quoted in Walter F. Wright, *Joseph Conrad* (Lincoln: University of Nebraska Press, 1964) 119.
15. Geoffrey N. Leech and Michael H. Short, *Style in Fiction* (London: Longman, 1981).
16. Quoted in Carter, *Political Theory of Anarchism*, 24.

6
John Cheever's *The Swimmer* and the Abstract Standpoint of Kantian Moral Philosophy

Rebecca Hughes and Kieron O'Hara

6.1 KANTIAN MORAL ABSTRACTION

In Kantian philosophy, morality demands that individuals be treated as deserving significant and equal respect. People should be seen as ends of moral behaviour, and not just as means to independently desirable outcomes. Morality is grounded on the categorical imperative, that 'I should never act except in such a way that I can also will that my maxim should become a universal law'. In other words, one may be subject to contradictory *desires* or *interests*, but these cannot be supported by *reason*.

In the second place, because any plausible moral maxim must be *universal*, particular individuals cannot be singled out for special (good or bad) treatment. A law cannot be universal if it only applies selectively. It may be desirable for me (or even for society as a whole) to receive specially good treatment in some way, but this cannot be a moral claim because reason will not support it. If I were morally entitled to reserve some good for myself, then by parity of reasoning, others would also be entitled to do the same. These individual selfish maxims would ultimately contradict each other.

The categorical imperative was Kant's attempt to ground morality in reason. His philosophy is an Enlightenment one, suspicious of earlier views in which patterns of behaviour were to be justified by an appeal to the world, either to entrenched practices or to metaphysical theories. For the sceptical Enlightened thinker, it was not enough to say that a practice was morally correct because it was implied by God's laws; a *reason* had to be given that was undeniable by any rational thinker. In Kant's analysis of morality and reason, only the categorical imperative could underlie our current moral behaviour in the right way (Kant's moral theory was conservative, and intended to respect the majority of moral judgements actually made). Under Kantian morality, because special treatment cannot be justified by reason, all (rational) individuals are deserving of equal respect, and for that reason should be treated as autonomous (i.e. as responsible for their own moral judgements and actions).

It is not our intention to examine, justify or criticise Kantian moral theory. We merely introduce it by way of providing a context for our discussion of the work of John Cheever and its contribution to moral philosophy. But note that this is not an arcane piece of exegesis. It is part of a live debate in philosophy and politics about the universality of morality. Newspapers are full of stories about the clashes between toleration and fundamentalism, and the preservation of cultural values against apparently malign forces. Moral judgements made from particular points of view tend to lead to intellectual gridlock between opposing groups of people who refuse (or are unable) to see each others' points of view. On the other hand, if one group *is* or *feels* entitled to impose its views on others, and is powerful enough so to do (e.g. in the imposition of Muslim law in Iran, say, or the suppression of Muslim elements in Algeria), the result is often an unacceptable restriction on individual liberty. The issue of whether character and culture are relevant to moral judgements is central to politico-moral discourse and one on which there is little consensus.[1]

Debate also continues in the academy along essentially Kantian lines. For example, in the influential work of John Rawls,[2] the contractarian theory of morality has been resurrected. On this theory, moral judgements should be made by examining how a rational agent would decide his or her best interests *in the abstract* about a moral issue. The abstractness of such a decision is essential to avoid special interest pleading, and to ensure a genuinely disinterested outcome. The moral thinker is to be placed behind what is rather poetically known as the 'veil of ignorance'.

> Among the essential features of this situation is that no one knows his place in society, his class position or social status, nor does any one know his fortune in the distribution of natural assets and abilities, his intelligence, strength and the like. I shall

> even assume that the parties do not know their conceptions of the good or their special psychological propensities. The principles of justice are chosen behind a veil of ignorance. This ensures that no one is advantaged or disadvantaged in the choice of principles by the outcome of natural chance or the contingency of social circumstances. Since all are similarly situated and no one is able to design principles to favor his particular condition, the principles of justice are the result of a fair agreement or bargain.[3]

In other words, behind such a veil of ignorance, moral maxims can be developed in good faith, without covertly working to any particular person's advantage. Behind the veil of ignorance, no individual would think that it was in his interests that, say, slavery was permissible, because there would always be the possibility that he could turn out to be a slave. This abstraction in moral discussions, designed to promote fairness, is a very Kantian strategy; the veil of ignorance performs the same task as the plea for universality did in Kant's original categorical imperative.

Many voices have been raised against this rarefied view of morality. For example Bernard Williams has argued that one's view of the good is often a constitutive part of one's identity and character, and that therefore to abstract from such a view can have the effect of removing all that is distinctively human from an individual:

> one reaches the necessity that such things as deep attachments to other persons will express themselves in the world in ways which cannot at the same time embody the impartial view, and that they also run the risk of offending against it.
>
> They run that risk if they exist at all; yet unless such things exist, there will not be enough substance or conviction in a man's life to compel his allegiance to life itself. Life has to have substance if anything is to have sense, including adherence to the impartial system; but if it has substance, then it cannot grant supreme importance to the impartial system, and that system's hold on it will be, at the limit, insecure.[4]

More recently, Bruce Brower has argued that failing to take account of others' conceptions of the good while making moral judgments is to fail to see them as autonomous individuals worthy of respect, by neglecting to consider the issues that they themselves view as most important in a moral context.[5] Bruce Ackerman claims that Rawls himself, in his later work on liberalism, can only preserve distinctively liberal views by jettisoning the veil of ignorance.[6]

Hence, Kantian moral abstraction is very much a live issue in current debates on morality and politics. As we say, we do not wish to resolve such disputes, even were we so capable. Our aim here is merely to provide the context for our discussion of the work of John Cheever, to which we will now turn.

6.2 AN ANTI-KANTIAN READING OF *THE SWIMMER*

We focus on *The Swimmer*, as one of Cheever's most famous reflections on identity and character.[7] The plot is simple yet horrific. The morning after a party, a group of well-heeled suburbanites assemble by the swimming pool, bemoaning their drinking of the previous night. Neddy Merrill, one of the guests, realises while drinking a gin that he could 'swim' the eight miles back to his home in Bullet Park via the swimming pools of his friends. This act assumes some symbolic importance for him.

> His life was not confining and the delight he took in this observation could not be explained by its suggestion of escape. He seemed to see, with a cartographer's eye, that string of swimming pools, that quasi-subterranean stream that curved across the county. He had made a discovery, a contribution to modern geography; he would name the stream Lucinda after his wife. He was not a practical joker nor was he a fool but he was determinedly original and had a vague and modest idea of himself as a legendary figure. The day was beautiful and it seemed to him that a long swim might enlarge and celebrate its beauty. (p. 777)

Initially he is welcomed on his journey by his friends, but gradually they become more sympathetic than friendly, commiserating with him about misfortunes he does not recognise as his own. He is snubbed by a family of social climbers and rejected by an ex-mistress. Finally he reaches his home and discovers that it is locked and empty, and in a state of disrepair.

The revelation of Neddy as a detested bankrupt clearly makes points about the superficiality of human relationships in the suburban society depicted by Cheever. Further, it has been convincingly suggested that the story acts as a parable of Cheever's own artistic position as a chronicler of American life.[8] But the story also has a psychological angle, and it is this that is most relevant to the problem of moral abstraction. For Neddy's experience provides, on a straightforward reading, a criticism of the Kantian abstractionism discussed in Part I.

Neddy's view of himself is as a man without a past, an abstract man who is to be judged on his current deeds. He is divested of clothes (he would prefer to swim the Lucinda River naked), and is, in his own mind at least, a heroic figure. His heroism is exemplified by his act of 'exploration' through the swimming pools of his friends. At the edge of the county, eight miles from home, they are willing to go along with the charade. But as we get closer to Bullet Park, his past actions – his snubbing of the Biswangers, his ill-treatment of Shirley Adams, his failed financial dealings – are held against him and finally we discover that, rather than being an abstract man, he is merely someone who has lost his place in society, by simultaneously alienating those who might have supported him through his troubles and squandering the money that is a prerequisite for social acceptance.

Hence the trip down the Lucinda River is at the same time a psychological trip into Neddy's heart. Superficially he is a hero, suave and welcome; but as we get deeper into his psyche, we discover the bad faith, selfishness, snobbishness and, ultimately, the emptiness at his core. Neddy's attempt to slough off these accretions, to become abstract, is too late; he only invites contempt.

The point against Kantian rationalism in this straightforward reading is now reasonably clear. A person's character and past *are* relevant to moral judgements. Pragmatically, it is difficult if not impossible for people's moral judgements not to be coloured by knowledge of a disreputable (or indeed reputable) character or past. But on a more idealistic level, Cheever seems to be challenging the claim that someone like Neddy *deserves* to be judged in abstraction from his earlier misdemeanours. He has not earned the right to be judged solely on the basis of his current actions; he has not *purged* his guilt.

6.3 DISCONTINUITY IN *THE SWIMMER*

The straightforward reading of the story depends on a continuity of events, heavily underlined by Cheever in the temporal and physical structuring of the story as a journey along a chain of swimming pools visited by the protagonist in a geographically plausible linear manner, and by a lack of explicit temporal marking other than from the perspective of the central character who sees the events of the journey as taking place on a single Sunday afternoon in Midsummer.

Nevertheless, the apparent continuity of events as seen through Neddy's eyes is subverted by significant background discontinuities and contradictions in the development of the dramatic journey 'home'. Not only is there a typical end-of-story 'twist' (i.e. the house which has been described as full of affluent family fun is in truth empty and decaying), but the reader is also sent back on a journey of discovery to reconsider the facts of the case in order to iron out, if possible, this final undeniable contradiction.

Therefore, on one level *The Swimmer* has the organisation of a 'classic' short story, relying on an apparently tight maintenance of the unities building up to a punchy ending within a single uninterrupted spatiotemporal line. However, since the climax is one of a twist in perspective and a contradiction between the narratorial stance of the central figure and that of the external context, the reader's reconsideration of the story also involves a reassessment of Neddy's status (both social and psychological). Cheever plays a temporal and physical context off against an atemporal and self-absorbed perspective which cannot permit discontinuity and change. Neddy's internal experience of time is severely at odds with events and surroundings he encounters on his journey. As such, the story is close to being a textual version of an optical illusion.

The story opens with an explicit time reference: 'It was one of those midsummer Sundays …' (p. 776). This is not presented from the internal perspective of the figure we come to distrust, but as an external statement of fact. Therefore, we feel secure in the knowledge not only of the day of the week, but also of the time of year. Neddy sits by the pool with a gin and conceives the plan to swim home, mentally mapping out the route which takes in 15 pools, including the public baths.

But things are not this simple. A number of dissonances with Neddy's understanding of events cause the reader to doubt the straightforward view. His wife to whom he talks about his project to swim to Bullet Park (p. 777) has disappeared from his life; a maple tree, which Neddy assumes must be blighted, is showing signs of Autumn (p. 780), as is a beech hedge (p. 783); the stars in the sky are the constellations of Autumn (p. 787); Neddy seems to have aged and lost weight during the day (p. 784).

But among the discontinuities, continuities are strung. A pile of cumulus cloud makes a number of appearances (pp. 776, 780), as does an aeroplane (pp. 779, 780). Together, the continuities and discontinuities disorient the reader, as does the closeness of the narrative stance to Neddy's subjective view when Neddy reveals uncertainties of memory (pp. 781, 785, 788), or when there is a bizarre reflection about the passengers of the evening train: 'He thought of the provincial station at that hour, where a waiter, his tuxedo concealed by a raincoat, a dwarf with some flowers wrapped in newspaper, and a woman who had been crying would be waiting for the local' (p. 780).

Neddy sets out in Midsummer and completes his swim in Autumn. Robert Slabey suggests the story compresses several years, presumably on the evidence of the conversation with the Sachses (pp. 784–5).[9] He sets out prosperous, youthful, if not young, and loved. He arrives bankrupt, weak, and despised. A single character cannot contain these contradictions, and something has to give.

6.4 CONTINUITY IN *THE SWIMMER*

In placing the discontinuous and incompatible elements to the story in the background, and simultaneously emphasising continuity, Cheever colludes in the foregrounding of the straightforward anti-Kantian reading of the story. It is easy to miss the significance of the blighted trees and changed constellations, since the author is at such pains to present a seamless surface. In this reading, Neddy is devalued by the stripping away of the circumstances which make him special: money, vitality, charm, the love and admiration of others. The easiest way out of the final contradiction of the empty house is to say that the man who thought the house was unchanged was deluded all along. That is to say, Neddy is confused from the outset, and since he develops into an unreliable commentator, we cannot judge whether his perceptions of anything were correct. The wintry aspect of the world may or may not be real, and as Cheever is careful to maintain his neutrality on this point we cannot judge. In this reading the contradictions take on symbolic connotations, rather than being pointers to the impossibility of the story's apparent temporal framework. The result is that we remain outside Neddy's crisis, which must, if the story is continuous, pre-date its beginning.

This is certainly a possible reading, and serious commentators have adopted it.[10] Furthermore, such a reading is explicitly adopted in the film version by Frank Perry and Sydney Pollack. The action of the film takes place in late Summer, while Neddy seems convinced that it is earlier in the year. There is little or no temporal discontinuity (save for a strange cut in the credits sequence). Most of the new events introduced in the film tend to confirm Neddy's self-deluding nature; for instance he appears to remember or imagine a splendid horse, which in the next shot is present before him. There are no objective witnesses to the horse's existence. Neddy races the horse and finishes level with it.

The chief difference between the film and the story is the initial situation. In the story, Neddy has been at the Westerhazys' party; he is drinking a gin in the morning after. His wife Lucinda is also present. This means that he is a socially successful man at the point at which he dreams up his scheme to swim home. In the film, however, Neddy comes (nearly) naked out of the woods, to surprise the Westerhazys, who greet him as a long-lost friend. Lucinda is not present. In their conversation, as Neddy dreams up the swimming scheme, it is already being hinted that all is not well with the Merrills. At the next pool, Neddy's claims that his daughters are playing tennis at home are met with astonishment and bemusement. This confirms that, on the continuous reading, the story postdates the crisis in Neddy's life, while on the discontinuous reading the crisis happens after the Westerhazys' party but before Neddy arrives home.

Hence, on the continuous reading, what we see is the impossibility of one man's illusion that he can retain his abstract 'legendary' status in the face of the fact of the loss of all the incidental factors which have gone to make up this character a project that is patently flawed since it is impossible to square the circle of his self-perception with the harsh facts of his real state.

On the discontinuous reading, however, the ill-fitting temporal framework serves to do more than highlight the delusions. If we take seriously the temporal markers in Cheever's story it cannot take place on the same Midsummer Sunday. The seamless presentation of the events places us in the same epistemological crisis as Neddy: we appear to begin and end a single journey on a single afternoon, but something of which we only have the briefest intimation has happened to shake the very foundations of the world to the point where everything is changed and we cannot trust our perceptions of the world around us or our understanding of the past. On this reading, the story plays out the struggle between abstraction and materialism dramatically before the eyes of the reader, placing us in the heart of the crisis as we waver between Neddy's efforts at abstracting himself from the detritus of his past, and the material facts which contradict and undermine this process. Neddy must build a wall of delusion between himself and the material world to maintain the vision of himself as hero.

Hence the difference in the initial conditions of the two readings entails the following: in the continuous reading (film) the cross-county swim is the conception of a man who has lost his reason; in the discontinuous reading (story) it is the conception of an (outwardly) successful man. In the continuous reading the 'explorer' discovers the hollowness of his own heart; in the discontinuous reading he is genuinely exploring a world, Cheever's strange suburban world. As his explorations continue, and as he loses the advantages of his social status, he disappears; the world becomes invisible to him, and he to it. His identity (or at least those aspects of his identity which he values most) is bound up very strongly with the accidents of his social success; when he loses them, he is thrown into crisis.

In the discontinuous reading, Neddy mistakes the accidents of social success for a heroic character. In the continuous reading, he attempts to replace his previous criteria of heroism and nobility (social success) with a more primitive idea of heroism based on physical perfection and an abstraction from history (a process aided by the casting of Burt Lancaster in the movie). He fails to see that heroic deeds involve a moral rectitude that he has never mastered or even understood. On the other hand, the discontinuous reading leaves his heroic status open; Neddy's ultimate failure still leaves it possible that he might have succeeded had he not been evicted from his Eden. The swim combined with his social success seems to underline his exceptional status within his own restricted society. Perhaps Neddy is no saint, but he still has a vision.[11]

In his private writings, incidentally, Cheever appears to be neutral between these two readings. In his journals for 1963, he seems to endorse the discontinuous reading.

> The Swimmer might go through the seasons; I don't know, but I know it is not Narcissus. Might the seasons change? Might the leaves turn and begin to fall? Might it grow cold? Might there be snow? But what is the meaning of this? One does not grow old in the space of an afternoon? Oh, well, kick it around.[12]

However, in a letter to his Russian translator Tanya Litvinov in 1966, he implies that the film's continuous reading is more or less faithful to his conception of the story.

> Eleanor Perry, who wrote the screen play has added a couple of scenes but she's followed the line and sense of the story precisely. There are no flashbacks, no explanations for his mysterious journey and it ends in an empty house in a thunder storm.[13]

The two readings, it seems, cannot be too far apart. Both readings are critical of the Kantian abstractionism discussed in Part I, the history and culture of an agent cannot simply be ignored when it comes to moral evaluations. But whereas the continuous reading gives us a reasonably straightforward criticism of moral abstractionism, the discontinuous reading is rather more subtle. In the discontinuous version, the abstraction that Neddy wants to perform is seen as part of his character and milieu, as something noble that the suburban hero is compelled to do. Hence abstractionism is not placed alongside and in competition with the other moral judgements that might be made about his snobbishness, promiscuity or (in the film at least) racism. In the discontinuous reading, the abstractionism is part of the suburban value system, an apparently tolerant moral maxim that in reality enforces cultural conformity.

All moral codes are culturally conditioned, hints the discontinuous reading. So, the Rawlsian rational agent hidden behind the veil of ignorance is in reality something like the rational economic man beloved of capitalism and the Chicago school of economics. The abstract man postulated by the Kantian categorical imperatives is compromised by immersion in a set of values.

> Consequently, [Kant] saw our moral life through a pair of spectacles ground to fit the eyes of an eighteenth-century, enlightened, Christian, Stoic moral teacher.[14]

One final point relevant to the decision between the two readings: in so far as the story is to be seen as a criticism of a disengaged moral rationalism, it is not enough simply to revel in its ambiguities. Many readers (maybe even Cheever, to judge from the quote from his journals) will sadistically enjoy the uncertainties of Neddy's plight, and marvel, properly, at Cheever's stylistic skill at bringing the ambiguity about. But taking the work as a piece of moral philosophy – and we naturally accept that it is much more than that – its engagement with Kantian ideas depends on taking one reading or another. This is not to say that either reading is the 'correct' one, whatever that may mean; neither is it to say that only one of the readings has philosophical force. It is only to say that, in a philosophical engagement, each reading needs to be precisely delineated, in order that their implications be clear.

6.5 PROSE, FILM AND IDEAS

Cheever's prose conveys Neddy's subjective world via the discontinuities of the temporal scheme and the ambiguities of the incidents reported. The film, however, denies itself access to these resources. *The Swimmer* is a relatively conventional Hollywood film, and tacitly accepts the conventions of the Hollywood cinema. We do not argue that the film-makers were *wrong* to use such a set of stylistic conventions, only that the use of such conventions subtly biases the story's message from an attempt to understand the social structures of the suburbs, to a criticism of their emptiness.

Standardly, such a film reveals events in the order in which they occur; they unfold from an opening. Flashbacks (well-flagged) are permitted as ways of revealing characters' memories gradually, but 'flashforwards' are very rarely used. Yet underlying the cohesion that is assumed by such conventions is the psychological process of temporal integration, the process of creating a coherent view from one's memories, current experiences and expectations. The success of this process depends very strongly on there being a coherent account of one's history and future available to the subject, and it is this that Cheever subverts by showing us Neddy's confusion from the inside. As David Bordwell puts it:

> The film which challenges this coherence [of the meanings of the past, present and future], a film like *Not Reconciled* (1964), *Last*

> *Year at Marienbad* (1961), or *India Song* (1975), must make temporal integration difficult to achieve. In the classical [Hollywood] film, however, character causality provides the basis for temporal coherence ....
>
> Psychological causality thus permits the classical viewer to integrate the present with the past and to form clear-cut hypotheses about future story events.[15]

This inhibition from undermining psychological causality would seem to rule out blurring the distinction between objective and subjective truth for the protagonists. For this reason, such a film tends to treat us to the objective, and tries to portray the subjective either by the quality of the acting, or in 'fantasy' sequences that are clearly marked as such (as in the sequence with the imaginary horse in *The Swimmer*). When it comes to the bulk of the imagery, the classical film has to come down on one side or the other of an ambiguity. For example, whereas Cheever can tease us with the revelation that Neddy can't make out the stars of Midsummer (which may or may not entail that they are there), the film has to take a firm decision to show us the foliage of late Summer.

The Hollywood film has often been derided for its lack of subtlety and ideological rigidity.[16] This derision is often overstated. For example, in the case of *The Swimmer*, the interpretation of the story, while less rich than the discontinuous reading of the prose, is neither impoverished nor obviously inadequate.[17] On the other hand, it is clear that the requirement for relative objectivity can result in the loss of shades of meaning, particularly from a situation where the characters' relationships, beliefs and values are inconsistent or unclear. The classical film often finds itself having to judge, to take a stand on issues which could be left open.

Thus, the classical Hollywood conventions might be said to be rather less sympathetic to the ideas underlying moral abstractionism, generally having to adopt a materialist stance by showing incidental detail. Not only are fantasy/dream sequences typically flagged, but also in both 'reliable' and 'unreliable' scenes, choices have to be made about, for example, which actor plays which role. In special circumstances, information can be withheld from an audience (e.g. with respect to the figure in the red coat in the Venetian scenes from *Don't Look Now*), but in general the creative effort is not made. This is not to say that film is necessarily incapable of conveying things that can be conveyed in prose; only that the set of classical Hollywood conventions tends to assume an Archimedean point from which events and actions can be assessed.

Furthermore, the Hollywood star system tends to mean that the actors in a movie carry with them the baggage of their career. This can be exploited subversively, as for instance with Leone's casting of Henry Fonda as the villain in *Once Upon a Time in the West*, but most of an actor's films will support the common view of him as hero, villain, boffin, cantankerous but lovable old man, or whatever. When Burt Lancaster was cast as Neddy, the chief association for audiences of the time was of the swashbuckling hero of *The Crimson Pirate* and *The Flame and the Arrow* (although the audience for *The Swimmer* would probably also be aware of his more ambiguous roles in films such as *Elmer Gantry*). Hence a star's previous career can be used to create expectations that are either confirmed or undermined. Again, this is not a criticism of the star system, merely a statement of one of its properties. But the fact remains that that casting of Lancaster makes it very difficult to approach Neddy Merrill on film without preconceptions.

6.6 CONCLUSIONS

We have developed two readings of Cheever's story, one where the action takes place continuously over a single day, and another where there are important discontinuities, invisible to the story's leading character. Neither reading is unproblematic, and each has some support from Cheever's private writings. The continuous reading has to deal with a number of inconsistencies, such as the increasingly Autumnal tone of the descriptions (these inconsistencies, of course, were simply written out of the film version, which followed this reading). The discontinuous reading, conversely, has to discount the prominent markers of temporal continuity.

The chief difference between the two readings is that Neddy's crisis must predate the events narrated in the continuous version, while it must be included within the timeframe of the discontinuous version. This creates a large gulf between the conceptions of Neddy's exploration that each reading will support. In the continuous version, the journey down the Lucinda River is the idea of the madman, the failure, and can perhaps most happily be seen as a Quixotic attempt to regain heroic status (on minimal resources). In the discontinuous version, however, the swim home is the scheme of a man at the height of his powers, who then attempts, at some unspecified later point, to retrace his steps or strokes as a straightforward, if doomed, way of recreating his former success.

In each case, the effects of the difference can be seen in the way in which the idea of the heroic quest interacts with and criticises the Kantian idea of abstract moral argument. In neither case does the reading support the abstract view of morality; Neddy's past transgressions are the key indices of his failure. But whereas the continuous reading simply shows that Neddy's attempt to raise himself above his former shallow self will forever be blighted by memories of the shallowness and vindictive superficiality, the discontinuous reading produces a more complex criticism of the Kantian imperative.

In the first place, the heroic quest is an indicator, not of an abstraction over the suburban society that Cheever is studying, but rather of a way of injecting mythic meaning into the more or less banal occupations of drinking, partygoing, golf, tennis, infidelity and so on (this is perhaps analogous to Cash Bentley's furniture-hurdling in 'O Youth and Beauty!'). But again, the attempt to rise above the sordid or banal is doomed by the immersion in the sordid or banal; a man cannot absolve himself from moral failures in the past by present performance of a ceremony that is judged on its own terms. The ceremony itself is born of the banal, is a product of the banal. Its only function is absolution, and it can only perform that function from the standpoint of its conception (i.e. within the sordid, banal society), and therefore it cannot be used to transcend that society. In the limit, as Bernard Williams claimed, the messy substance of life has a greater hold than the impartial moral system.

Notes

1. Immanuel Kant, *Foundations of the Metaphysics of Morals*, trans. Lewis White Beck, 2nd edn (New York: Macmillan, 1990).
2. John Rawls, *A Theory of Justice* (Oxford University Press, 1972); *Political Liberalism* (New York: Columbia University Press, 1993).
3. Ibid., 12.
4. Bernard Williams, 'Persons, Character and Morality' in Amélie Oksenberg Rorty, ed., *The Identities of Persons* (Berkeley: University of California Press, 1976) 197–216; 215.

5. Bruce W. Brower, 'The Limits of Public Reason', *Journal of Philosophy*, 91 (1994) 5–26.
6. Bruce Ackerman, 'Political Liberalisms', *Journal of Philosophy*, 91 (1994) 364–86.
7. John Cheever, 'The Swimmer' in *The Stories of John Cheever* (London: Vintage, 1979) 776–88. All subsequent references to this edition are given in parentheses in the text.
8. Eugene Chesnick, 'The Domesticated Stroke of John Cheever' in R. G. Collins, ed., *Critical Essays on John Cheever* (Boston: G. K. Hall, 1971) 124–39; 135.
9. Robert M. Slabey, 'John Cheever: The "Swimming" of America' in R. G. Collins, ed., *Critical Essays on John Cheever* 180–91; 183.
10. Chesnick, 'Domesticated Stroke', 135–6, and, arguably, Michael D. Byrne, *Dragons and Martinis: The Skewed Realism of John Cheever* (San Bernardino: Borgo Press, 1993) 72.
11. Byrne, *Skewed Realism*, 16–17, 70–2.
12. John Cheever, *The Journals* (London: Vintage, 1991) 187–8.
13. Benjamin Cheever, ed., *The Letters of John Cheever* (London: Vintage, 1988) 235.
14. Roger J. Sullivan, *An Introduction to Kant's Ethics* (Cambridge University Press, 1994) 141.
15. David Bordwell, Janet Staiger and Kristin Thompson, *The Classical Hollywood Cinema: Film Style and Mode of Production to 1960* (London: Routledge, 1985) 43.
16. See the discussion in Bordwell *et al.*, *Classical Hollywood Cinema*, 3–11.
17. We get an analogous result in our analyses of the films *Under the Volcano* and *The Dead*; see Rebecca Hughes and Kieron O'Hara, 'The Filmmaker as Critic: Huston's *Under the Volcano* and *The Dead*' in Patrick A. McCarthy and Paul Tiessen, eds, *Joyce/Lowry: Critical Perspectives* (Lexington: University Press of Kentucky, 1997) 177–96.

Part III
Literature, Interpretation and Ethics

7

Understanding and Ethics in Coleridge: Description, Evaluation and Otherness

David P. Haney

Students of literature have always been concerned with the relationship between description and evaluation, which is perhaps why the distinction between 'fact' and 'value', the relation between what 'is' and what 'ought' to be, is a natural concern of literary critics who turn their attention to ethics. In the early part of this century the distinction appeared in the division of labour between scholars who described texts and critics who evaluated them.[1] Then we began to evaluate the merits of texts based on how well they could be described within a formalist and subsequently a deconstructive paradigm. Lately we have begun describing and evaluating with a vengeance: history has returned, descriptions have become 'thick' and anecdotal – but just as authoritative – and evaluation has moved from the aesthetic to the political.

Despite many permutations, the structural relationship between the 'is' of description and the 'ought' of evaluation remains fairly intact throughout this history, even though the usefulness of that distinction in ethical philosophy was brought into question as early as Hume.[2] A good example of how the fact/value distinction can be invoked in the name of description and evaluation (even as the objectivist version of the distinction is critiqued) is Barbara Herrnstein Smith's characterisation of the relativist as a moral agent. After noting that relativism entails 'no particular moral stance', she characterises that non-stance rather particularly: 'The relativist's social and political choices and actions are "compelled", then, ... by the specific, contingent *conditions* in which she operates as an agent, as she perceives, interprets, and considers these conditions – or, in short, *evaluates* them.'[3] This view suggests that as moral agents we 'evaluate' conditions that we can describe (or at least 'perceive' and 'interpret'), but that we already recognise as contingent, and that are therefore subject to no higher law than our own act of evaluation, which Smith is careful to dissociate from autonomous subjectivity,[4] but which operates within an economic model of social interaction. Smith's model of evaluation is ultimately literary-aesthetic,[5] which implies the very questionable assumption that a simple transfer of literary-critical skills to other areas of life will produce good moral agents.

The is/ought, fact/value, description/evaluation pair is problematic on both sides, though I will argue later that the very persistence of the pairing in literary studies has its own necessity and value. Literary theorists who reduce moral agency to evaluation – particularly aesthetic evaluation – often miss Julius Kovesi's point that 'evaluation', in which we make judgements based on the description of an 'is' (as when we call someone a good liar) 'is quite neutral to morals. We can and do evaluate both what we value and what we detest.'[6] Bernard Williams argues that ethical theorists, particularly those who see ethics as embedded in language, import distinctions such as that between 'fact' and 'value', when what they should be finding are 'thicker' notions of both reflective and non-reflective ethical knowledge.[7] The fact/value distinction has often been invoked as a way of grounding ethics in universal principles, but it also appears in postmodern arguments for these terms' incommensurability. For example, in 'Levinas's Logic', Lyotard invokes the difference between denotation and prescription as inevitable: 'But when the initial message is prescriptive, it seems inevitable that the commentary, being denotative, displaces the message's own genre.'[8]

The fact-value debate is further complicated by the historical conditions in which it has occurred. Not only do moral choices and debates about them occur within what Charles Taylor calls 'inescapable moral frameworks' that change over time,[9] but the terms we use often depend for their meaning on contexts that we no longer consider viable. G. E. M. Anscombe argues, for example, that the very term 'ought' is bound to be incoherent in ethical debate since Hume because it is meaningful only in the context of divine law issuing an unquestionable imperative.[10] Alasdair MacIntyre adds that we have impoverished our sense of agency by discarding, in addition to divine law, the moral psychology that would ground a theory of virtues and the good as we embrace a scientific empiricism. The result has been an incoherent division between reductive notions of fact and choice – we establish the 'facts', then make 'choices' – when in fact moral choices are not independent of how we see the facts.[11]

How facts are seen is itself problematic: Christopher Norris has recently raised some cogent objections to what he calls 'descriptivist' thinking, according to which 'the act of reference – of picking out an object – is a matter of applying the appropriate criteria as given by some current conceptual scheme or system of intra-linguistic representation'. This thinking begins with 'the *sense* of the referring expression' as a linguistic phenomenon rather than its '*reference*' to the world.[12] Norris points out that, although descriptivism is not necessarily anti-realist, its exaltation of linguistic representation has led to the relativism of Lyotard and Foucault, who have used the priority of linguistic 'sense', defined in Saussurean terms as arbitrary, to argue for the incommensurability and fictionality of discourses. Norris claims that these arguments entail illegitimately relativistic readings of the history of science as dependent on arbitrary and shifting paradigms; such readings, which are often invoked in support of a general historical relativism, ignore science's referential success even given the incompleteness of its paradigms. Norris is emphatically not arguing against the fact/value distinction – in fact, part of his project is to reinforce Kant's distinction between 'truths of experience' and aesthetic or ethical judgements[13] – but his analysis nonetheless suggests a problem with the way the 'fact' side of the fact/value distinction is presented in some recent literary theory.

In addition to suffering these logical difficulties, the fact/value, description/evaluation distinction does not do a very good job of accounting for the relation to others, and one must live according to either an unrealistically transcendental or an unrealistically internal code to be ethical all by oneself. 'Otherness', however, is a seriously problematic and clichéd term; as Norris points out, it becomes a mere 'rhetorical place-filler' if it confronts us with the false dilemma of choosing between the other as 'an involuntary construction out of our own discourse' or 'a locus of absolute alterity' before which we must refuse 'any common ground of insight or mutual understanding'.[14] Such is the case with the theories that remain tied to a descriptivist paradigm that leaves only two options – either the other can be fitted into our conceptual paradigm, or he/she cannot – and that reduces the world to a textual field.

However, partly because he does remain tied to a 'causal realist' argument, and thus to some of the restrictive binarism of the fact/value distinction, Norris perhaps underestimates the specificity and value of discussions of 'otherness' in the post-Heideggerian hermeneutic tradition of Hans-Georg Gadamer and Emmanuel Levinas,[15] to which group I will add Paul Ricoeur, who in my view can together provide an important bridge between literary interpretation and ethical thought. They offer, in different but importantly compatible ways, ethically concrete concepts of human otherness that permit us to do more than merely describe and evaluate people, relationships and situations. One of Gadamer's main objects of critique in *Truth and Method* is the kind of binarism that informs the descriptivist aspect of the fact/value distinction, specifically the view of language that sees meaning as constructed by systems of signs set in a representational opposition to the world.[16] According to Kovesi's critique of the is/ought pair, 'moral notions and judgments', instead of being evaluations based on separable descriptions of the world, 'are about our life insofar as our life is constituted by these very notions, judgments, concepts, and descriptions'.[17] This is a hermeneutic point; according to Gadamer, 'when we interpret the meaning of something', as opposed to when we indicate something semiotically, 'we actually interpret an interpretation'.[18] 'Presence' for Gadamer is in this sense not a matter of the representational presence that the early Derrida finds at the heart of meaning, but rather the presence of one person to another in a 'conversation' or 'game' in which subjects put their prejudices at risk in pursuit of a truth that is 'neither mine nor yours and hence so far transcends the interlocutors' subjective opinions that even the person leading the conversation knows that he does not know'.[19]

Gadamer and Levinas are very different, of course; Gadamer affirms the possibility of dialogic understanding and Levinas describes the human ethical situation that is prior to such thematisation, objecting in particular to the fundamentality of reciprocal dialogue in Buber.[20] However, they provide usefully complementary perspectives on our relation to the Other with whom we engage both ethically and historically. Embracing the interpersonal implications of Heidegger's emphasis on human finitude, both shift the focus from a problem of detached, conceptual, representational knowledge that starts with the subject to the scene of responsible human interaction. For Levinas, the proximity of the other in conversation overwhelms and thereby grounds subjective conceptuality: 'to approach the Other in conversation is to welcome his expression, in which at each instant he overflows the idea a thought would carry away from it. It is therefore to *receive* from the Other beyond the capacity of the I, which means exactly: to have the idea of infinity'.[21]

As Gadamer pointed out to Derrida, hermeneutics is not necessarily ethical: '[e]ven immoral beings try to understand one another'.[22] However, his thought owes a great deal to Aristotle's ethics,[23] and his concept of understanding is dependent on a modified version of the Levinasian ethical bond: 'the person who is understanding does not know and judge as one who stands apart and unaffected but rather he thinks along with the other from the perspective of a specific bond of belonging, as if he too were affected'.[24] Thus even 'self-understanding [*Selbstverständnis*] is, in all its forms, the extreme opposite of self-consciousness [*Selbstbewusstsein*]'.[25] To understand a text, as Gadamer put it in an interview (using very Levinasian terms), is to 'allow it to obsess us and lead us beyond our own horizon'.[26] Levinas describes the welcoming of the Other in terms of a more radical obsession: the 'obsession by the other, my neighbor ... reduces the ego to a self on the hither side of my identity, prior to all self-consciousness, and denudes me absolutely'.[27] Ricoeur is right to note that Levinas's conception of otherness reduces it to the otherness of other people, excluding, for example, the otherness of one's own flesh and one's ancestors.[28] Gadamer's expansion of otherness to the historical text is one answer, not without its own difficulties, to that objection.[29]

Levinas's notion of otherness does not, as Norris argues, require 'the suspension of all pre-existent concepts and categories'.[30] His point is rather that such concepts and categories, to the extent that they stem from an instrumental rationality under the control of a 'free' autonomous subject, need to be grounded in the very real, 'in your face' world of human contact: 'To identify the problem of foundation with the knowledge of knowledge is to forget the arbitrariness of freedom, which is precisely what has to be grounded.'[31] In *Otherwise than Being*, where Levinas distinguishes ethics – the absolute, non-conceptualized proximity of the other – from justice, in which the presence of a third party generates 'control, a search for justice, society and the State, comparison and possession, thought and science, commerce and philosophy, an outside of anarchy, the search for a principle', he stresses their interdependence as well as their difference: justice is a 'betrayal' of ethical proximity, but also its necessary expression, and thus '[i]n no way is justice a degradation of obsession, a degeneration of the for-the-other'.[32]

This is a circuitous route to some suggestions about how this kind of phenomenological and hermeneutic thought can connect the interpretive (as opposed to the descriptive/evaluative) work of literary criticism to an exploration of the ethical relation to a concrete sense of the other, with specific application to Samuel Taylor Coleridge. I have argued at length elsewhere for the relevance of Gadamer's hermeneutics to interpretive issues in Romanticism,[33] and Coleridge's place in the hermeneutic tradition has been argued by Elinor Schaffer and Pierre Mileur, but it still may seem perverse to argue for the ethical relevance of Coleridge in these terms; for example, one of the few points of agreement between Norris and the New Historicists is that Coleridge is responsible for an 'aesthetic ideology' (what Romanticists, after Jerome McGann, call the 'Romantic Ideology')[34] that would confuse the realms that Kant divided.[35] Coleridge does, at the beginning of a tradition that runs straight to Gadamer, ground the world in language by stressing the *Logos* of John's Gospel, but that does not necessarily lead either to an aestheticisation of the world or to a relativistic hermeneutic circle, as is made clear by Coleridge's refusal to follow the lead of Schelling in resolving either theology or reality into art. To take the most familiar examples, the distinction between Primary and Secondary Imagination clearly differentiates artistic creation from general perception, and 'Kubla Khan' narrates the disastrous consequences of assuming that Kubla Khan's historical actions can be assimilated into a work of art.

Coleridge's intense engagement with Kant and his very failure to achieve his desired synthesis of philosophy, theology and politics force him to confront some fundamental problems of descriptivism, the fact/value distinction and of the ethical relation to the other. In *The Friend*, he distinguishes between mere 'verbal truth', by which 'we mean no more than the correspondence of a given fact to given words' and the higher 'moral truth', which operates in the hermeneutic context of a speaker's expectations regarding the understanding of his intention: 'we involve likewise the intention of the speaker that his words should correspond to his thoughts in the sense in which he expects'.[36] The former, lesser kind of truth is 'merely' descriptive; the stakes are not very high in its demand for adequate correspondence between words and facts, signs and the world: 'distinct *notions* do not suppose different *things*'.[37] Coleridge was not at all sceptical about science, as the *Theory of Life* and other works attest, but in order to encompass natural science he needed to reject both the descriptivism inherent in merely 'verbal' truth that would pretend to adequately describe the world and what he saw as an atomistic world that would lend itself to such description.

Sabina Lovibond suggests that the eighteenth-century 'segregation of "reason" and "sentiment"' is 'perpetuated in the "fact/value distinction" of modern analytical philosophy'.[38] Coleridge's attempts to bridge this gap between the sentimental ethics of Shaftesbury and the rational ethics of Kant can thus help to illuminate the twentieth-century effects of the fact/value distinction,[39] even though many would now reject Coleridge's theology and even more would reject his anti-atomism. The same kind of reasoning that enables Coleridge to critique descriptivism while preserving empiricism allows him to preserve a strong sense of 'ought' without depending on the 'fact/value' distinction (though he did acknowledge its force)[40] or falling into Lyotardian paradox. If Being is the expression of God's willed ethical act, and if human perception is a 'repetition in the finite mind' of the divine act of self-consciousness,[41] then it looks as if, far from deriving ethical 'oughts' from statements about how the world 'is', Coleridge sees the 'is' as an expression of a super-'ought'; as Levinas would have it, ethics is prior to ontology and epistemology.

This is not, however, a simple reversal of the fact/value distinction, because ultimately, as for Kant, both are rooted in the unconditioned realm of pure Reason; Coleridge once rewrote the First Commandment as 'Unconditional Obedience of the Will to the pure Reason, or Conscience ... the *Reality* of which is *God*'.[42] This position is supported by Coleridge's hermeneutic view of the world; if language, defined on the finite level in terms of cultural dialogue, shares in the constitutive status of ideas, on the analogy, for him, of the creative force of God's Word, then to understand what 'is' by engaging in that creative language shares in the ethical *and* ontological force – not reducible to a separable 'ought' – of both language's ethical/cultural constitution and God's creative decree.

Lockridge makes a convincing case for Coleridge's other-centred ethics, arguing that, despite his attraction to a formalist ethics, Coleridge not only expands Kant's directive to treat people as ends rather than means into an affective other-centred morality, but also sees the relation to another as essential for self-consciousness.[43] Coleridge sees 'conscience', defined as the ethical relation to others, as the ground for the continuity of consciousness: '*From* what reasons do I believe a *continuous* <& ever continuable> *Consciousness*? From *Conscience*! Not for myself but for my conscience – i.e. my affections & duties toward others, I should have no Self.'[44]

However, Coleridge struggles with two notions of 'otherness', one of which engages Levinas's sense of the ethical proximity of the absolutely other and the other of which suggests the alternative view of 'oneself as another' put forth by Paul Ricoeur in his book of that title. Ricoeur, partly in explicit opposition to Levinas's location of ethics in the approach of the other person, gives the self an active role in the dialectic between '*ipse*'-identity or 'selfhood' and '*idem*'-identity or 'sameness'. *Idem*-identity is the 'I' as a stable object of reference in the world.[45] *Ipse*-identity, on the other hand, 'implies no assertion concerning some unchanging core of the personality', but instead engages 'the dialectic of *self* and *other than self*'.[46] Ricoeur's terms fit Coleridge's familiar theological interpretation of Schelling's dialectical description of the self,[47] and Coleridge almost seems to be echoing Ricoeur when he says (in Anthony Harding's translation of Coleridge's Latin): 'to be conscious is to be aware of both myself and of another at the same time – therefore, self-consciousness is to be aware of myself *as if I were another*'.[48] This conception of the self is based on the notion of God as a creatively self-othering 'Deus Alter et Idem'.[49] Coleridge's theology translates quickly to the human because of his emphasis on the originary status of the 'Person' at both levels, which enables him to address the still problematic issue of the inevitable conflict between 'person' as an abstract, universal category and as designating unique individuals.[50]

This very Christian sense of God and self in terms of the self-othering *Logos* is in tension with a Hebraic, Levinasian sense of the absolutely other. This second kind of otherness can be traced to Coleridge's refusal, contra Schelling, to see polarity as foundational; behind the notion of God as self-othering Logos or 'Ipseity' (in the sense used by both Coleridge and Ricoeur) must be a concept of God as 'the absolute will' or 'Identity' absolutely other to the human.[51] (This creates some complex ethical problems, such as the fact that while unrealised Will is the definition of God's absolute divinity and goodness, unrealised human will is the definition of absolute evil.)[52] Like Levinas, Coleridge translates this notion of a commanding, unconditioned otherness into the human imperative of an other-oriented 'conscience'. Levinas also sees 'conscience' as foundational: 'in conscience I have an experience that is not commensurate with any *a priori* framework – a conceptless experience'.[53] Coleridge often implies a Levinasian sense of the other as that which confronts and overflows our conceptual categories, as when, in the *Rime of the Ancient Mariner*, the Mariner confronts the Wedding Guest and calls him to responsibility, after the Mariner himself has had his ego, in Levinas's striking phrase, 'cored out' by an experience of absolute otherness.[54]

The most poignant combination of the two senses of otherness comes in Coleridge's infatuation with Sara Hutchinson, where he compounds the difficulty by defying Kant and giving love a primary ethical status. Love is an 'element' rather than a compound, and demonstrates a noumenal act of will at the foundationally ethical level of 'conscience' though it is below 'consciousness':

> What Kant affirms of Man in the state of Adam, an ineffable act of the will choosing evil and which is underneath or within the *consciousness* tho' incarnate in the *conscience*, inasmuch as it must be conceived as taking place in the [*homo noumenon*], not the [*homo phaenomenon*] – something like this I conceive of *Love* – in that highest sense of the Word, which Petrarch understood.[55]

After Kant's exclusion of the affective realm from rational ethics and Freud's assertion of a conflict between love and 'the interests of civilization' philosophy has found it difficult to use human love as a paradigm for ethical relations.[56] Of course love, as a synthesis of *eros* and *agape*, plays a central role in the Augustinian tradition of Christian ethics.[57] For Coleridge, whose thoughts on love combined Augustinian theology and his hopeless infatuation with Sara Hutchinson, love is both 'the only Perpetuator' and 'the strongest antagonist' of 'desire'.[58] To the extent that this paradoxical formulation gives desire an ethical function, both Williams and Ricoeur give philosophical reasons for why this should be so. Williams points out that '[d]esiring to do something is of course a reason for doing it', and is thus involved in the ethical question of what one 'should' do.[59] Ricoeur points out that desire is not necessarily egoistic: 'the good man's own being is desirable to him; given this, the being of his friend is then equally desirable to him'. Part of Ricoeur's notion of 'solicitude' depends on a self-love that is a love of 'the best part of oneself';[60] Coleridge puts forth a similar, though much more theological argument that in a self-love directed toward the 'unindividual nature of the idea, Self or Soul', consideration of the 'course of action' that 'will purchase heaven for *me*, for my Soul, involves the thought, all men who pursue that course'.[61]

In the depths of his anguish over Sara in 1807, Coleridge suggests that her existence as an other *and* as a version of the self is the ground of his own moral subjectivity: '[i]t must be one who is & who is not myself – not myself, & yet so much more my Sense of Being'.[62] This is not only a subjectivity defined in relation to an other, as Ricoeur would have it, but also a suggestion of the Levinasian subject whose authenticity depends on accepting responsibility for the other as 'conscience', beyond any coherent image or form of self-consciousness: Sara is 'herself & the Conscience of that self, beyond the bounds of that form which her eyes behold'.[63] This is 'desire' as Levinas defines it in opposition to 'need': 'in need I can sink my teeth into the real and satisfy myself in assimilating the other; in Desire there is no sinking one's teeth into being, no satiety, but an uncharted future before me'.[64] The Levinasian sense of an otherness that 'cores out' the ego is particularly evident in the notebook entries written en route to Malta in 1804,[65] as Coleridge undertook a journey from which he did not expect to return, a journey, like that which Levinas prefers to the circular myth of the *Odyssey*, reminiscent of 'the story of Abraham leaving his homeland forever for a still unknown land'.[66]

The very subjectivity of Coleridge's definition of all life (that is, the equation of the world's creation with God's subjectivity) means that the first-person speaking subject is the 'limit of the world' in Ricoeur's phrase[67] only insofar as he cannot see beyond his own consciousness. But that very limitation suggests a subjectivity beyond that limit, a subjectivity by definition inaccessible to consciousness – Coleridge's version of Kant's Unconditioned, which he defines in several places, with different emphases, as the 'absolute self'.[68] In 'What is Life', dated near the end of his stay in Malta (16 August 1805) though later dismissed as juvenilia, the notion that subjective life transcends consciousness emphasises the self's vulnerability to its own transcendent potential:

Resembles life what once was deem'd of light,
Too ample in itself for human sight?
An absolute self – an element ungrounded –
All that we see, all colours of all shade
By encroach of darkness made? –
Is very life by consciousness unbounded?
And all the thoughts, pains, joys of mortal breath,
A war-embrace of wrestling life and death?[69]

This is the down side of what, in the notebook entry quoted above, was later seen as a universalisable subjectivity that validated a kind of Ricoeurean 'self-love'. Here, Coleridge offers something different from both Levinas and Ricoeur, though it shares the problematics of both. Unlike Ricoeur, Coleridge sees the first-person self as possibly *not* the limit of its subjective world, and thus vulnerable not only to the approach of the other but also to the 'absolute self', potentially '[t]oo ample in itself for human sight'. If this is subjective idealism, it carries a high price, because the conscious ego is attacked on two flanks: the ego is on the one hand potentially too subjective, and must suffer the Levinasian 'coring out' of the ego suggested by the Mariner's and Coleridge's own experience. On the other hand, the conscious ego may be not subjective enough, if consciousness is a mere darkening of the 'absolute self' instead of its 'bound'. Thus he cannot enjoy Ricoeur's confidence that solicitude for others, expressed in the dialectic of *ipse* and *idem*, is an essential and supportive structure of the self, because the *idem* beyond the *ipse* is not only objective continuity, but also unconditioned transcendence (ultimately, the divine Identity), whose absolute otherness to the conscious self threatens the ego. But neither can he enjoy Levinas's confidence that peace can be achieved through a dissolution of the ego and a responsible welcoming of the other person's proximity because, as a consequence of the conscious ego's incompleteness relative to the 'absolute self' – the necessary incompleteness of self-understanding that Gadamer sees as resulting from our existence as historical beings[70] – transcendent otherness assaults one from within as well as from without.[71] Here Coleridge approaches Heidegger's notion that '[*i*]*n conscience Dasein calls itself* .... The call comes *from* me and yet *from beyond me and over me*', and perhaps Kristeva's sense that 'the foreigner lives within us' as 'the hidden face of our identity'.[72]

I have tried to sketch a hermeneutic reading that discusses

Coleridgean ethics from outside the descriptive/evaluative, fact/value, is/ought mode with whose difficulties I began. However, literary interpretation may tend to embrace that mode because it is inherent in narrative itself, however problematic an opposition it may be for ethical thought in general. If evaluation is 'quite neutral to morals' in general, the fact/value pair in which evaluation occurs is essential to the ethics of autobiographical conversion narratives, of which the *Rime of the Ancient Mariner* is a strange example. Geoffrey Galt Harpham argues that 'ought' is derived from 'is' as the result of 'a repressive force that … drives the primary text down to a position of secondary dependence: the truth of the primary can only be delivered by a secondary text that represses the "evaluation" that constituted the primary text'.[73] The Ancient Mariner's experience can be described in these terms: the secondary text of the Mariner's moral injunction to the Wedding Guest represses the moral ambiguity of the experience at sea (turning it into an 'is' available for moral evaluation), and the marginal gloss repeats the process of repression in an even more overt process of analysis.[74] This process is in tension with the fact that the narrative's 'is' – the 'content' of the story – is a world of strange and unpredictable 'oughts' wildly disconnected from any known 'is'. This world is directed by powers appearing from nowhere, in which the empirical causality assumed by the crew's contradictory interpretations of the Mariner's act (lines 91–102) is exposed as absurdly inappropriate. 'Ought'-related acts – killing birds, propelling ships, dicing for a human life, blessing snakes – take priority over any describable reality. It is such a frightening world to visit and such a difficult world to return from partly because the Mariner must speak a language in which the necessary narrative progression from 'is' to 'ought' is forcibly contradicted by an experience that denies such a progression.

In complaining to Coleridge that his poem lacked a moral, Mrs Barbauld wanted him to produce, in effect, an aesthetic ideology. Coleridge, who knew, tragically, that art could not structure life, refused, complaining that the poem had too much of a moral.[75] The poem itself suggests both the narrative inevitability and the experiential insufficiency of the description/evaluation, is/ought pair, and thus the poem's real moral for us may be to suggest what literary interpretation can and cannot tell us about ethics.

Notes

1. See Barbara Herrnstein Smith's discussion of 'Fact and Value in the Academy' in *Contingencies of Value: Alternative Perspectives for Critical Theory* (Cambridge, MA: Harvard University Press, 1988) 17–29.
2. See David Hume, *A Treatise of Human Nature*, Book 3, Part 1, Section 1, quoted in Bernard Williams, *Ethics and the Limits of Philosophy* (Cambridge, MA: Harvard University Press, 1985) 123.
3. Smith, *Contingencies of Value*, 161, 163–4.
4. Ibid., 11, 30–2.
5. Ibid., 44.
6. Julius Kovesi, 'Against the Ritual of "Is" and "Ought"', in *Studies in Ethical Theory*, ed. Peter E. French, *et al.*, *Midwest Studies in Philosophy*, 3 (1978) revised reissue (Minneapolis: University of Minnesota Press, 1980) 5–16; 14.
7. Williams, *Ethics and the Limits of Philosophy*, 129–52.
8. Jean-François Lyotard, 'Levinas's Logic', trans. Ian McLeod, in *The Lyotard Reader*, ed. Andrew Benjamin (Oxford: Blackwell, 1989) 275–313; 282.
9. Charles Taylor, *Sources of the Self: The Making of the Modern Identity* (Cambridge, MA: Harvard University Press 1989) 3–24.
10. G.E.M. Anscombe, 'Modern Moral Philosophy', in *The Is-Ought Question: A Collection of Papers on the Central Problem in Moral Philosophy*, ed. W.D. Hudson (New York: Macmillan, 1969) 175–95; 180–1.
11. Alasdair MacIntyre, 'Moral Philosophy: What Next?', in *Revisions: Changing Perspectives in Moral Philosophy*, ed. Stanley Hauerwas and Alasdair MacIntyre (Notre Dame, IN: University of Notre Dame Press, 1983) 1–15; 11–12.
12. Christopher Norris, 'New Idols of the Cave: Ontological Relativity, Anti-Realism, and Interpretation Theory', *Southern Humanities Review* 30, 3 (Summer 1996) 209–45; 218.
13. Christopher Norris, *What's Wrong With Postmodernism: Critical Theory and the Ends of Philosophy* (Baltimore, MD: Johns Hopkins University Press, 1990) 275.
14. Christopher Norris, *Truth and the Ethics of Criticism* (Manchester University Press, 1994) 73.
15. For Norris's view of Levinas, see *Truth and the Ethics of Criticism* 47–51; for Gadamer, see *What's Wrong With Postmodernism*, 94, 114.
16. See Hans-Georg Gadamer, *Truth and Method*, 2nd revised edn, translation revised by Joel Weinsheimer and Donald G. Marshall (New York: Crossroad, 1990) 413–18.
17. Kovesi, 'Against the Ritual of "Is" and "Ought"', 14.
18. Hans-Georg Gadamer, 'Composition and Interpretation', in *The Relevance of the Beautiful and Other Essays*, trans. Nicholas Walker, ed. Robert Bernasconi (Cambridge University Press, 1986) 66–73; 68.
19. Gadamer, *Truth and Method*, 368.
20. Emmanuel Levinas, *Totality and Infinity: An Essay on Exteriority*, trans. Alphonso Lingis (Pittsburgh, PA: Duquesne University Press, 1969) 68.
21. Ibid., 51.

22. Hans-Georg Gadamer, 'Reply to Jacques Derrida', trans. Diane Michelfelder and Richard Palmer, in *Dialogue and Deconstruction: The Gadamer–Derrida Encounter*, eds, Diane Michelfelder and Richard Palmer (Albany, NY: State University of New York Press, 1989) 55–7; 55.
23. Matthew Foster emphasises this side of Gadamer in *Gadamer and Practical Philosophy: The Hermeneutics of Moral Confidence* (Atlanta, GA: Scholars Press, 1991). See especially pp. 60–9 on Gadamer's debt to Aristotelian ethics. Another study of the ethical implications of Gadamer's hermeneutics is P. Christopher Smith, *Hermeneutics and Human Finitude: Toward a Theory of Ethical Understanding* (New York: Fordham University Press, 1991), which emphasises the ethical role of *Sittlichkeit* and tradition in Gadamer.
24. Gadamer, *Truth and Method*, 323.
25. 'Letter to Dallmayr', in *Dialogue and Deconstruction*, eds, Michelfelder and Palmer, 93–101; 95.
26. Quoted in Foster, *Gadamer and Practical Philosophy*, 16. Gadamer speaks approvingly of Levinas ('Letter to Dallmayr', 97 and 'Hermeneutics and Logocentrism', in *Dialogue and Deconstruction*, eds Michelfelder and Palmer, 114–25; 119), and Donald G. Marshall argues for the consistency of Gadamer's and Levinas's notions of dialogue ('Dialogue and Écriture', in *Dialogue and Deconstruction*, eds, Michelfelder and Palmer, 206–14; 212–13).
27. Emmanuel Levinas, *Otherwise than Being or Beyond Essence*, trans. Alphonso Lingis (The Hague: Martinus Nijhoff, 1981) 92.
28. Paul Ricoeur, *Oneself as Another*, trans. Kathleen Blamey (University of Chicago Press, 1992) 352–3.
29. Gadamer's hermeneutic approach to history has, as Habermas and others have noted, and as Gadamer himself has intimated, the danger of limiting the conversation with the past to a specific and exclusionary tradition. (See Jürgen Habermas, 'A Review of Gadamer's *Truth and Method*', trans. Fred Dallmayr and Thomas McCarthy, in *Hermeneutics and Modern Philosophy*, ed. Brice R. Wachterhauser [Albany, NY: State University of New York Press, 1986] 243–76, and Gadamer's admission of his own Romantic roots in 'Text and Interpretation', trans. Dennis J. Schmidt and Richard Palmer, in *Dialogue and Deconstruction*, eds, Michelfelder and Palmer, 21–51; 24–5). But, as Gadamer says in response to Habermas, 'the idea that tradition, as such, should be and should remain the only ground for acceptance of presuppositions (a view that Habermas ascribes to me) flies in the face of my basic thesis that authority is rooted in insight as a hermeneutical process' (*Philosophical Hermeneutics*, trans. and ed. David E. Linge [Berkeley: University of California Press, 1976] 34).
30. Norris, *Truth and the Ethics of Criticism*, 47.
31. Levinas, *Totality and Infinity*, 85.
32. Levinas, *Otherwise than Being*, 161, 159.
33. See David P. Haney, *William Wordsworth and the Hermeneutics of Incarnation* (University Park, PA: Penn State University Press, 1993);

'Nuptial Interruption: Marriage and Autobiography in Wordsworth's "A Farewell"', in *Autobiography and Post-Modernism*, ed. Leigh Gilmore, *et al*. (Amherst: University of Massachusetts Press, 1994) and 'Viewing "The Viewless Wings of Poesy": Keats, Gadamer, and Historicity', *Clio*, 18 (1989) 103–22.

34. See Jerome J. McGann, *The Romantic Ideology: A Critical Investigation* (University of Chicago Press, 1983).
35. Norris, *What's Wrong With Postmodernism*, 262–70.
36. Samuel Taylor Coleridge, *The Friend*, ed. Barbara E. Rooke, Vol. 4 of *The Collected Works of Samuel Taylor Coleridge*, 2 vols. (Princeton University Press, 1969) 1: 42.
37. Ibid., 1: 177 n.
38. Sabina Lovibond, *Realism and Imagination in Ethics* (Minneapolis: University of Minnesota Press, 1983) 22.
39. On Shaftesbury's and Kant's relation to the Romantics, see Laurence S. Lockridge *The Ethics of Romanticism* (Cambridge University Press, 1989) 50–8, 74–81.
40. Coleridge's argument in the *Opus Maximum* in favour of the is/ought distinction is summarised in Lockridge, *Ethics of Romanticism*, 150.
41. Samuel Taylor Coleridge, *Biographia Literaria*, eds James Engell and W. Jackson Bate, Vol. 7 of *The Collected Works of Samuel Taylor Coleridge*, 2 vols. (Princeton University Press, 1983) 1: 304.
42. *The Notebooks of Samuel Taylor Coleridge*, eds Kathleen Coburn and Merle Christenson, 4 vols to date (Princeton University Press, 1957–) 3: 3293.
43. '[T]o be conscious of oneself as a *self* requires a synchronous commitment to the reality of another' (Laurence S. Lockridge, *Coleridge the Moralist* [Ithaca, NY: Cornell University Press, 1977] 124–5). See also Anthony John Harding's discussion of Coleridge's other-centred ethics in *Coleridge and the Idea of Love: Aspects of Relationship in Coleridge's Thought and Writing* (London & New York: Cambridge University Press, 1974) 121, 144–6, 188–92.
44. Coleridge, *Notebooks*, 2: 3231.
45. Ricoeur, *Oneself as Another*, 116–18.
46. Ricoeur, *Oneself as Another*, 2, 3.
47. This is the 'subject which becomes a subject by the act of constructing itself objectively to itself; but which never is an object except for itself, and only so far as by the very same act it becomes a subject' (Coleridge, *Biographia Literaria*, 1: 273).
48. Samuel Taylor Coleridge, *Collected Letters*, ed. Earl Leslie Griggs, 6 vols (Oxford: Clarendon Press, 1956-71) 4: 849. See Harding's discussion of this letter in *Coleridge and the Idea of Love*, 144–5.
49. Samuel Taylor Coleridge, *On the Constitution of Church and State*, ed. John Colmer, Vol. 10 of *The Collected Works of Samuel Taylor Coleridge* (Princeton University Press, 1976) 84 n.
50. See Bernard Williams's analysis of this conflict in 'Persons, Character and Morality', in *The Identities of Persons*, ed. Amélie Oksenberg Rorty (Berkeley: University of California Press, 1976) 197–216, and in *Ethics and the Limits of Philosophy*, 114–15.

51. For one of Coleridge's many formulations of this distinction, see 'On the Trinity', in *Shorter Works and Fragments*, eds H. J. Jackson and J. R. de J. Jackson, Vol. 11 of *The Collected Works of Samuel Taylor Coleridge*, 2 vols. (Princeton University Press, 1995) 2: 1510–11. In a different context, Coleridge applauds the beauty of 'the Hebrew idea of the world as at enmity with God' (quoted by J. Shawcross, in the Introduction to S. T. Coleridge, *Biographia Literaria*, 2 vols. [London: Oxford University Press, 1907] 1: xi–xcvii [lxxxv]). For a full explication of Coleridge's relation to Schelling on this issue, see Raimonda Modiano, *Coleridge and the Concept of Nature* (Tallahassee: Florida State University Press, 1985) 168–73 and Mary Ann Perkins, *Coleridge's Philosophy: The Logos as Unifying Principle* (Oxford University Press, 1994) 163–8.
52. 'For pure Evil what is it but Will that would manifest itself as Will, not in Being' (Coleridge, *Notebooks*, 4: 5076). This makes theological sense, since man's greatest sin is to pretend to Godhood. See Lockridge, *Coleridge the Moralist*, 65 on this point.
53. Levinas, *Totality and Infinity*, 100–1.
54. Levinas, *Otherwise than Being*, 64, 181.
55. Samuel Taylor Coleridge, *Marginalia*, ed. George Whalley, *et al.*, Vol. 12 of *The Collected Works of Samuel Taylor Coleridge*, 3 vols to date (Princeton University Press, 1980–) 3: 265.
56. See, for example, Kant's critique of moral 'feeling' in *Groundwork of the Metaphysic of Morals*, trans. H. J. Paton (New York: Harper and Row, 1964) 110; Sigmund Freud, 'Civilization and Its Discontents', in *The Complete Psychological Works of Sigmund Freud*, trans. James Strachey, *et al.*, 24 vols. (London: Hogarth Press, 1955–74) 21: 64–145; 103.
57. See Paul Tillich's discussion of the synthesis in *A History of Christian Thought From Its Judaic and Hellenistic Origins to Existentialism*, ed. Carl E. Braaten (New York: Simon and Schuster, 1968) 115–16, and Saint Augustine's discussion of good and bad love in *City of God*, Book 14, Section 7 (trans. Philip Levine, Loeb Classical Library, 7 vols. [Cambridge, MA: Harvard University Press, 1966] 4: 287–93).
58. Coleridge, 'Love and Desire', in *Shorter Works and Fragments*, 1: 284.
59. Williams, *Ethics and the Limits of Philosophy*, 19.
60. Ricoeur, *Oneself as Another*, 186, 184.
61. Coleridge, *Notebooks*, 3: 4007.
62. Ibid., 2: 3148.
63. Ibid., 2: 3146.
64. Levinas, *Totality and Infinity*, 117.
65. For example, Coleridge describes 'these frightful Dreams of Despair when the sense of individual Existence is full and lively only <for one> to feel oneself powerless, crushed *in* by every power – a stifled boding, one abject miserable Wretch/yet hopeless, yet struggling, removed from all touch of Life, deprived of all notion of Death/strange mixture of Fear and Despair – & that passio purissima, that mere Passiveness with Pain (the essence of which is perhaps Passivity – & which our word – mere Suffering – well comprizes –)' (*Notebooks* 2: 2078).

66. Emmanuel Levinas, 'The Trace of the Other', trans. Alphonso Lingis, in *Deconstruction in Context*, ed. Mark C. Taylor (University of Chicago Press, 1986) 345–59; 348.
67. Ricoeur, *Oneself as Another*, 51.
68. In Chapter 12 of *Biographia Literaria*, when Coleridge temporarily accepted Schelling's notion of a polarity at the heart of the concept of God, the term 'absolute self' is equated with 'the great eternal I AM' (1: 275), but, in opposition to Fichte, Coleridge sharply distinguishes the absolute self from divinity itself, stating the relation thus, commenting on Fichte's *Grundlage der Wissenschaftslehre*: 'Im absoluten Ich erkennt man Gott – nicht – im Gotte erkennt man das absolute Ich' [In the absolute I one recognises God – no – in God one recognises the absolute I] (*Marginalia* 2: 623).
69. Samuel Taylor Coleridge, *Poetical Works*, ed. Ernest Hartley Coleridge (1912; London: Oxford University Press, 1967).
70. Gadamer, *Truth and Method*, 302.
71. Gadamer acknowledges the theological origins of his historical-hermeneutic notion of the necessary incompleteness of self-understanding: 'The statement "I don't understand myself" expresses a primal religious experience within Christianity. Indeed, human life is a matter of the continuity of one's self-understanding, but this continuity consists in constantly putting oneself into question and a constant being-other' ('Hermeneutics and Logocentrism' 119).
72. Martin Heidegger, *Being and Time*, trans. John Macquarrie and Edward Robinson (New York: Harper and Row, 1962) 320; Julia Kristeva, *Strangers to Ourselves*, trans. Leon S. Roudiez (New York: Columbia University Press, 1991) 1.
73. Geoffrey Galt Harpham, *Getting It Right: Language, Literature, and Ethics* (University of Chicago Press, 1992) 142.
74. Jerome McGann distinguishes 'four clear layers of development' by the time of the 1817 text, which form successive layers of interpretation: '(a) an original mariner's tale; (b) the ballad narrative of that story; (c) the editorial gloss added when the ballad was, we are to suppose, first printed; and (d) Coleridge's own point of view on his invented materials' ('The Meaning of the Ancient Mariner', in *Spirits of Fire: English Romantic Writers and Contemporary Historical Methods*, eds. G. A. Rosso and Daniel P. Watkins [Rutherford, NJ: Fairleigh Dickinson University Press, 1990] 208–39; 221). See also Martin Wallen, 'Return and Representation: The Revisions of "The Ancient Mariner"', *The Wordsworth Circle*, 17 (1986) 148–56, and Frances Ferguson, 'Coleridge and the Deluded Reader: "The Rime of the Ancient Mariner"', in *Post-structuralist Readings of English Poetry*, eds. Richard Machin and Christopher Norris (Cambridge University Press, 1987) 248–63, for the implications of these layers of interpretation and revision.
75. Samuel Taylor Coleridge, *Table Talk*, ed. Carl Woodring, Vol. 14 of *The Collected Works of Samuel Taylor Coleridge*, 2 vols. (Princeton University Press, 1990) 2: 100.

8

Derrida, Rushdie and the Ethics of Mortality

Chris McNab

Jacques Derrida's *The Gift of Death* offers both a distinctive moment in the genealogy of his thought on responsibility, and a potential groundwork for a postmodern ethics of mortality. The exact nature of the allegiance between Derrida and postmodernism has always been a hazy connection; one which tends to be resolved in an acceptance of their *de facto* relationship within contemporary theoretical discourse. I shall claim that a more definite link can be made between Derrida and postmodern fiction in the ethical preoccupation with mortality. This focus, however, manifests some distinct problems for the plurality and play central to the postmodern theoretical canon. For postmodern writing and Derridean deconstruction lead us not to the recognition of irreducible alterity or unending difference, but instead produce a distinctly metaphysical and rather questionable attempt to generate an ethics on the basis of our own inevitable death.

The Gift of Death analyses the historical philosophy of Jan Patocka, a Czech intellectual who died under police torture in 1977 for his promotion of the Charta 77. Derrida's concern is with Patocka's *Heretical Essays on the Philosophy of History*, where Patocka traces the lengthy associations between religious responsibility and European history under the twin giants of Platonism and Christianity. The examination of Patocka's text is notable not only for its assertion that deconstructive thought is compatible with ethical relevance, but also for Derrida's most conspicuous gravitation towards a religious vision. For *The Gift of Death* sees Derrida utilising the apophatic icons of death and the *mysterium tremendum* in an ethical perspective which questions the anti-metaphysical stance of post-structuralist theory.[1]

At the heart of European history, for Patocka, is the 'demonic', the 'secret', or the 'orgiastic': a non-definable space of compulsion towards the irrational and the subversive. This unpredictable void is a perpetual counter force to ethical discipline, with its effects being continually re-encountered in the practices of revolution and rationality initially meant to provide the escape to order. Patocka argues that Platonism and Christianity have provided successive strategies of disciplining the orgiastic into a coherent responsibility, though it is only by Platonic 'incorporation' and Christian 'repression' that the orgiastic becomes an ethical property.

Yet – and this is essential to the direction of Derrida's thought – Patocka is reluctant to dispense with the creativity of the demonic, its ability to disrupt what Erazim Kohak calls the 'profane' self-concern that is as much a threat to conscious responsibility as the erratic motions of the hedonistic and the protean.[2] Responsibility amounts to the disciplining of the orgiastic while recognising that the demonic remains beneath the ethical act:

> The secret of responsibility would consist of keeping secret, or 'incorporated', the secret of the demonic and thus of preserving within itself a nucleus of irresponsibility or of absolute unconsciousness, something Patocka will later call 'orgiastic responsibility'.[3]

While Patocka recognises that responsibility partially overcomes the irrational, he also perceives in the orgiastic the primary material of ethical demand. Consequently, Patocka is wary of responsibility's absorption into rationalism, and Derrida concurs that to subsume ethics within reasoned codes is to denude responsibility of the singular relationship between a *particular* individual and a *particular* action. Derrida criticises legislative ethics for its detraction from the independence of the ethical act. It is from this position *outside* of rationalistic morality where Derrida is able to posit a morality of death.

Death is that which is irrevocably our own. No-one can die for us, even in the act of sacrifice, for our unique moment of death forever remains a matter of non-substitution. Expanding upon Heidegger's theorisations of mortality, Derrida sees death as revealing and isolating our absolute responsibility as a consequence of our absolute singularity. From death the individual becomes aware that mortality confers total responsibility, as it presents the 'gift' of our obligation to self and other which no-one can perform as our substitute, a gift which cannot be displaced onto a general, codified responsibility: 'It is from the site of death as the place of my irreplaceability, that is, of my singularity, that I feel called to responsibility. In this sense only a mortal can be responsible' (Derrida, *Gift*, p. 41). Death may communicate the existential isolation of ethical performance, but it is less appreciable as to how this solitary consciousness provides an ethical response to the other. To overcome this problem, Derrida seems to reapply Rudolph Otto's *mysterium tremendum* as an apophatic motif of the *presence* of justice. Patocka sees the awe of the *mysterium tremendum* as the primary example of how Christianity disciplines the orgiastic under the imperious demand of the other. For Derrida, the numinous acts as an awareness of the gaze of absolute alterity itself, a gaze that always surrounds our solitary ethical moment with the gift of death. As our mortality opens us to the singular freedom of our responsibility, that freedom becomes a silent demand that is from the infinite Other and the others that physically surround us. The ethical numinous comes not so much from a God (though Derrida's relation to theology in *The Gift of Death* is distinctly ambiguous), but from an alterity whose aura of ontological confrontation and moral ineffability steps directly out of religious tradition.

The whole tenor of Derrida's argument is a shift away from ethics as compliance with a social norm, towards ethics as cast within the deviance of 'irresponsibility'. While Patocka by no means wants the hegemony of a sterile rationalism, he does see the orgiastic as requiring control for a mindful social order. Derrida, however, sees the presence of ethical codes and prescriptions as a distraction *away* from the genuine complexities of ethical decision. Thus Derrida revisits the Abraham and Isaac myth to demonstrate how moral activity is based upon absolute silence rather than the voices and opinions of an ethical mean. Abraham obeys the command to sacrifice Isaac not *because of* the demand of ethics, but *contrary* to ethics. Abraham's actions follow the singularity of his relation to the *mysterium tremendum*: the silence of Abraham's isolation under the gaze of the Other. The intention to kill Isaac runs against the social prohibition of infanticide. So, Derrida points out, for Abraham ethics actually function as a 'temptation' *away from responsibility*, a temptation which must be resisted to preserve his non-mediated relationship with morality. The irresolvable space between the codified and the absolute results in an ethics which assaults moral norms yet also has a practical familiarity. 'This is ethics as "irresponsibilisation", as an insoluble and paradoxical contradiction between responsibility *in general* and *absolute responsibility*' (Derrida, *Gift*, p. 61). Derrida's ethics of 'irresponsibility' offer a moral domain constantly wrestling within its own limitations and urges.[4] What makes this theory distinct from simple realism is that moral failure becomes intrinsic to the whole expression of responsibility. Derrida later enters a polemical voice when he attacks moral complacency, which he sees as ignorant of the fact that responsible decisions always involve irresponsible effects either through bad decision or inevitable exclusion.

Yet we must start to question Derrida's consistent use of religious models and iconography in *The Gift of Death*. *The Gift of Death* is perhaps Derrida's most solid engagement with religion, with a significant welding together of religious universality and the mortal gift into a paradoxical ethical model. In the end, Derrida, as one would expect, does not clearly suggest a divine reality as an identifiable origin of responsibility. What does occur through a strange mixture of Heideggerian, Levinasian and Judaeo-Christian associations is the allusion towards the alterity of death equalling a common, and transcendent, property in the same way as the *mysterium tremendum*. The alterity of the absolute other is descriptively located as a centre of humankind's ethical determinations. So Derrida is able to see the story of Abraham and Isaac as more than just an individualistic message:

> The sacrifice of Isaac belongs to what one might just dare to call the common treasure, the terrifying secret of the *mysterium tremendum* that is a property of all three so-called religions of the Book, the religions of the races of Abraham. (Derrida, *Gift*, p. 64)

The 'common treasure' to which Derrida 'dares' to refer is that which cannot be contained in scriptural doctrine. The gift of death extends the alterity within ethics to a figure in itself, a 'terrifying secret' whose equation with God transfers alterity into a brooding presence which emerges from the space beyond life and language. Derrida uses the silent God in a way that implicitly defies his contention that deconstruction should not be equated with a negative theology. In many ways *The Gift of Death* re-embraces the silent god of Kabbalistic and Rabbinical Judaism and celebrates an ethics whose apophatic source is an encounter with 'fundamental ontology' at its most extreme.

Derrida perhaps follows Patocka's lead in trying to show how religion has not been 'thought through' to some of its genuine conditions. The example of Abraham's moral dilemma shows that there 'is no longer any ethical generality that does not fall prey to the paradox of Abraham' (Derrida, *Gift*, p. 78). The gift of death is a common gift whose presence, like that of ineffable Yahweh, constantly returns morality to silence and secrecy. Derrida extends the commonality of this gift beyond the confines of a Judaic, Christian or Islamic ancestry to embrace all others in the relationship to the other. For the gift of death 'stands for Jews, Christians, Muslims, but also for everyone else, for every other in its relation to the wholly other. We can no longer know who is called Abraham, and he can no longer tell us' (Derrida, *Gift*, p. 79).

Abraham becomes unidentifiable because he disappears within the apophatic spaces of morality. Derrida's transformation of Abraham into anonymity attempts to prevent the re-scripting of his ideas on the structures of logocentric religion. Yet what remains is a sense in which the alterity of death performs the same role as the face of God hidden from Moses: there is the promise of meaning while deferring the resolution of meaning. So when Derrida reappraises Christianity through the perspective of irresponsibility, he sees it as no longer in need of the event of revelation, but only the deferred possibility of that event:

> It [Christianity] needs to think the possibility of such an event but not the event itself. This is a major point of difference, permitting such a discourse to be developed without reference to religion as institutional dogma, and proposing a genealogy of thinking that doesn't amount to an article of faith. (Derrida, *Gift*, p. 49)

By insisting on the *possibility* of revelation, rather than revelation itself, Derrida describes a religion with a deferral at its 'centre' which maintains moral urgency within the secrecy of death and the infinite. Derrida goes on to say that the gift of death '"repeats" the possibility of religion without religion' (Derrida, *Gift*, p. 49) as the *mysterium tremendum* gestures to that which religion cannot contain. Thus the *mysterium tremendum* functions as what Derrida calls the 'ghost of the undecidable', a ghost that 'deconstructs from within any assurance of presence, any certitude or any supposed criteriology that would assure us of the justice of a decision'.[5] While

Derrida does attempt to resist the reconstruction of a faith, he is only partially successful. What frequently emerges from *The Gift of Death*, and, I shall argue, from much postmodern fiction, is the movement towards alterity as a presence in itself. This presence is similar to that of the divine in negative theology, where a system of meaning is generated around something which cannot be directly addressed. Derridean and postmodern alterity lead us not into an irreducible play of difference, but give a focused motif for the confrontation with death, God and morality. So alterity has become a communicable element of discourse within postmodernism, something which demarcates meaning rather than exploding such meaning.

Derrida's presentation of the gift of mortality is a peculiarly relevant way of reinterpreting the haunting sense of loss written into many postmodern texts. The pluralities and fragmentations of postmodern fiction are often seen as generating an environment in which foundations cannot survive interpretative motion and temporal priorities. However, Derrida unwittingly demonstrates how alterity can find a physical presence in death. The negativity that results within much postmodern fiction need not be relegated to the opposite pole from moral and ontological foundations, but may actually increase the priority of these foundations within any search for meaning.

Taking irresponsibility as a common gift, it seems that much postmodern literature reproduces on a literary level the ethical effect of the gift of death and the *mysterium tremendum*. It is my argument that postmodern textuality emphasises the mortality within the act of reading and thereby increases our ethical responsibility to the interpretative act. As textual indeterminacy appears to break the metanarrative quest, responsibility shifts away from complicity with an overarching theme to responsibility in the life span of an interpretative, and temporal, performance. Yet we must be aware that alterity, once prioritised through a conspicuous textual indeterminacy, becomes a visible trope whose ethical directive returns the demand for meaning and, in effect, foundations. This is because the *thematic* alterity of postmodern texts centres absence in an absolute relation to being, existence and language. Alterity, in effect, becomes implicitly offered as the truth of being, a space which commands both our ethical response and our philosophical expansion. Otherness is not that which unsettles totalisation but is a thematic presence in postmodern discourse which replays theological absolutes and reinforces ontological isolation and individuality. Such a series of claims means that, in effect, we must look at alterity not as a disruption, but a convention which is at heart a repetition of theological ideas.

My selection of Salman Rushdie to illustrate the practical outworking of the above theory is partly arbitrary. There are many postmodern authors who write with what I have called the mortality of the text. Yet the novels of Rushdie, and here I shall focus mainly on *The Moor's Last Sigh*, are especially relevant for their strong sense of ethical demand and their distinct consciousness of death. What I shall claim is that Rushdie attempts to create a space for reader 'irresponsibility' that transfers metanarrative ethics into the flux of *possible* ethics. In attempting this project, however, Rushdie utilises a vision of death as a new ethical metanarrative which commands an acute sense of self and a repetition of ontological metanarratives. In effect, the plurality of Rushdie's ethics is restrained by its figuration in death and the re-prioritisation of the self-determining subject.

The ethical confrontations that emerge from Rushdie's novels are born out of paradox. On the one level there are the moral challenges in the crossover space between history and fiction. In *Midnight's Children* the deteriorating body of Saleem Sinai, irrevocably linked to the national condition of India from Independence to Indira Gandhi, is a fiction which continually leaps beyond the pages of the book and compels the reader to admit, to take responsibility for, the extra-textual history where people *are* killed and bombs *do* explode. And yet Rushdie is noted for his qualification of the real. His constant digressions, admissions of authorial fallibility and deliberate chronological error, all enforce a relation to history not as fixed entity but as shifting act of narrativisation.

The consequence is a familiar one within postmodernism. Our sense of textual responsibility is continually scattered across fragmented routes and displaced subjects. We receive clear ethical demands from Rushdie's novels, yet we are denied a secure position through which to stabilise the fictional world in relation to a 'real world' generality. Yet the resulting 'ethics of alterity' seem to operate in an identical way to metanarrative ethics by attributing to alterity both indescribability *and* influentiality. The effect is a haunting not dissimilar to the ethical function of the *mysterium tremendum*, as alterity forces a confrontation between the self and an absence which possesses a universal ethical demand. Alterity performs a U-turn from a general responsibility to the Book to a general responsibility towards a discursively distinct Other. In effect, my argument is that postmodern ethical strategies buttress the theme of moral foundationalism by turning the aporetic into a universally influential absence, one which is further mystified in the rhetoric of indescribability. What we see in *The Moor's Last Sigh* is the way that ethical strategy can be read as a simple dialogue upon death, rather than an opening up to a world of 'irresponsibility'. To examine this proposition, I shall discuss how Rushdie disrupts stable subjectivity through certain narrative themes and techniques, but then seems to return to such a subjectivity through the preoccupation with death.

The Moor's Last Sigh initially promises the coherent teleology of a life. The novel opens with the narrator, Moraes Zogoiby, known as the 'Moor', closing the futurity of the narrative in retrospection. Fleeing from the imprisonment of Vasco Miranda's fortress, in which the Moor has written his life story under duress, he nails the pages of his narrative to objects that lead through the path of his escape. The effect is reminiscent of the opening retrospection of *Midnight's Children*. For *The Moor's Last Sigh* seems to start with the end of the narrative vision as the Moor deterministically places himself at the end of a long line of causality:

> I have turned the world into my pirate map, complete with clues, leading X-marks-the-spottily to the treasure of myself. When my pursuers have followed the trail they'll find me waiting, uncomplaining, out of breath, ready. *Here I stand. I couldn't have done it differently.*[6]

The Moor asserts the equality between his written life and his actual life in a moment of completion and permanence, positing a chain of cause and effect which promises the following text a chronological confidence. As the novel progresses this confidence is supported by the development of Aurora Zogoiby's artwork. Aurora, the Moor's mother, starts her painting career at the age of fourteen and exposes a skill which will take her through both national fame and ignominy. Her first painting, effected on the walls of the room in which she has been imprisoned by her father Camoens da Gama, is a colossal work in which ancestral, personal and national histories collide in what Camoens describes as 'the great swarm of being itself' (Rushdie, *Moor's*, p. 59). Aurora's work seems somehow to enclose being in its comprehensiveness; to list, define and shape multiplicity rather than permit its defiance. The Moor's voice assures us that 'this endlessly metamorphic line of humanity was the truth' (Rushdie, *Moor's*, p. 60); the painting preserves the metamorphic qualities of Indian culture in a mimetic relation with the social reality. As Aurora's creativity develops, art and life combine into the telos of the novel, with art's metaphors unearthing, even creating, what is the governance beneath the events. Nationally, her painting tracks and exposes the resistance to the government of Nehru, the confusion of myth and reality in Indian culture and the destructive return to power of Indira Gandhi. Personally, Aurora's paintings also pursue the life of the Moor himself showing his various failures and transformations under the partisan influences of business, family and nation.

The interaction between Aurora's art and the novel's characters continues what the Moor starts in the first pages of the novel. The Moor seems to initiate a text of existential revelation, with our responsibility being towards unearthing the general thematic of a life. Such can explain Aurora's last painting, *The Moor's Last Sigh*, which reveals the image of her killer, her husband Abraham, when the top layer of paint is removed. The detective-style denouement combined with the predestinate feel of the Moor's introduction and the sequential style of narrative, all conspire to make us conscious of the two covers that seemingly delimit our responsibility within the authority of the Book. Our response to the very real themes of state and individual and the prevalence of faction and corruption in recent Indian history, becomes more a matter of exegetic process, digging through the lines of metaphor to find what the Book actually *means*. Thus in many ways *The Moor's Last Sigh* would seem to place the reader in a general responsibility to the Book both on the level of interpreting characterisation and on the level of discerning its broader context.

However, a different perspective could lie in the moments where Rushdie disrupts dependent strategies of reading by focusing on our singular relation to a *mortal text* rather than our ethical displacement onto the eternity of the Book. For as much as Rushdie gives the teleology of the Book, which in turn leads to a general responsibility, he also strives to reveal the limits of such responsibility. Returning to the beginning of the novel we also find denials of general thematic expectations:

> But after a not-so-long (though gaudily colourful) life I am fresh out of theses. Life itself being crucifixion enough. (Rushdie, *Moor's*, p. 4)

The implication of the Moor's statement seems more than just a moody fatalism with which to open the novel. We are faced with the intense ambiguity of what 'life itself' actually means outside of 'theses' and conceptualisation. Is it experience, emotion, pain, passivity? What the Moor seems to suggest is that what will follow will be underwritten by the absence of summation and conclusion, because the 'theses' do not have an independence outside of the actual moment of writing and the silence that surrounds the present tense of the novel's introduction. Thus reaching to the end of the novel, we see the Moor declaring that the 'world was a mystery, unknowable [...] The present was a riddle to be solved' (Rushdie, *Moor's*, p. 413). This statement is important because the Moor recognises the absence beneath the narrative act, and the 'mystery' of a world without trans-historical referent. The significance of this moment extends throughout the novel, as the text reminds us that our responsibility lies within the individuality of an interpretative act.

The questioning of the general ontological premise of the narrator is mirrored in the novel's social deliberations. If we were to extract a central theme out of *The Moor's Last Sigh* it might be the destabilisation of post-independence India under the factions of commercial interest and corrupt politics. The da Gama/Zogoiby family tree that dominates the novel is polarised from the very beginning in the respective pro- and anti-British positions of Epiphania and Francisco da Gama. This tendency towards division passes through generation after generation, leading, after Francisco's demise, to intense and violent infighting between the families of Epiphania and her daughter-in-law Carmen. The conflict literally results in the house being divided and a litany of murder, destruction and imprisonment. *The Moor's Last Sigh* frequently repeats such disharmony throughout the novel in a whole series of oppressive balances. The pluralities of Camoens da Gama are opposed by the schizophrenic personalities of Uma Sarasvati, whose origins are ironically split between the two halves of the former Bombay state, themselves frozen into repetitive violence. Likewise Aurora is split from her son, the Moor, and the former loving husband Abraham turns out to be Aurora's killer.

These personal factions mirror national dissensions, with Raman Fielding's pro-Hindu mafia, the brutal secrets within the Bombay Central jail and the 'invisible' sub-class of the exploited all gathering into a consciousness which, like Aurora's 'black and white period', shows the impossibility of the union of opposites.

The splits which are apparent throughout *The Moor's Last Sigh* drive the narrative of the novel, yet there is an epistemological caution about forging a general theory on this basis and setting about defining the social or political foundation of such conflict. The Moor on several occasions gives explanations of social violence which, though providing us with certain ethical particulars, centre more on the *condition* of ethical difference. For example:

> there is a thing that bursts out of us at times, a thing that lies in us, eating our food, breathing our air, looking out through our eyes, and when it comes out to play nobody is immune; possessed, we turn murderously upon one another, thing-darkness in our eyes and real weapons in our hands, neighbour against thing-ridden neighbour, thing-driven cousin against cousin, brother-thing against brother-thing, thing-child against thing-child. (Rushdie, *Moor's*, p. 36)

This enigmatic 'thing-darkness' provides violence with both objectification and ambiguity as it moves through the possibilities of demonic haunting to psychological property, from a familial trait to an individual bent and primordial influence. The melodramatic supernaturalism of this passage is typical within Rushdie's brand of magic realism, which plays amongst possible worlds to question the security of textual realism. Rushdie undoubtedly gives a precedence to the injustices created by India's factions, yet this theme is placed within such an amorphous mixture of genetics, politics, personality and history that it is in danger of dissolving into an interpretative aporia that produces a *general ethics of alterity* unable to transfer itself into particular codes.

The problem of turning ethical alterity into ethical praxis is a perennial discomfort for postmodernism, a discomfort reflected in the Moor's moral considerations. The Moor does not deny that there is moral reasoning. Yet, as is shown in his evaluation of Sammy Hazaré, the explosives terrorist of Raman Fielding's brotherhood, reasons ultimately run into absence:

> Hazaré was a Christian Maharashtrian, and had joined up with Fielding's crew for regionalist, rather than religious reasons. O, we all had reasons, personal or ideological. There are always reasons. You can get reasons in any chop bazaar, any thieves' market, reasons by the bunch, ten chips the dozen. Reasons are cheap, cheap as any politicians' answers, they come tripping off the tongue: *I did it for the money, the uniform, the togetherness, the family, the race the nation, the god.* But what truly drives us [...] is not to be found in any bazaar-bought words. Our engines are stranger, and use darker fuel. (Rushdie, *Moor's*, p. 312)

Reasons, like the Moor's later treatment of their partner, Facts, are insubstantial and deceptive and are rarely adequate to the needs of justification (Rushdie, *Moor's*, pp. 22–5). Rushdie is not saying that money, the family, the nation or god are not genuine influences on social life – such would be unthinkable, especially in novels such as *The Satanic Verses* and *Shame*. Instead, it seems that Rushdie strives to disrupt the *complacency* of reasons and their tendency to make the individual, in this case Sammy Hazaré, absent within a generality. Rushdie does not instruct the reader in a total vision of Indian society, but leaves its ethical demands under the alterity of a text which presents a multitude of ethical possibilities ceaselessly ranging from the psychological to the social. What must be addressed, indeed what must be asked of all postmodernism, is whether the attempt to express an ethical alterity is at its heart a metaphysical project which obfuscates ethical mobility rather than promotes social activity?

The characterisation and incidents of *The Moor's Last Sigh* seem to live under an ethical 'irresponsibility' which plays between the individual and the social, the general and the absolute. This paradoxical moral alterity appears as a sphere of possibility which is an imponderable mixture of the general referential text and the absolute solitude of the interpretative process. Yet the primary effect of this alterity is to make absence into an absolute by placing the individual *before* alterity in a situation of massive ontological isolation. Postmodern alterity reaffirms the metaphysical primacy of the subject because it impersonates traditions similar to the divine confrontation with the self. For like Moses's confrontation with otherness on Mt Sinai, alterity is presented as the absolute quality which should disrupt our entire sense of being and yet re-empower the way we see the world and our identity. Perhaps we could simply say that alterity affirms ontotheology by continually offering itself as something *profound*, rather than as the proclamation of indeterminacy. Turning to the theme of death in *The Moor's Last Sigh*, we can see death presented as both a recognition of the void within existence and language, yet also as an event which gives a singular definition to our individuality and a possessive relation to meaning.

Throughout *The Moor's Last Sigh* the Moor's constant references to his own mortality seem to generate the alterity of the death that qualifies permanent ontological presence. Rushdie roots the novel in a narrative that shares in the mortality of the narratorial life and so implies that the text will not always be; it is as ephemeral and contingent as the interpretative life which sustains it. It is useful at this point to remind ourselves of Derrida's contention that 'It is from the site of death as the place of my irreplaceability, that is, of my singularity, that I feel called to responsibility. In this sense only a mortal can be responsible' (Derrida, *Gift*, p. 41). Derrida presents an ethics which can only exist when Being is framed by the fact of its own mortality. Such a relation to self is recurrent in *The Moor's Last Sigh* from the very first page, when the narrator casts the shadow of his approaching demise at the hands of his pursuers across the futurity of the text. As the novel progresses the Moor speculates increasingly on the fragility of his self and its relation to meaning. At the beginning of Chapter 4, when Moraes ponders the strain of his asthmatic attempts to sleep, he equates his Being with the breath that only just sustains his life:

> I am what breathes. I am what began long ago with an exhaled cry, what will conclude when a glass held to my lips remains clear. It is not thinking makes us so, but air. *Suspiro ergo sum.* I sigh, therefore I am. The Latin as usual tells us the truth: *suspirare* = *sub*, below, + *spirare*, verb, to breathe.
>
> *Suspiro*: I under breathe.
>
> In the beginning and unto the end was and is the lung [...] and beyond the airless,
>
> silent void. (Rushdie, *Moor's*, p. 53)

The Moor's revision of Descartes realigns Being with respiration, with the fragility of the lung which is always under-breathing, hovering over its own collapse and the glass that will remain clear. The move away from the transcendent realm of thinking to the mortality of the individual lung signals a self-identity whose Being is not the general relation to humanity, but a unique consciousness aware of the mortal hesitancy of its own breath. Such a viewpoint leads the Moor to realise that the combination of Being and breath offers a demand on his, and our, responsibility:

> A sigh isn't just a sigh. We inhale the world and breathe out meaning. While we can. While we can. (Rushdie, *Moor's*, p. 54)

The Moor's ethical statement moves from the individual lung to the collective breath. Our creation of meaning, our reception and integration with the world, is more of an exigency under the apprehension of death than in the search for our independence from our mortal processes. Thus throughout the novel the Moor creates mottoes which unite the solitary responsibility towards life with the expectations of imminent demise: '*I must live until I die*' (Rushdie, *Moor's*, p. 169), '*So you made it today. Will you still be here tomorrow?*' (Rushdie, *Moor's*, p. 340). Under the conscious mortality of the narrator the text becomes framed in the demise of the source and the existence of the text. This awareness is extended to reader responsibility by the recognition that our reading is not sustained by a transcendent authority but by the alterity of a narrator in death. As a result we accept our obligation to the meaning of the Book, but also to the alterity that will never secure itself in meaning.

The problem with Rushdie's, and indeed Derrida's, attempt to create an ethics of mortality is twofold. Firstly, alterity and death function by challenging basic ontological assumptions, yet this challenge seems curious in that alterity produces a subject conscious of her own lack of stable identity. The paradox is that alterity becomes a self-reflexive tool for the deepest ontological awareness. The otherness in our selves and in the world becomes a visible space demanding the reorganisation of the way *we look* at ourselves and the world. Moreover, the awareness of the singularity of death and the individual responsibility for meaning following from the confrontation with death, posits an individual with the freedom of a high degree of self-determination. The second problem of the ethics of mortality is perhaps more morally significant than the first. The ultimate problem of an incomprehensible source of ethics seems to be that others become pointers towards otherness and alterity, rather than designating themselves. So instead of encountering those who are marginal or abused, we are instead given a metaphysics which contextualises others within a discourse of otherness. Both Derrida and Rushdie reach towards an encounter with alterity *itself* through the comprehension of death, and as such give otherness the presence which they seek to avoid. So the Moor, and Derrida's Abraham, become emblems of otherness, stranded in their alterity rather than being defined by their own actions in a definable social environment. The Moor may always be alluding towards the conditions of postwar Indian society, but the ethical message emerging from these allusions is always within the remit of a discourse *upon* the ethics of death rather than the ethical situation of those who die.

This problem not only characterises much postmodern fiction, but also dominates postmodernity itself. It has always seemed rather trite to accuse postmodernism of establishing its own totality, as postmodernism has always acknowledged that it cannot escape metaphysical terms. Yet perhaps, in these days when postmodernity is tending towards the anachronistic, we no longer seem afraid of offering voices which are not anti-foundational, perhaps because the exigencies of the world around us demand such voices.

Notes

1. Poststructuralism is not, strictly speaking, *anti*-metaphysical, but rather aims itself at disrupting the confidence of metaphysical foundations. However, my argument will be that deconstruction does not even *disrupt* metaphysical language, but clearly focuses its discourse into metaphysical tropes which actually repress the insistence upon difference.
2. Erazim Kohak, *Jan Patocka: Philosophy and Selected Writings* (Chicago and London: University of Chicago Press, 1989) 125.
3. Derrida, Jacques, *The Gift of Death*, trans. by David Wills (Chicago and London: University of Chicago Press, 1995) 21. Hereafter quotations from this edition will be cited in the text.
4. Zygmunt Baumann gives a similar description of postmodern morality as 'incurably *aporetic*', where 'few choices [...] are unambiguously good' (Zygmunt Baumann, *Postmodern Ethics* [Oxford: Blackwell, 1992] 11).
5. Jacques Derrida, 'Force of Law: The Mystical Foundation of Authority', in Drucilla Cornell, Michel Rosenfeld and David Gray Carlson, eds, *Deconstruction and the Possibility of Justice* (New York and London: Routledge, 1992) 24–5.

6. Salman Rushdie, *The Moor's Last Sigh* (London: Jonathan Cape, 1995) 3. Hereafter, quotations from this edition will be cited in the text.

9
'Role Models', Conversation and the Ethical Drive

Ian MacKillop

'What is the use of a book,' wondered Alice, 'without pictures and conversations?'

Lewis Carroll, *Alice's Adventures in Wonderland* (1865)

9.1 PICTURES AND CONVERSATIONS

I am going to start with pictures and go on to conversations. By pictures I mean the creation of human figures in outline, or what might be called verbal statuary in literature. There are many connections between ethics and literature: we seek and find in literature dramatisation of ethical issues, sometimes in straightforward ways as in, say, *The Merchant of Venice* (which plays through *summum jus summum injuria*). More subtly, there is ethical interest tangled intricately into the art of fiction. One such involvement is in the pictures, the figures of social types in fiction which satisfy our ways of ethical rumination about 'what we are supposed to do'.

I shall deal briefly with pictures and the creation of model roles in literature, doing so in an affirmative spirit, believing that our need for these ethical pictures is an endearing one. Then I will turn to conversations and say there are less wholesome connections between readers and literature, because we readers may be too often *ethically driven*: we seek dramatisation of our sense of moral value or we make art into material in which we can do the dramatisation for ourselves. As 'textualists' we may be unconscious of our ethical drives. We may (conceivably) deconstruct to propagate a silent ethics, veiled in the sanctimony of theory. Art is vulnerable to ill-usage: it can be all-too-easily hoovered up by the ethical drive. Our need to feel at home with the value-systems of a fiction, or the discourse within which a fiction resides, can slow down our appreciation of *its* drives or *its autonomy* – to use a word favoured by Hans-Georg Gadamer. This part of my paper will be, *pace* Alice, about conversations because I think we might damp down our ethical drive if we become more aware of conversation in fiction, more aware of the devices in which art can fulfil *itself* rather than us. Part of this paper will be about Henry James's *The Golden Bowl*, a natural candidate for any discussion of literature and ethics. A few other examples are chosen deliberately from motley sources because it seems to me that discussion of literature and ethics tends to have a predictable field of reference, 'literature' in this context being somewhat narrowly or even preciously defined. The other reason for choosing odd scraps of illustration is that I would like to make quick points, ones which are not held back by responsibility to works of great complexity.

I will start with a picture of Auguste Rodin. In 1914 the elderly sculptor visited some friends in Essex, accompanied by his partner Rose Beuret, with whom he had maintained an uneasy *ménage* for many years. In England he encountered Henry James who reported the meeting to Edith Wharton, describing 'Rodin and his never-before-beheld and apparently most sordid and *inavouable* little wife, an incubus proceeding from an antediluvian error, and yet apparently less displeasing to the observer in general than the dreadful great man himself'.[1] James detested Rodin's self-presentation as great man, the 'dreadful great man himself'. His cruel disgust at the sight of Rodin and Beuret was perhaps fuelled by James's feeling that Rodin worked, to public acclamation, in the same line as himself as a creator of monumental groups, for James was also a specialist in tableaux, though in words. He may have thought Rodin's monumentalism was exasperatingly simple when compared to his own. What is manifest here is his distaste, and disgust or visceral recoil is certainly relevant to ethics. (The ethical interest of negative emotions has been well shown, for example, by Amélie Oksenberg Rorty in her essay on 'Jealousy, Attention and Loss'.)[2] What is also interesting in this case is James's dislike of the part that Rodin seemed to play, his way of being 'an artist'. Art and ethics have long come together in an interest in the parts we can and have to play. This relationship has celebrated classical authority in a passage in Horace's *Ars Poetica*, once hackneyed, then forgotten, now conceivably in line for recuperation:

> qui didicit patriae quid debeat et quid amicis,
> quo sit amore parens, quo frater amandus et hospes,
> quod sit conscripti, quod iudicis officium, quae
> partes in bellum missi ducis, ille profecto
> reddere personae scit convenientia cuique.

> He who has learned what he owes his country and his friends, what love is due to a parent, a brother, and a guest, what is imposed on a senator and judge, what is the function of a general sent to war, he [the poet] surely knows how to give each character his fitting part.[3]

This is not to say art gives job-descriptions, but we and it cannot but be emotionally interested in 'what we are supposed to do'. Inevitably we profess to be 'mother', 'lover', 'teacher'. The word 'role' has been spoiled by having been embedded in a dull phrase, 'role model', but we still think of roles, and think ethically because in a role duty and desire are peculiarly combined. Jane Austen in *Pride and Prejudice* plays with thoughts of what it can mean to be a 'soldier', as does Mary Wollstonecraft in Chapter 2 of *A Vindication of the Rights of Woman* when she says that women are glamorised, possessing 'strong weakness', much in the same way as the military. John Ruskin was later to think in the first Essay of *Unto This Last* about what a 'businessman' or 'merchant' could be by reference to what 'soldiers' are.

There is a distinction basic to ethics between behaviour which is on one side determined by the available courses of action and on the other hand determined by the available concepts of role. So literature gives pictures of roles which cannot but tangle with our own sense of imperatives. G.K. Chesterton wrote well about art and morality in his book on G.F. Watts, the leading late Victorian painter of moral allegories. 'A didactic poem was a thing known indeed among the ancients and the old Latin civilisation, but as a matter of fact it scarcely ever professed to teach people how to live the higher life. It taught people how to keep bees.'[4] Literature may be more ethically practical than Chesterton believed. In its creation of human roles and puzzlement over them it can actually show

how to *keep* bees as against keeping *bees*. This is one of the ways literary art satisfies our fascination with ethical issues.

9.2 THE ETHICAL DRIVE

We are fascinated by ethical issues, as human being and as readers, but less attractively we can be *ethically driven* to the detriment of art. (Fascination with ethical issues, either in life or in life-and-literature, is not usually the source of the ethical drive.) I will sketch what I mean by reference to a capsule-review of the film of Irvine Welsh's *Trainspotting*.

> A scabrous, shocking, painfully subjective trawl through the Edinburgh heroin culture of the 1980s. Audaciously punching up the pitch-black comedy, juggling parallel character strands and juxtaposing image, music and voice-over with virtuosity. *Trainspotting* the movie captures precisely Irvine Welsh's insolent, amoral intelligence. Nihilism runs deep in this movie, but the anarchic, exhilarating rush of the highs can't drown out the subsequent, devastating lows.[5]

The passage is saturated with value-terms: it is a hymn to romantic ethics with which the writer feels at home. 'Feeling at home' with a value-system is one way in which the ethical relationship works in literary matters; it makes a tribal bond between the work of art and the person who experiences it. That we have such dense concerns in our theoretical, our pedagogic and in our merely descriptive activities is undeniable. But reading can be improved if we damp down the ethical drive. I suggest that a simple way of doing so is to play up attention to one particular trope by *looking at the conversations*. This suggestion begs many questions. (Quite apart from the puzzle of what conversation is, anyway, in real life.) It might be argued that, even if literary texts are divisible, conversation is not a discrete element and may not even be a discernible trope at all. But, pragmatically, we do know what conversation is in literary art. I only wish to say that it *may* differ in kind from other textual elements and that to focus on it *may* be a salutary heuristic because it may counter the ethical drive and reveal the energies of art the more fully.

The ethical drive makes literature suit the values of various tribes; it encourages readers to process art, preferring its ethics to its autonomy, the word used by Hans-Georg Gadamer in his 1978 paper, 'Aesthetic and Religious Experience'. He wrote about what he called 'the proper text', which 'holds together in such a way that it "stands" in its own right and no longer refers back to an original, more authentic saying, nor points beyond itself to a more authentic experience of reality. Wherever that happens without the support of legal or ecclesiastical practices, we have an *autonomous* text.'[6] (It is possible that Emmanuel Levinas's idea of 'seeing' as against 'saying' – '*noesis* without *noema*' – could help to explain this autonomy.)[7] The work of art desires autonomy. Its desire can be discovered and described by observing some of the devices it uses to attain it, and conversation, I suggest, is one such device, but one which has been relatively neglected in literary studies, though it has, of course, received much attention elsewhere, in the work and the wake of Erving Goffman.

On the face of it conversation might seem the least plausible site in which art works towards autonomy. Surely when the artist creates a conversation he or she is *least* autonomous? The artist is committed to the verisimilitudes of speech, tied to what people *can* say. This might be true if I were specifying 'talk' as a device for consideration. But conversation is different from talk; it is artifice as stylised as stichomythia, but artifice borrowed from the inexhaustible fund of artifice in real-life human interaction. Crudely, conversation has two features, the aesthetic and the forensic. Conversation is *aesthetic* talk, talk aware of its own art. Conversation is also *forensic* talk, investigative talk: what we do while driving home from a dreadful meeting or party. Conversation can be brief, as in this example which combines both the aesthetic and the investigative.

> FREUD: Do you love your little sister?
> HANS: Yes.
> FREUD: Do you wish she were dead?
> HANS: Yes.[8]

'Conversation' is, in a sense, an escape from the 'text', the soup of textuality. Conversation though 'inside' the text can, indeed, make us aware of the text going on autonomously outside it, for instance, in the little 'Ambo' refrain at the end of 'The Nut Brown Maid', or indeed in the whole of the poem. There is a very interesting example of conversation as interview in Dan Jacobson's novel *Hidden in the Heart*, forming the whole of Chapter 8.[9] There are examples in the fictions in which characters talk about the books they have been in, like Robert Louis Stevenson's story 'The Persons in the Tale' in the collection, *The Strange Case of Dr Jekyll and Mr Hyde*. Authors may do the same, as in the case of Molière's appearance in his *L'Impromptu à Versailles*, talking about the reception of *L'Ecole des femmes*. Both characters and author (though not *the* author) appear in Howard Barker's recent *(Uncle) Vanya*. These are not cases simply of (stale) reflexivity and they rather amusingly fly in the face of polyphony. But I must say they are specialised cases, meant to sketch what conversation can mean. I am here simply concerned with the *duets* of literature (actually as common in verse as in prose) and how attention to them might put a brake on the ethical drive. I am going to take one example, from Henry James's *The Golden Bowl*.

9.3 WHY *THE GOLDEN BOWL*?

I have three reasons. First: it is a classic ethical fiction. We have to talk about it in a collection on literature and ethics, just as the winning parliamentary candidate at a British General Election must, in his or her acceptance speech, thank the police and the electoral returning officer. Second: *The Golden Bowl* has received excellent treatment from a leading commentator on literature and ethics, Martha C. Nussbaum. Third: the conversations are so *good* in this novel in which James continues his pioneering work on talk in *The Awkward Age*. Let me say a word about two of these reasons.

The Golden Bowl is irresistibly a classic of ethical concern for a specific reason. It is one of those works from a generic group about family and notional incest, the conflict between so-called blood-roles and personal roles. The genre includes the *Oresteia*, *Hamlet*, *The Nibelung's Ring*. Like them, it is *frontier* drama, and *The Golden Bowl* does, indeed, contain its reference to the Wild West. It is about the acclimatisation of foreigners. (An important scene actually occurs in the Foreign and Commonwealth Office in Whitehall.) It is about aliens, fighting for their livelihoods, with Maggie Verver possessing some of the qualities of an extra-terrestrial: 'She had always had odd moments of striking him ... as a figure thus simplified, "generalized" in its grace, a figure with which his human connexion was fairly interrupted by some vague analogy of turn and attitude, something shyly mythological and nymph-like.' *The Golden Bowl* is truly about the making of roles, as Fanny Assingham recognises: 'I quite hold ... that a person can mostly feel but one passion – one *tender* passion, that is, at a time, only that doesn't hold good for our primary and instinctive attachments, the "voice of blood", such as one's feelings for a parent or a brother.'[10]

Secondly, treatment of *The Golden Bowl* is a way of ushering Martha C. Nussbaum into the arena – necessary but dangerous for my argument, because she has shown the ethical drive in such an admirable and subtle form that I have to wonder whether I should be arguing that we need to put a brake on it.

In *Love's Knowledge* (1990) Nussbaum has three essays which use *The Golden Bowl* for illustration: 'Discernment', Finely Aware' and 'Flawed Crystals'.[11] 'Discernment' deals with the long passage at the end of the novel in which Maggie Verver considers how she should urge the Prince, her husband, to meet again with Charlotte Stant, the wife of her father, even though Charlotte has been the Prince's lover. Maggie has successfully extricated her husband from the liaison, but believes the Prince has a debt to pay Charlotte. 'Finely Aware' has, in particular, valuable commentaries on two passages. One is Adam Verver's semi-vision of his daughter as a sea-creature; the other is about a confrontation which occupies two chapters between the couple who have a choric function in the novel, Bob and Fanny Assingham (pp. 150–1, 158–9). Nussbaum's treatments are very rewarding. The sea-creature metaphor is one of the stylistic devices, the full battery of which gives the novel its autonomy as art, though this device is not related to conversation. The discussion between the Assinghams represents conversation; it is made up of some segments of conversation and could be said ideally to illustrate what happens in real-life conversation, though here Nussbaum is not concerned with conversation as device. 'Flawed Crystals' deals with the kind of understanding, a 'high' understanding, attained by Maggie Verver, what might be called the 'involved' understanding of James and his style. This cast of mind, according to Nussbaum, accepts uncertainty, elects to avoid what James himself called 'the mere muffled majesty of irresponsible "authorship."' *Ir*-responsible authorship, in this context, means *over*-responsibility, the presumption of omniscience (p. 144).

There are many insights delivered in these pages. Nussbaum comes straight out and asks just how can fiction make us cleverer or better at knowing ourselves and being in the world. *The Golden Bowl*, she says, explores 'significant aspects of human experience' (p. 138), but she asks why we need *its* text, rather than a simpler version of its discoveries? In what ways is James's definition in *The Golden Bowl* of 'decision theory' or 'deliberation', his dramatisation of a type of philosophically unusual intuition? She daringly says that novels like this train us because, difficult though James is, it is easier for us to read him than ourselves: 'We find here love without possessiveness, attention without bias, involvement without panic' (p. 162). She is good on what I mentioned as one item on the ethical agenda, the definition of roles, and on the novel-reader relationship (novel-as-friend). She is interesting on the dynamics of the influence of fiction on the reader: how it can act on one like a 'tip', for which she uses a hint from Wittgenstein.

I return often and respectfully to *Love's Knowledge*. If fiction doesn't matter, in a way at least resembling this one, then it doesn't matter. But I return because I stray, not feeling completely at home. I must say I hesitate to attempt a full critique of Nussbaum on James, but I would like to propose some re-orientation. I will quote a passage in which I think Nussbaum indulges a refined form of ethical drive. In doing so she makes James's Maggie worshipful, but makes *The Golden Bowl* less good than it really (and autonomously) is.

> It is not only, then, the novel's capacity to explore the length and breadth of a life, but the combination of this exploratory power with the presence of a character who will count as a high case of the human response to value, that creates the telling argument James tells us emphatically that the moral claims of his texts depend centrally on the presence inside them of such high characters, both agents and interpreters of their own lives, whose readings of life we will count as high exemplars of our own.

There are worries here, but hardly ones that Nussbaum does not make allowance for elsewhere. She knows her taste for 'high' novels sounds snobbish: we have a long note recognising the claims of 'minorities and oppressed groups in our own society'. If we want to question the 'height' of Maggie's consciousness as character and James's as novelist, Nussbaum can remind us Maggie is all too human in the limits of her understanding – she has to be cruel and knows it, and to be wrong. But the worries are not easily dispelled. With the 'high' character we seem to be in the world of early twentieth-century poetic justice: the supposed redemption of King Lear 'through suffering', a quantity of understanding that the reader breathlessly acquires. For me the biggest worry resides in the fact that Nussbaum deals almost exclusively with what is *in* a person, *in* a consciousness. James, she avers, is rendering a consciousness, a rich consciousness, in the 'late' style. Maggie's thinking and James's style become for Nussbaum *exemplary* consciousness, observant, vulnerable, reactive. The novel becomes too much like this description by Nussbaum of Maggie, as she thinks about how her husband should have a final meeting with his mistress: 'She allows herself to explore fully the separate nature of each pertinent claim, entering into it, wondering about what it is, attempting to do justice to it in feeling as well as thought .... First she considers .... Then, while she is nearly overwhelmed ...' (p. 89).

Such consciousness, Maggie's, is eminently to be desired: the ethical drive propels Nussbaum to fasten upon the signs of it in *The Golden Bowl*. She makes it, I fear, Maggie's book. But the novel has more to it (ethically more to it, even) than such passages of deliberation, elements which do not readily feed the ethical hunger and elements which establish its autonomy as art; these elements even free it from the now-rather-deplorably established category of 'late James'.

To explain what *else* there is in the book I will now come to an example of conversation in it.

9.4 *THE GOLDEN BOWL*

In Chapter 30 there is a conversation which resists the ethical drive. Maggie Verver challenges Fanny Assingham about the relationship between her husband, the Prince and Charlotte, her father's wife.

> What awfulness, in heaven's name, is there between them? What do you believe, what do you *know*?

About two-thirds of Chapter 30 consists of their conversation, an investigative passage, in which Maggie seeks what Fanny knows, and the other way about. Amerigo and Charlotte are weekending together, having been encouraged to do so by Maggie. For them to have stayed at home would have been to expose their guilt to her.

The conversation between Maggie and Fanny, like all conversations, has phases: Fanny is at first dominant – when sitting, she is once said to be 'enthroned'; when moving, she is self-assured, permitting herself on one occasion 'a graceful little frisk'. But, in the wonderful old phrase, the tables turn.

I will quote from a watershed passage. Fanny has said, 'I see no "awfulness" – I suspect none. I'm deeply distressed ... that you should do anything else', a statement which draws from Maggie 'a long look' and 'You've never even *imagined* anything?' This is followed by a 70-word sentence of bluster from Fanny ('poor woman') which ends with 'He wouldn't hurt a hair of your head.' It produces from Maggie 'the most extraordinary expression' and a blank statement:

> 'Ah, there it is.'

From her there is now a 'strange grimace' and a speech. The speech is followed by an exchange, containing 'shadowing' or interrogative repetition. This segment concludes with the statement, repeated, by Maggie:

> 'For love.'

I think *for love* is pivotal, or rather it could be said that the pair of statements, *for love* and (earlier) *ah, there it is* frame what is happening. To use another simile, they are the key-strokes in the rally, a crucial one in the game, and in the set. Here is the rally I have just summarised:

> He wouldn't hurt a hair of your head
>
> It had produced in Maggie, at once, and apparently in the intended form of a simile, the most extraordinary expression.
>
> 'Ah, there it is.' But her guest had already gone on.
>
> And I'm absolutely certain that Charlotte wouldn't either.
>
> It kept the Princess, with her strange grimace, standing there.
>
> No – Charlotte wouldn't either. That's how they've had again to go off together. They've been afraid not to – lest it should disturb me, aggravate me, somehow work upon me, as I insisted that they must, that we couldn't all fail – though father and Charlotte hadn't really accepted; as I did this they had to yield to the fear that their showing as afraid to move together would

> count for them the greater danger: which would be the danger, you see, of my feeling myself wronged. Their least danger, they know, is going on with all the things that I've seemed to accept and that I've given no indication, at any moment, of not accepting. Everything that has come up for them has come up, in an extraordinary manner, without my having by a sound or a sign given myself away – so that it's all as wonderful as you may conceive. They move among the dangers I speak of – between that of their doing too much and that of their not having any longer the confidence, or the nerve, of whatever you may call it, to do enough.
>
> Her tone, by this time, might have shown a strangeness to match her smile; which was still more marked as she wound up: 'And that's how I make them do what I like!'
>
> It had an effect on Mrs. Assingham who rose with the deliberation that, from point to point, marked the widening of her grasp. 'My dear child, you're amazing.'
>
> 'Amazing – ?'
>
> 'You're terrible.'
>
> Maggie thoughtfully shook her head. 'No; I'm not terrible, and you don't think so. I do strike you as surprising, no doubt – but surprisingly mild because – don't you see? – I *am* mild. I can bear anything.'
>
> 'Oh, "bear",' Mrs. Assingham fluted.
>
> 'For love, said the Princess.
>
> Fanny hesitated. Of your father?
>
> 'For love.'

The exchange is of ethical interest. It is so because it is about ethics, but not in any technical novelistic way: the passage shows people talking about an ethical question and one of them proposing an idea – that there is an unusual type of love, one somewhat different from what is normally meant by the word in the world and so meant up to now in the novel. Maggie is saying something about the *use* of the word 'love'. How this use differs from other uses in an ethical problem. We are introduced to the concept of 'love' *pur*, or sheer love as love, not love *for*, but love 'itself', the idea of 'love', one might say. James was writing of the period just before the demise of philosophical idealism. The discussion discloses an idea about the presence of a value in the world, and thus the utterance of an ethical proposition.

But the passage is, of course, not only a discussion. That is what is so good about the scene. The conversation dramatises something happening between Maggie and Fanny, dramatises, perhaps, what Sharon Cameron in *Henry James and Thinking* calls consciousness *between* people rather than consciousness *in* a person – and that, surely, is conversation?[12] It also, at the behavioural level, dramatises a new stage in Maggie and Fanny's relationship to each other, a sort of reunion. The method of the conversation is balletic: actions dominate, words are bold, but inarticulate or actually disingenuous. So we are alert to make deductions, ordered away on to a treasure-hunt across our knowledge of the book in which suddenly seekable incidents present themselves as fascinating quarries. We are urged to search, to rapid-reverse, an activity more exciting, more appropriate to art, than the rather passive pleasure unleashed when the ethical drive is given its head. I do not mean that this activity is something special to 'late James'. I mean something perfectly simple: that we are dispatched around the book by surprises in this conversational set. One surprise is in the type of thing Maggie says. Her statements are rather puzzling: we are accustomed to her saying emotionally refined things, but not intellectually difficult ones. It is Charlotte who is the thinker, the intellectual stowaway in the plush galleon of Ververian curatorial conquest – and thus Maggie's deviation from her norm sends us in a quest of a comparison with Charlotte. After all, Charlotte *reads*. Books are involved in two key episodes in the drama. (In the second episode, when Maggie takes the opportunity to take the right volume of a three-volume novel out into the garden to Charlotte, an act which shows that Maggie cannot really conceive of anyone re-reading something.) Maggie also speaks here in an unusual way for her and so we are reminded of the difference of Charlotte's speech. Other figures in the novel flood in, or new voices are woven into the discourse: what I called the ballet of conversation energises the discourse. This is *a capella* singing, not Jamesian rumination, or reverie, or Nussbaum's 'deliberation'. One might almost say it is 'fun' (something associated with Fanny Assingham early in the novel).

Chapter 30 ends with a more direct assimilation of Maggie and Fanny, or *vice versa*. They embrace. 'I've convinced you it's impossible?' cries Fanny.

> She held out her arms, and Maggie, after a moment, meeting her, threw herself into them with a sound that had its oddity as a sign

> of relief. 'Impossible, impossible,' she emphatically, more than emphatically, replied; yet the next minute she had burst into tears over the impossibility, and a few seconds later, pressing, clinging, sobbing, had even caused them to flow, audibly, sympathetically and perversely, from her friend.

Maggie embraces *Fanny*, not merely the speaking puppet of this scene, but Fanny of the book. I hesitate to use the expression 'O my America, my new found land', but am tempted, because the embrace is of something so large, so alien that perhaps it can only be expressed in a topographical simile: Fanny as a land mass, a tropical region equatorially distant from the nun-like Maggie. The conversation provokes the embrace, and the embrace throws us into memories of what is being embraced: we realise that this is a Conradian confrontation, for Fanny is like a creature 'formed by hammocks and divans, fed upon sherbets and waited upon by slaves. She looked as if her most active effort might be to take up, as she lay back, her mandolin, or to share a sugared fruit with a pet gazelle' (p. 23).

Nussbaum's Maggie is a long way from the world of mandolins and sherbet. It is a Maggie deprived of the embrace with Mrs Assingham; her exposition is only concerned with a 'Maggie person' and other separate persons. It is weakened by the presumption that it is a book of separate figures, Maggie doing or being this, Charlotte doing or being that. Indeed, much commentary on *The Golden Bowl* has 'hers and hers' paragraphs, Maggie's and Charlotte's. But the creations are really interdependent, made to merge (in our minds) at key moments such as this. When Fanny gives way to weeping after Maggie's sobs, we are looped back to her own tears (p. 247) in her own husband's arms, Maggie thus supplanting Colonel Assingham. Their embrace is ghosted by yet another embrace at an earlier chapter's end, that of the adulterers, the Prince and Charlotte – Charlotte who in Chapter 17, her face 'rain-freshened', addresses the Prince with her love 'as with the whizz and red light of a rocket' (p. 192). I think the best of James's art shows how different beings move and merge together. These American women may as well be alien to each other, so different are they. In the embrace of Fanny and Maggie the collocation of east and west, as T. S. Eliot might say, is not accidental. It is part of the grosser, kinetic drama of *The Golden Bowl*.

This is autonomous art, the best kind in the book and what James meant to be the best part. Liking the book for this is better than giving it over to the quiet solemnities of ethical drives.

Notes

1. Ruth Butler, *Rodin: The Shape of Genius* (New Haven, CT: Yale University Press, 1993) 496.
2. For other negative emotions, see Amélie Oksenberg Rorty, 'Jealousy, Attention and Loss', in *Mind in Action: Essays in Philosophy of Mind* (Boston: Beacon Press, 1988).
3. 'Ars Poetica, or Epistle to the Pisos', ll. 312–16, *Horace: Satires, Epistles, Ars Poetica*, with an English translation by H. Rushton Fairclough, The Loeb Classical Library, 194 (London: Heinemann; New York, Harvard University Press: 1926; rpt 1970) 476–7.
4. G. K. Chesterton, *G. F. Watts* (1904; London: Duckworth, 1920) 120–1.
5. 'T. C.', *Time Out* (London), 22–9 May 1996.
6. See Hans-Georg Gadamer, *The Relevance of the Beautiful and Other Essays*, trans. Nicholas Walker, ed. Robert Bernasconi (Cambridge University Press, 1986).
7. See Emmanuel Levinas, 'The Servant and Her Master', in *The Levinas Reader*, ed. Seán Hand (Oxford: Blackwell, 1989) 157. The relation between Levinas, Gadamer and Derrida is valuably documented by Simon Critchley, *The Ethics of Deconstruction: Derrida and Levinas* (Oxford: Blackwell, 1992) 49–50.
8. 'Analysis of a Phobia in a Five-Year-Old Boy', in *The Complete Psychological Works of Sigmund Freud*, trans. James Strachey, *et al.*, 24 vols (London: Hogarth Press, 1955–74) Vol. 10.
9. Dan Jacobson, *Hidden in the Heart* (London: Bloomsbury, 1991).
10. Henry James, *The Golden Bowl*, Everyman edn. (London and Melbourne: Dent, 1984) 257–8. (Subsequent references to this text will be given in parentheses.) There are other relevant ideas around these statements: '"Can't a man be, all his life then", he almost fiercely asked, "anything but a father?"' (p. 146); 'I somehow feel, as if he were *her* father-in-law too.' (p. 174); 'They were husband and wife – oh, so immensely!' (p. 429).
11. Martha C. Nussbaum, *Love's Knowledge: Essays on Philosophy and Literature* (New York and Oxford: Oxford University Press, 1990). References to this work will be given in parentheses in the main text. The full titles of the essays are: 'The Discernment of Perception: An Aristotelian Conception of Private and Public Morality'; 'Flawed Crystals: James's *The Golden Bowl* and Literature as Moral Philosophy'; '"Finely Aware" and "Richly Responsible": Literature and the Moral Imagination'.
12. See Sharon Cameron, *Thinking in Henry James* (Chicago and London: University of Chicago Press, 1989). The following is interesting: 'So in my view – in my experience – a living, other partner argues,

disagrees, lovingly or angrily points out that he or she is also there, that you are merely you, that one is only one – in other words, that a couple is more, far more, than just two' (Simon Gray, *Fat Chance* [London: Faber, 1995] 123–4).

Part IV
Sympathy for the Other

10

Feminist Ethical Reading Strategies in Michèle Roberts's *In the Red Kitchen*: Hysterical Reading and Making Theory Hysterical

Susan Rowland

This essay will examine the ethical encounter with the Other in a contemporary feminist novel: *In the Red Kitchen* by Michèle Roberts.[1] I will argue that the novel is designed not only to display an ethical field structured around gender paradigms in the social realist content of the novel but also that it is crucially concerned with ethics in its narrative form. Such a narrative form problematises realism while exposing and challenging theories of psyche implicit in historical categories of gender. In short, the text demands that the reader formulate ethical reading strategies which stage an encounter with the Other under the auspices of feminism. *In the Red Kitchen* makes direct ethical claims upon the reader and these ethical claims are feminist in two modes: first at the level of social realism by depicting life for female narrators in Ancient Egypt, Victorian and modern London, and secondly at a theoretical level. The theoretical stratum of the novel challenges male generated theories about the feminine, that of hysteria by Sigmund Freud,[2] and of femininity by C. G. Jung,[3] in ways that inhabit and organise the novel's narrative structure. As a result the reader is offered two models of absorbing the text: that of reading as murder of the Other (where that Other is aligned with the feminine in the novel's narrative form), and of reading hysterically. Reading hysterically means shifting subject position to respect difference in a move that simultaneously makes male theories, at the genesis of psychoanalysis, hysterical.

First we need some account of the narrative structure. *In the Red Kitchen* has a fragmented narrative form because it has five female narrators whose stories reflect and comment on each other as characters but whose narratives do not add up to a coherent tale. Significantly, they do not read each other's writing but offer conflicting accounts both of events and motives. A good example is the novel's opening in the form of a letter denouncing one of the major narrators, Flora Milk. We later learn that this was written by her sister and rival in love, Rosina.

> Flora Milk is a monster in silk skirts. She looks like a woman, but she's a devil underneath, the part you can't see .... She doesn't *look* vicious of course. Her trick is to charm you. Everyone falls for it at first. You did, sir, just a little, didn't you? Just like all the others. (p. 1)

This immediately positions the reader as one who can be tricked, who can fall for it, and interestingly as one who can take a 'masculine' position, erotically enchanted by the all-female narrators.

Three of the narrators are involved in Spiritualism in Victorian London. Flora Milk is a successful young working class medium aided by her sister, Rosina, who may be helping her to fake psychic phenomena. Rosina tells us of '[c]ollapsible rods to make spirit arms, trick slates with messages already written on them, rubber gloves to feel like spirit hands ...' (p. 1), but we later learn that Flora marries Rosina's young man George so casting doubt on Rosina's objective status as a witness. Rosina's letters to the sceptical psychic investigator, Mr Redburn do become an erotic exchange ending in her marriage to him and her escape into a middle class existence. Flora is meanwhile patronised by Minnie Preston, middle-class wife of Sir William Preston, physicist and psychic investigator. He experiments with Flora, eventually taking her to Dr Charcot's Salpetrière to be exhibited as an hysteric. Sigmund Freud famously learnt hypnosis, a treatment for hysteria (predominantly a female disease) at Charcot's clinic in Salpetrière.[4] The novel traces the transition between psychic symptoms in women being absorbed by the discourse of Spiritualism, at its height in the 1870s, to being later incorporated into the paradigms of hysteria.[5] This transition forms a pretext for the genesis of psychoanalysis. Sir William Preston and Flora Milk are modelled on a real psychic investigator and medium: Sir William Crookes and Florence Cook. The novel makes use of the inconclusive Victorian speculation about their relationship (see 'Author's Note' to *In the Red Kitchen*).[6] Certainly, *In the Red Kitchen*'s Flora seems to suffer sexual interference from William but the real Crookes never subscribed to the belief that a medium's symptoms could be defined as hysteria. Fictional Flora ends up labelled as either an hysteric or a fraud or both by William and Minnie when she alleges sexual misconduct and returns from Paris, pregnant. Minnie Preston's relations to Flora, the medium are determined by her desire to contact her dead daughter, Rosalie, about whose demise Flora's spirit voice makes some interesting claims. In the seance, Flora's Other becomes the voice of the murdered daughter:

> *Mother. Smother. Mother, you smothered me. Mother, you smothered me.* (p. 94)

Mediumship links the three main narrators of *In the Red Kitchen* who are Hat, Pharaoh's daughter and later Pharaoh in Ancient Egypt, nineteenth-century Flora and a contemporary woman called Hattie who seems to be living in Flora's house in 1980s London. Hattie is making a life with her male lover, only known as 'you', the object of her autobiographical writing and another erotic masculine position for the reader. Flora's spirit-guide could either be Hat or Hattie or both. Hat ends her narrative in Ancient Egypt by projecting herself forward as a ghost, 'searching for a faithful scribe … [o]ne whose hand will dance to my spelling' (p. 133) while contemporary Hattie sees a ghost who may be the child, Flora, and records fantasies of being a king in Ancient Egypt. It is clear from this that literal mediumship is not the only way of understanding the links between these three main narrators. There are in fact three ontological possibilities: one, that they are mediums mutually summoning and operating as ghosts; two, that all are figures for the Other's unconscious, loosely drawing upon the theories of C. G. Jung; and thirdly, that they are all in some sense fiction makers, creative writers, figures for the female artist.

Let me say a little more about the latter two possibilities. Michèle Roberts has creatively used Jungian ideas in her novels up to and including *In the Red Kitchen*.[7] Jungian theory is deployed strategically for feminist purposes to represent female identity as authentic (if in process with patriarchal forces), to figure the female artist and female art. The female narrators of *In the Red Kitchen* are Others to each other in the Jungian sense in that they stand for an autonomous, meaningful and creative unconscious. The narrators as Other promote a sense of female identity at one level simply structurally, by having the other as feminine, so suggesting a kind of feminine autonomy. At a Jungian level, female identity is presented through a conjunction with the unconscious which can develop a sense of self and promote artistic expression, here writing. This does not necessarily replace a cultural model of the female self in patriarchy. Although the Jungian unconscious is creative and autonomous, it manifests itself through images shaped or 'coloured' by culture. Therefore a patriarchal culture will still oppress women defined as inferior, but a Jungian model of a pro-active unconscious allows Roberts to propose a positive engagement with the Other which may heal the psychological damage of patriarchy and can figure the female artist as involved with her culture but in part creative of her own sense of self, not wholly subject to received gender paradigms. I am not saying that the novel suggests a kind of whole achieved identity that the post-modern project has brought into grave doubt. Rather, that Jungian ideas allow the novel to figure a sense of autonomy through interaction with a creative unconscious that is far from complete and, in this novel, still subject to patriarchal oppression. The quest model of identity as something achievable in a fully satisfying structure modelled on romance is perceptible in Roberts's first three novels but Jungian ideas do not necessarily form such a paradigm, containing as they do the powerfully deconstructive concept of the shadow.[8]

Here, it is possible to see how the formation of the mediums as each other's unconscious Other in the novel is coherent with the modelling of the female artist as Jungian and/or medium. The Other that each medium contacts is a figure for her (Jungian) unconscious and/or a spirit. However cultural *fictions* are another possibility for defining the connection between Egyptian Hat, Victorian Flora and contemporary Hattie. Pharaoh Hat's discourse of spirits may well be her and her culture's need to mythologise their regal power, which resembles Freud's family romance. Hat marries her father and bases her later claim to be Pharaoh and immortal on a fantasy of removing her despised female gender to become male. Much or even all of Flora's spirit manifestations may be tricks or fictions designed to gain her power and money in a society where she has few opportunities to earn a living. Contemporary Hattie's fantasies in her childhood of being 'Hat' in Ancient Egypt as well as her perception of the ghost Flora as sobbing child may well be her creative responses to abuse from an 'uncle'.

> 'At night, in my narrow white bed encircled by white curtains, I escaped into another country called Egypt where I was King'. (p. 35)

The feminist ethical claim that all five narrators make at the level of social realism is that all of them are suffering from patriarchal oppression which materially, psychologically, and spiritually impacts upon their lives. Where Hat strives to live out a patriarchal religious and monarchical myth, contemporary Hattie is still traumatised by the abuse that no one believed at the time and Flora, desperate for money, is later also victimised by male discourses of hysteria. Nineteenth-century hysteria, pre-Freud, defined women as pathological and/or morally inferior liars.[9] Even the relentlessly patriarchal Minnie Preston is oppressed by her husband's sexual demands and fears death through excessive childbearing. Unlike feminist utopian fictions and all Roberts's earlier novels, *In the Red Kitchen* does not provide a feminist ethical model of social living: there is no female support group, group of friends or manifesto solidarity. The narrators are by contrast divided by time, history, class and culture differences. Although much of the direct opposition between the three Victorian narrators is structured by patriarchy, there remain real issues of difference between women, of class, culture and sexuality. Even the sisters by blood are not 'sisters' in the feminist sense. Flora steals Rosina's lover for reasons that are both erotic and prudent and it is not until she is an old woman that she regrets the loss of her sister and that she valued her daughter less than her dead son. I would like to suggest that the novel makes two feminist ethical moves here: on the one hand we have a feminist politics of respecting difference, the otherness of the Other, but on the other hand, the feminist support group, denied in the novel's techniques of social realism, re-convenes in the mind of the reader. The reason that these very different voices may structure a *feminist* support group lies in the recognition that they are all oppressed by patriarchy, if in different ways and that they are all needy. The narrative structure of the novel is driven by female desire formed through and against patriarchal modes and the resulting pain. Even Hat, who would appear to win in that she becomes Pharaoh, cannot succeed in eradicating her female gender that marks her as Other to the symbolic of her culture. The writing that embodies the immortality of the male pharaohs will be erased in her case.

> She says: 'The tomb is the first book; the house of life; the body that does not decay because it is written ….' (p. 24)

But in her case:

> Now that my name has been hacked off the walls … the sign of my kingship has been broken off me. I am lacking. I am a lack … I am female … (p. 133).

The shade of Lacanian theory lurks here as some kind of ironic feminist joke in Egyptian culture's religion of divine phallogocentrism in ways that suggest both theory's ability to account for history and history's ability to suggest that theories may be historical manifestations structured through patriarchy. The novel makes one other ethical claim at the level of narrative content which is fashioned for feminist purposes. It is that patriarchy operates upon a binary system where the dominant term seeks to suppress the Other as absolute Other, and that Other, in this novel, is aligned with the feminine. Binarism haunts the text and is most explicit in Flora's medium practice, where the medium's body becomes home to the absolute Other, the dead.

> I see the half-dead medium shudder with cold …. She is the point at which opposite charges, opposite impulses, spark and meet: life explodes into death, heat into cold, past into future. (p. 94)

So the novel challenges the ethical validity of binary systems of thought and makes that challenge *feminist* by the way it identifies subordination of the Other with female experience. In its most acute form, the patriarchal identified women, King Hat and Minnie, both appear to kill other women under the pressure of trying to live out Egyptian monarchical theology and a Victorian marriage respectively. Minnie may well have killed her daughter and Hat can allow no rivals for her father's love so she announces her plan to kill her father-god's favourite concubine the day after she marries him (p. 85). Hat and Minnie's violence is not negated but is identified as being structured through patriarchal pressures.

Flora too, wished her mother dead and suppressed the knowledge that her father desired her unborn self not to live.

> Admit it, admit it, my tears insist: you wished your mother dead. You wanted her out of the way. You wanted her killed. (p. 128)

Roberts's treatment of heterosexual romance in *In the Red Kitchen* is to show it structured through and against patriarchy and as a possible response to fear. It is a cultural critique of romance (and ultimately of Freud's female Oedipus complex) that is a feminist ethical condemnation of patriarchy in various historical manifestations.

Having considered the feminist ethical dynamics of the proto-realist content of *In the Red Kitchen*, I want to turn to the ethical challenge to theory and to the effects of the fragmented narrative form. If the novel aligns suppressing Otherness with oppressing the feminine, then what is distinctive about this novel is that this method is incorporated into reading strategies and into investigations of literal and metaphorical modes of understanding. *In the Red Kitchen* identifies patriarchal thinking with a literal mode of understanding formed through rigid binary oppositions. To King Hat in Egypt, writing *is* life in perpetual opposition to death while to William Preston, Flora's spirits are real spirits *or*, if this ontology cannot be sustained, she is a fraud *or* diseased. The feminine is placed as a sliding signifier which can occupy only one signified at a time: Flora is a medium *or* an hysteric *or* is criminally alleging (or is a victim of) sexual abuse. The novel offers a counter ontological mode: that of a literal-metaphorical continuum where the narrators are Others to each other in a field which includes the possibility of spirits, the creative unconscious or fiction-making. Here the feminine is not confined to one definition which would structure it as purely Other to patriarchy's medical, erotic and occult discourses. At one point also in the novel, this literal-metaphorical mode of reading is particularly stressed. When Flora is exhibited in Salpetrière as a medium now collapsed into an hysteric, so rigidly defined under the patriarchal mode as pathological, she has to puzzle out or 'read' what the male doctors are saying about her.

> When Dr Charcot starts to speak, William whispers to me that it's all technical medical details, too complicated to translate. I understand one word. It recurs often enough for me to grasp it,

> turn it over in my hand. *Isterry*. History? And then *famm*. History and women? (p. 124)

Impoverished Flora, whose culture, class and gender have given her no opportunities to learn French, thinks that the male doctors are talking about history and women. What happens next is what Flora call a performance. She witnesses a parade of female hysteria patients acting out their patriarchally defined pathology under the orchestration of Charcot, who is variously named 'magician', 'ring-master', 'God', and 'great artist' (pp. 124–5). In this scene, *In the Red Kitchen* indicts medicine, religion and art's appropriation of the feminine as Other, including the art of the realist novel with its 'detached' and 'objective' narrators.

Returning to Flora's (mis)reading of *Isterry*, at this point the two modes of understanding (the literal binary union of signifier and signified identified in the novel with patriarchal methods and the poststructural literal-metaphorical continuum in opposition to the former), these modes are identified with reading strategies. For, the educated reader, who may have heard of Charcot and Salpetrière with his famous performances of hypnotised hysteria patients, is here tempted to overrule Flora's interpretation of '*Isterry*' as history and conclude that she has mistaken the word for *hysteria*. A simple over-ruling of Flora here has two ethical consequences: it aligns the reader with the doctors and the male gaze of their theory, so subordinating Flora into the despised Other, and secondly, it represents a *choice* to adopt the literal mode of reading where a word can only stand for one concept, a mode that the novel identifies with patriarchy. Previously, some narrative forms have suggested a male erotic subject position for the reader, for example in Hattie's writing, always addressed to 'you', a male lover and Rosina's opening artful constructions. Now, in Salpetrière, the ethical consequences of adopting *solely* a male gaze, now aligned with masculine theory, are exposed. The reading position is now a *choice* because the novel has by now set up the opposing mode of reading poststructurally, the literal-metaphorical continuum where 'Isterry' can stand for hysteria but also credence can be given to Flora's construction of 'history and women'. Such a reading strategy is explicitly feminist because it is designed to rescue the Other from outside signification, to give the Other a voice from within the 'objective' (in two senses) gaze of male theory. To read in the literal patriarchal mode *only* is to miss the feminine voice hystericising male theory of hysteria by suggesting that symptoms of Otherness could also be understood as the history of women's lives.

What the novel does not do, of course, is to suggest that there are female and male modes of reading. *In the Red Kitchen* is not an essentialist text. It structures a patriarchal literal mode of reading and thinking opposed by a poststructuralist version which is feminist here because the subordinated Other it recuperates is aligned with the feminine. Women can try to operate in the patriarchal mode in order to try to erase their own Otherness from the symbolic order as King Hat and Minnie seek to do. Ultimately, they are unable to overcome patriarchy's situating them as bodies outside phallogocentrism but their collaboration gains them precarious temporary power at the expense of exterminating Otherness as other women: they kill. So I am arguing that *In the Red Kitchen* makes reading an explicitly ethical process by offering two alternatives: reading as hysteria or reading as murder.

Let me take reading as murder first. If the reader succumbs to the temptation to overrule Flora on the meaning of 'Isterry' and hence of the scene at Salpetrière, she adopts the masculine position offered earlier in the text as romance, eros, but now formed as masculine theory defining women as the untrustworthy Other. This not only places the reader with William and Charcot but also with Minnie in her middle class determined adherence to patriarchal norms at the expense of working class Flora. In Flora's account of their relationship, Minnie has murdered her daughter, so the novel formulates an ethical argument that leads straight back to the reader: by allowing no Otherness to interpretation, binding a signifier to one signified, what is Other is then expelled, repressed, ultimately murdered by being cast out into the wastes outside the symbolic. To underline the point we have a further patriarchal-identified woman operating in the literal mode, Hat, who kills in order to secure her place in the erotic political romance that is her union with her father-god. Even so, Hat cannot retain the masculine power she later assumes since her body is to be cast out from patriarchy after her death. The reader in the literal mode adopts the 'masculine' position occupied by patriarchy's repressive impulses and murderous patriarchal women.

Minnie, however, represents a further temptation to the reader to murder part of the possibilities of the novel. She is truly ghastly rather than ghostly in her self-justifying, simpering narrative that makes Flora's portrayal of her as a self-deceiving, adulterous child murderer all too sympathetic and plausible. Her usual tone is of sickly childish compliance addressed to her 'Mamma'.

> You are much too good to your naughty child, spoiling her with so many affectionate remembrances and kind messages. (p. 20)

> I would not be your daughter if I did not retain a strong feeling of *my duty*. (p. 6)

Outwardly all patriarchal submission, Minnie's own narrative suggests that tricks and fictions to evade patriarchal surveillance are not confined to the medium. A result is that the liberal leaning feminist minded reader is tempted to murder this voice and to throw all belief onto the side of Flora. It is worth noting that the novel deliberately structures a conflict between these two female narrators. While Minnie describes her kind patronage of the young medium who repays her benefactress by ludicrous allegations against her god-like scientist husband, Flora tells a history of devious manipulation, erotic attentions from Minnie, adultery, bribery and the revelation of Minnie's murder of daughter Rosalie (see pp. 90–8).

Yet, if reading as murder of the Other is ultimately a patriarchal tool, the ethical arguments against it must apply to Minnie as well. She too, is terrified. She too is a victim, here of her husband's sexual demands that put her life at risk through excessive childbearing. If her simpering history of her daily life cannot generate sympathy, then her record of her own Otherness in the unconscious, her dreams, demonstrates fear.

> In the dream … I wait, in dread, for the approach of some monstrous being that lurks behind one of the toppled colonnades; I smell his rank smell, I hear the scrape of his claws and the grinding of his foul jaws. (p. 11)

If the reader chooses to downgrade Minnie's account in order to support Flora and to construct some coherent logical story rather than alternative possibilities, then this is the reader's choice, to murder some of the Otherness in the conflicting narrative voices. What *In the Red Kitchen* does is to make the reader examine her own desires and prejudices on feminist ethical grounds. Minnie Preston's role is a critique of class oppression and a tempting of the reader to exact a reciprocal revenge. It is also an attempt to give a voice to a female child murderer who is also oppressed. The practice of reading as murder of the Other is allied to patriarchal suppression of the feminine but the novel offers an alternative: reading hysterically.

If hysteria can be described as the failure to find a secure subject position then hysteria is the practice of the ethical feminist reader of *In the Red Kitchen.* All the narratives conflict at some points and so hysteria is the only way of escaping the temptation to erect a hierarchy of narrative voices. Such a hierarchy would murder some of the Otherness and is structurally allied with patriarchy. The ethical feminist reader needs to *learn* to shift subject position between the narrators: the novel exposes the temptation to mutilate in order to construct a coherent story. If the novel has some of the elements of a detective story – the whodunit – then it is the reader who done it, if we decide that 'Isterry' means *only* 'hysteria' or that Minnie is *just* a detestable child murderer. The reader becomes the murderer of Otherness in the text where Otherness can signify other possibilities and meanings. Reading hysterically, on the other hand, respects female difference while simultaneously re-convening the feminist support group in the mind of the reader. The reader shifts between narrators in the same way that the text shifts between the discourse of mediumship, the unconscious and creative fictions. Reading hysterically is constructed in *In the Red Kitchen* as a specifically ethical response to patriarchy's binary oppositions. Now it is worth exploring further the effect of hysterical reading on masculine theory.

Reading hysterically also mounts a feminist ethical challenge to the male gaze and to masculine theory of the feminine. In the first place, the term 'hysteria' marks a positioning of and a challenge to Charcot's and later Freud's theories of hysteria. Freud took from Charcot the practice of hypnosis and notions that hysteria was a pathology concerning the interaction of body and mind with particular emphasis on sexuality.[10] Neither Charcot nor Freud believed that hysteria was an exclusively female disease although the vast majority of patients of the late nineteenth century were female. Freud famously changed his aetiology of hysteria from real repressed sexual trauma to sexual fantasy and formed his female and male versions of the Oedipus complex.[11] Where Freud does appear to be more liberal than Charcot is in his listening to the stories of his female patients, but he practised the literal *or* metaphorical mode of understanding. What they described was sexual abuse *or* then fantasy; there was no literal-metaphorical continuum. *In the Red Kitchen*'s hysterical reading hystericises the genesis of psychoanalysis with its crucial transition in the definition of hysteria: taking it from the realm of abuse to the realm of fantasy. The formation of ethical reading strategies in the novel offers a site from which the Otherness of male theory, the challenge to its empirical and objective claims, can speak. Hysteria is also about history and women.

There is a similar hystericising of Jung's theories of the feminine. I have argued that *In the Red Kitchen* uses Jungian ideas of the unconscious productively for feminism, to represent the female artist. It also offers a criticism of Jung's definitions of a female nineteenth-century medium described in a key early work, his doctoral thesis published in 1902.[12] In Jung's text, the medium is described in terms coherent with Freudian definitions of dreams and their relation to the unconscious (as a fantasist disturbed by sexuality). Additionally, Jung's later theories displace the medium role from the feminine to appropriate it exclusively for male subjectivity. The male subject becomes medium-like, interacting with psychic 'ghosts', and the feminine is collapsed into a figure standing for the male unconscious, called the 'anima'. *In the Red Kitchen*'s hysterical reading practice interrogates the so-called objectivity of the male theorist while simultaneously claiming back the medium position for women, as one shifting site where women can speak for themselves in the literal-metaphorical continuum. To read Roberts's novel alongside Jungian writings is to witness the fictional text offering a critique of the gender politics of Jungian theory: the displacement of authentic subjectivity from feminine to masculine positions as female occult mediums become Jungian 'masculine' subjects with the feminine as (unconscious) object.

Finally, if there is any underdeveloped structuring of the Other in the narrative form it is that figured by the colonial politics of fictionalising an Egyptian princess. The Owen essay used by Roberts does record the existence of 'black' spirits summoned by nineteenth-century female mediums.

> Miss Wood, who began her public career at the age of 18, was renowned for her little black sprite, 'Pocha', whose favourite tricks were stealing money from sitters and sitting on the laps of the gentlemen.[13]

In the Red Kitchen retains little trace of ethnic identities in the novel, where the emphasis is on class, cultural and historical differences. Minnie reports that William tells her that Hattie is 'aristocratic' (p. 96) and 'majestic' (p. 97) in pure contrast to the working class Flora. Similarly Flora recalls that William enjoys class difference.

> Then he liked Hattie to move freely, to dance even, if she felt like it; he thought that was what I was like amongst my own people in Hackney, he expected a certain coarseness. It excited him. (p. 108)

Indeed, the blonde Flora models for Hattie in William's photographs with no suggestions of any incongruity. Hattie, the spirit, moves around so William makes Flora pose in Hattie's positions and sexually exploits both of his female subjects.

> He lays Hattie on the rug in front of the fire, her knees apart, her robe rucked up over them to show her plump white thighs, the golden tuft at the top. (p. 122)

This passage deliberately mystifies 'Hattie' and 'Flora' so that we do not know when Hattie is Hattie or when she is Flora modelling Hattie or if the materialised Hattie is always Flora tricking William. Similarly there is no suggestion that contemporary Hattie is dark skinned yet she too can be the 'Hattie' that Flora sees. Racial difference is not signalled in the text, perhaps in the cause of promoting the translatability of the three main narrators so that they can be literal and metaphorical, distinct mediums of Other cultures, Jungian Others, and fictions or tricks. The narrators can impersonate each other where racial difference would mark them as discrete.

On the one hand, Roberts's Jungian spiritualism can be defended as a postcolonial critique because the retention of fiction-making or fraudulence means that this is no full appropriation of the Other. The fantasy element in co-opting African experience is inscribed in the structure of the novel. Indeed *In the Red Kitchen* draws attention to spiritualism as a colonial discourse with its mimicking of Other voices in its claim to embody the absolute Other, the dead.[14]

On the other hand, Victorian spiritualism was a bleaching of the Other as contemporary photographs show whitened figures very similar to their mediums.[15] Some traces of this bleaching of the

Other seem to operate in *In the Red Kitchen* in the way racial difference is blanked out in favour of the fictional and the ability of medium narrators to impersonate each other. Such impersonation is designed to serve feminist ends as the reader's ability to structure these 'histories' as fantasies and fictions of each other is a mode to structure female sympathy and solidarity across cultural boundaries. It is possible that the feminist drive in the novel partakes of a Victorian colonial paradigm inhabiting spiritualism.

In the Red Kitchen demonstrates an aspect of contemporary fiction which could be called 'critical novels' by which I mean texts deliberately engaging with current controversial cultural, ethical and theoretical debates. Roberts's novel stages an ethical encounter with the Other within narrative structures that offer, but do not determine, an active feminist role for the reader. The reader too is an ethical subject in this text both by how she is treated and the demands placed upon her. *In the Red Kitchen*'s reader is granted responsibility and choice: the responsibility to be hysterical, the choice of exterminating the Other. By situating *In the Red Kitchen* at the genesis of psychoanalysis in the erotic, psychological and occult field of ideas about femininity, the novel employs the concepts of both Freud and Jung for feminist purposes. It does this by simultaneously offering a feminist critique, through situating male theory culturally and historically, and by suggesting fictional and erotic components to empirical claims. By evolving a feminist reading practice of hysteria, male theory can be made hysterical on ethical grounds, to respect the Others, to murder none.

Notes

1. Michèle Roberts, *In the Red Kitchen* (London: Methuen, 1990). All further references to this edition are incorporated into the essay.
2. For Freud's changing views on hysteria, see *Selected Essays* Vol. 2, *Studies on Hysteria*, especially, 'Katharine', 125–34, *Selected Essays* Vol. 3, 'The Aetiology of Hysteria', 191–221 and *Selected Essays* Vol. 7, 'Dora – Fragment of an Analysis of a Case of Hysteria', 1–122. For the Oedipus complex, especially the female version, see *The Pelican Freud Library*, Vol. 7, *On Sexuality: Three Essays on the Theory of Sexuality and Other Works*, translated from the German under the General Editorship of James Strachey, compiled and edited by Angela Richards (London: Pelican Books, 1977) 371–8.
3. For a full range of Jung's treatments of the feminine, see C. G. Jung, *Aspects of the Feminine* (London: Ark Paperbacks, 1982).

4. See Elaine Showalter, *The Female Malady: Women, Madness and English Culture, 1830–1980* (London: Virago Press, 1987). For the career of Charcot, see 147–55; for Freud and Charcot, see 147–8. Roberts acknowledges Showalter as a source in an 'Author's Note' at the front of *In the Red Kitchen*.
5. For a comprehensive history and discussion of the various definitions of hysteria, see Showalter and *Hysteria Beyond Freud*, essays by Sander L. Gilman, Helen King, Roy Porter, G. S. Rousseau, Elaine Showalter (Berkeley, Los Angeles and London: University of California Press, 1993).
6. The 'Author's Note' also cites an essay discussing women in Victorian Spiritualism in general, and Sir William Crookes and Florence Cook in particular: Alex Owen, 'The Other Voice: Women, Children and Nineteenth-Century Spiritualism', in Carolyn Steedman, Cathy Urwin and Valerie Walkerdine, eds. *Language, Gender and Childhood* (London: Routledge & Kegan Paul, 1985) 34–73; later reprinted in *The Darkened Room: Women, Power and Spiritualism in Late Nineteenth Century England* (London: Virago Press, 1989).
7. Michèle Roberts confirmed to me in a phone call on 9th July 1994, that she had used Jungian ideas in novels before *In the Red Kitchen* as well as in this work.
8. See Andrew Samuels, Bani Shorter and Fred Plaut, eds, *A Critical Dictionary of Jungian Analysis* (London and New York: Routledge, 1986).
9. See Showalter, *Female Malady*, Owen, 'The Other Voice' and *Hysteria Beyond Freud*.
10. See Showalter, *Female Malady*, for Freud and Charcot.
11. See note 2 for the Oedipus complex.
12. Jung's doctoral thesis, *On the Psychology and Pathology of So-Called Occult Phenomena*, originally published Leipzig 1902, now in *Psychiatric Studies, Collected Works*, Volume One, trans. R. F. C. Hull (London: Routledge & Kegan Paul, 1957) 3–88.
13. Owen, 'The Other Voice', 59.
14. There is comparatively little research on Spiritualism as a colonial discourse in the Victorian period. Wendy R. Katz does consider Spiritualism to be imperialist but she is mainly concerned with a slightly later period and does not consider séances or mediums. See Wendy R. Katz, *Rider Haggard and the Fiction of Empire: A Critical Study of British Imperial Fiction* (Cambridge University Press, 1987) 108–30. Patrick Brantlinger also considers Spiritualism as a frame for imperialist drives under the general heading of the occult but does not analyse the dynamics of séances. See Patrick Brantlinger, *Rule of Darkness: British Literature and Imperialism, 1830–1914* (Ithaca NY: Cornell University Press, 1988) 227–53. The 'bleaching' argument is my own.
15. See Owen, *The Darkened Room*, 171 for photographs of 'white' or 'bleached' spirits similar to their mediums.

11
Sensibility and Suffering in Rhys and Nin

Andrew Gibson

This chapter will partly contend that it is time for a revival of the concept of sensibility in literary theory and criticism, and that the concept itself is of ethical importance. The term is a richly suggestive one. On the one hand, in its philosophical sense, from Kant onwards, it designates the power or faculty of feeling, the capacity of sensation and emotion together as distinguished from cognition and will. But from the early eighteenth century onwards it also meant quickness or acuteness in apprehension or feeling; a particularly keen susceptibility to emotional influence. It indicated, not merely a capacity for emotion, but a specific kind or quality of emotional capacity. In the later eighteenth century, of course, this sense of the term engenders another that is familiar in English literature from Sterne to Austen: sensibility as what Mackenzie refers to, in *The Man of Feeling*, as 'the soft sense of the mind' and regards as feminine or feminising.[1] This is sensibility as a capacity, in particular, for refined or delicate emotion, crucially including compassion for suffering. Taken together, these three senses of the word lend it a peculiar power, point and effectiveness at the present time. An elaborated theory of sensibility, for instance, might question, perhaps even serve to limit what always threatens to prove to be a hegemony of cognitive assumptions and values in literary theory and criticism. Furthermore, it might arguably do so without advocating a relapse into doctrinaire irrationalism, any naive celebration of supposedly innocent responsiveness. The concept of sensibility implies an education in feeling; or, better – providing that we deny the term any architectonic connotation – *Bildung*, the formation of feeling. At its best, the concept of sensibility invokes a subtilisation or complexification of feeling, a mode of feeling in the midst of feelings. But, at the same time, the term is surely useful only insofar as we recognise it as properly designating an ethical faculty. Sensibility is to be understood as distinct from cognition in that it does not direct itself at an object with the intention of mastering it but is rather characterised by a mode or modes of openness and attentiveness. Sensibility is a power of being affected, even a capacity for being mastered. The term denotes a receptiveness which precedes cognition and makes cognition possible. It is precisely as such that sensibility is ethical and interests me.

11.1 A BRIEF HISTORY OF MODERN SENSIBILITY

But there is a problem with reviving the concept of sensibility, at least within the Anglo-American tradition, and that is the very currency of the term in Anglo-American criticism from the 1920s to the late 1960s. The principal source of the modern concern with 'sensibility' is of course T. S. Eliot's 1921 essay 'The Metaphysical Poets', in which Eliot coined the famous phrase 'dissociation of sensibility'. Eliot was outlining a theory of the evolution of English poetry in the seventeenth century. The gist of this theory was that the poetry of the first half of that century was characterised by a 'unification of sensibility'. In the second half, however, a 'dissociation' set in, as a result of which the eighteenth- and nineteenth-century poets 'thought and felt by fits'.[2] In Middleton, Tourneur, Webster, Donne, Marvell, thought and feeling are one. In Milton and Dryden, however, they have lost their unity, and a Gray, a Tennyson or a Browning can only either feel or think, never both together. Eliot's theory spawned innumerable articles over four decades which argued the case for or against a dissociation of sensibility in the work of innumerable writers. But its popularity represented, not a new valuation of sensibility in the senses I listed earlier, but precisely a new abstraction of the concept of sensibility itself, and thereby a decisive gain for the cognitive intellect within modernity. For there is no question but that Eliot privileges cognition over sensibility in its earlier sense. This is even evident in his choice of metaphor, as in his description of the earlier seventeenth century as 'a period when the intellect was immediately at the tips of the senses'.[3] So too for Eliot a unified sensibility is one which always thinks in and through feeling, one in which a 'mode of feeling' is always 'directly and freshly altered' by 'reading and thought' ('The Metaphysical Poets', p. 286). The point is still clearer in the apparent source for Eliot's concept of sensibility, Remy de Gourmont's *Le Problème du Style*, where de Gourmont argues for 'le raisonnement au moyen d'images sensorielles' as opposed to 'le raisonnement par idées' – not so much categorically distinct activities as distinct modes of the same activity, reasoning. Indeed, the preferable mode – 'raisonnement au moyen d'images sensorielles' – is to be preferred partly because it actually involves a repudiation of feeling in the service of intellect: 'le sentiment inutile', writes de Gourmont, 'est rejeté comme une cause de trouble et l'on obtient ces merveilleuses constructions qui semblent de pures oeuvres intellectuelles'.[4]

What we see, then, from de Gourmont to Eliot and subsequently through Middleton Murry and Herbert Read to the numberless hordes of Eliot's followers is not a new valuation of sensibility within modernity, but rather a triumph over and subjection of sensibility, a modern transformation, intellectualisation, even professionalisation and thereby a comprehensive derogation of sensibility that takes place virtually everywhere in Anglo-American letters. The meaning of the term undergoes a shift that denies it any possible ethical significance and neutralises its potentially disruptive power. We might think of this shift as part of a larger movement of thought that, on the one hand, gives us the code of the new 'toughness', of Empsonian rigour and discipline, analysis as 'hard' interrogation; and, on the other hand, finally produces the scholarly blockbuster, research as information overkill and/or pre-emptive strike, as in the work of Richard Ellmann. Yet at the same time, the word 'sensibility' *also* retains something like its older sense. It is in fact in widespread use in literary criticism of the same period as (still) designating a faculty of unalloyed sensation and feeling. Insofar as it is used in this way, however, it takes on a new negativity. For it now designates a faculty of feeling after the fall, as it were, what remains of feeling after the cataclysm of dissociation, an altogether cruder and more negligible faculty. This is sensibility as recalcitrant to thought and intellect, a difficult and dangerous force. The double meaning of sensibility in the modern period is nowhere more evident than in Leavis, who repeatedly and shamelessly oscillates between the two senses. On the one hand, there is sensibility as in 'the line of wit' – Jonson, Donne, Marvell and so on – unified, urbane, mature, poised, fine and complex, 'supremely civilized', 'toughly reasonable', endowed with 'a spirit of good sense'.[5] On the other hand, there is 'sensibility' as in Shelley: 'ecstatic dissipation', 'emotion in itself, unattached, in a void', 'the kind of inspiration that works only when critical intelligence is switched off', and so on.[6] This is a 'sensibility' antipathetic 'to any play of the critical mind' and thus given over to 'viciousness and corruption', to 'the grosser, the truly corrupt gratifications' (*Revaluation*, pp. 202, 207). Here, certainly, sensibility has an ethical significance. But what is in question is sensibility as dangerous lure, sensibility as a chronic and disastrous weakening of will and intellect.

Whether sensibility is assimilated to intellect, however, as it is within the Eliotic tradition or within one strand of the Leavisite project, or represented as a force for degradation, as it is elsewhere in Leavis's criticism, the effect is always the same: a relegation of sensibility in relation to cognition and critique. In fact, in a number of different ways, sensibility – the power to be affected – repeatedly turns out to be the problematic other of criticism as will to power, a will that is actually that of criticism itself, but that it insistently descries in the literary work itself. The advent of theory, which changes so much in Anglo-American letters, hardly changes this configuration at all. Rather, the modern subjection of sensibility is precisely accomplished or completed by theory, at least in its dominant forms. This, however, is not so much or, at least, not only because of the triumphant prioritisation of intellect in the theoretical discourses dominant in the seventies and eighties. Theory itself has not been without its theory or theories of the emotions. But in Foucault, Derrida, Deleuze and (at least, early) Lyotard, again and again, whether as 'force' or 'libidinal economy', emotion is repeatedly theorised in post-Nietzschean, Dionysian, invariably virile terms as an active violence, a movement outwards towards an object. It is seldom conceived of as passive susceptibility, affectivity or openness to the event. The advent of theory, then, has not produced a revival of the concept of sensibility. Rather the reverse: theory presides over an eclipse of sensibility. The term virtually vanishes from all but the most conservative critical discourses for two decades and more. If it is now begging for a postmodern reinstatement, that is surely, above all, because it finds an explicit articulation in Levinas's work.

For Levinas, the concept of sensibility is intimately linked to what, in *Otherwise than Being*, he calls a notion of the subject 'independent of the adventure of cognition, and in which the corporeality of the subject is not separable from its subjectivity'.[7]

'As a sensibility of flesh and blood', he writes, we are 'on the hither side of the amphibology of being and entities', 'non-thematizable' and 'non-unitable' by synthesis (*Otherwise than Being*, p. 79). Sensibility, then, has a pre-phenomenological anteriority. Sensibility comes before cognition, and what is apprehended by sensibility lies 'on the hither side' of ontology. It is precisely thus that Levinas reverses the *modern* formulation of sensibility as it appears in the work of Eliot and Leavis, and it is for this reason that Levinas's concept of sensibility may be thought of as a post-modern one. In Levinas's earlier work, however, and specifically in *Totality and Infinity*, sensibility is conceived of as ungenerous. It does not 'make its way outward'.[8] Indeed, for the early Levinas, it is precisely in that respect that sensibility differs from thought. Sensibility is rather the very '*mode* of enjoyment', the mode in which 'the sensuous element ... is savoured, is assimilated', as Levinas puts it in *Existence and Existents*, before that element is 'taken as so much data for cognition'.[9] Sensibility is not open to the infinite, but is rather a movement that 'comes incessantly from me'. It is thus not only 'essentially naive', but fundamentally and irreducibly self-sufficient, 'the very narrowness of life' (*Totality and Infinity*, p. 138). It is the mode in which the ego wraps itself up in itself. It belongs to the order 'of sentiment, that is, the affectivity wherein the egoism of the I pulsates' (p. 135). In the later Levinas, however, in particular in *Otherwise than Being* and the essay 'No Identity', the concept of sensibility undergoes a radical transformation. Fulfilment now no longer constitutes 'the ultimate sense of the sensibility' (*Otherwise than Being*, p. 72). Something like the reverse is true. Levinas now thinks of sensibility, not as a closure of the self upon itself, but as 'a pre-originary susceptibility', a 'pre-original involvement'.[10] It is 'the incessant event of subjection to everything'. As sensibility, 'one is always *coram*, disturbed in oneself to the point of no longer having any intention' (*Otherwise than Being*, p. 92). This means that sensibility does not and cannot 'congeal into a structure' (p. 82). It is irreducible to a state and not conceivable as an entity. One way of putting the point would be to say that sensibility is *always moved*. It appears, thus, as a 'for the other' that is 'total gratuity', a 'breaking of interest' (p. 96). But this 'for the other', says Levinas, is not exactly 'the psychological event of compassion' (*Collected Philosophical Papers*, p. 146). It is rather a constant 'exposure to the other', an exposure made ineluctably, 'without holding back', as in the act of saying (*Otherwise than Being*,

p. 15). It is characterised by an 'immediacy on the surface of the skin' (p. 64). In *Otherwise than Being* and, above all, perhaps, in 'No Identity', Levinas will associate it with 'uncovering' (*Collected Philosophical Papers*, p. 146), exposure to wounds, *vulnerability*: vulnerability, however, explicitly construed, not as a passive reception of stimuli, but as a positive 'aptitude' (ibid.). Hence sensibility cannot be distinguished from the power of suffering. Sensibility, writes Levinas, in 'No Identity', is 'the nakedness of a skin presented to contact, to the caress, which always ... is suffering for the suffering of the other' (*Collected Philosophical Papers*, p. 146). A substitution for the other, then, is 'proper to sensibility' (*Otherwise than Being*, p. 77), and the latter has 'the very modality of dis-interestedness, the form of a corporeal life devoted to expression and to giving' (p. 50). Thus sensibility is ethical as thought, consciousness, the reflective ego can never be. Indeed, it is opposed to the 'scornful subjectivity' of the ego (*Collected Philosophical Papers*, p. 146), to the 'imperialism of consciousness' and its intransigent grasp of the world (*Otherwise than Being*, p. 92). Indeed, finally, in Levinas's ethics, and above all in 'No Identity', in the concept of sensibility, we witness both an insistence on the death of the subject and the birth of a new subjectivity. For sensibility itself becomes 'the subjectivity of the subject' – a subjectivity, however, which also paradoxically involves 'a defection or defeat of the ego's identity' (*Otherwise than Being*, p. 15). As sensibility, writes Levinas, we find no protection in any consistency or identity of a state (p. 75). It is precisely as sensibility that 'no one is at home', that the ego is always a hostage, that there is a 'non-coincidence of the identical' (*Collected Philosophical Papers*, p. 147). Here, subjectivity has only the fragile, ambivalent status of a being that never returns to itself.

The beauty of Levinas's conception of sensibility seems to me to be hardly contestable. It is remarkable not least for its emphasis on bodily apprehension (surely more compelling than the better known Levinasian stress on the 'face', so readily open to feminist questions about specularity, to Heideggerian or Rortean interrogation as resorting yet again to the metaphor of the view). The Levinasian concept of sensibility is profoundly ethical whilst also devoid of any strain of Eliot's or Leavis's Anglo-Saxon puritanism. Its implications for literary ethics – for ethical reading – are far-reaching. The questions proliferate at once: how might sensibility be described insofar as it manifests itself in literature? How does it thus manifest itself? What are the modes of its insertion into literary texts? How does it manifest itself differently in different texts? How is sensibility articulated against other modes of relation to the world – not least cognition – in literary texts? Do the differences between these articulations involve questions of ethical value? What kinds of transformation are needed in our theoretical and critical discourses in order for us to be able to articulate questions of sensibility?

11.2 SUFFERING AND 'STAGING' IN RHYS

Elsewhere, I have tried to give some preliminary indication of how such questions might be answered in an analysis of Austen's *Sense and Sensibility*.[11] Here, however, rather than considering the value of any of the myriad relations sensibility enters into in a literary text or texts, I want initially to reflect on how far the value of sensibility if itself relational. There are various different perspectives from which such a reflection is possible. But a feminist perspective has a peculiar and powerful relevance, in this context, and it is that perspective that will concern me for the rest of this essay. For, in the end, it seems to me that the beauty of Levinas's conception of sensibility needs both to be profoundly sustained and, if not interrogated, set in certain proportions or given certain limits. One obvious problem with it is its apparent universalism. To put the point simply: Levinas never appears to ask the question 'Whose sensibility?' What difference might context or positionality make to the ethical value of sensibility? Does not an ethics that privileges vulnerability run the risk of acquiescing in and confirming the violence, exploitation, immiseration and oppression to which vulnerability may be subject? Is not Levinas's ethics of sensibility an ethics of more importance to oppressor than victim; in fact, a *partial* ethics? Equally, in literary theory and criticism, will not all the familiar questions of positionality enter into any adequate reflection on the place and value of sensibility in any given literary text? To focus specifically on gender relations: feminist scholars like Tina Chanter and Catherine Chalier have discovered in Levinas a wholesale feminisation of philosophy. Such a view of his work is both attractive and worrying. Chanter suggests, for instance, that Levinas is of crucial importance in conferring a philosophical positivity on the invisibility and suffering that have historically been women's.[12] Is she not in danger, in the very act of an ethical valuation, of freezing that invisibility, that suffering and the power relations that produce them in place, as though they cannot be changed, only revalued? Irigaray, of course, has written of women's 'derelection', that destitution or lack of an identity that has still to be made. For Irigaray, one of the ways of negotiating 'derelection' is the 'masquerade', a play of provisional identities as part of a progress forwards.[13] A Levinasian ethics, by contrast, an ethics which collapses identity *into sensibility*, would seem to be an ethics of 'derelection' itself, an ethics of some importance insofar as it might be assumed by men, but one which, at the same time, might arguably threaten to confirm women in a position of subordination and deprivation.

For the present, then, there is surely a final and insurmountable undecidability to the value of sensibility. On the one hand, as contrasted with the understanding of the term in the Eliotic and Leavisite traditions and the modern criticism that has developed in their wake, Levinas's might be thought of as a 'feminised' conception of sensibility. In contradistinction, again, to Eliot and Leavis, insofar as it is made into an ethical value, it will therefore also tend to privilege a canon of female writers. On the other hand, there is at once a danger, not only of hypostasising sensibility as 'essentially female', but, in doing so, of actually yielding to an order in which sensibility is likely to be proportional to impotence. In other words, in the modern period, at least, there is always a problematics of sensibility. This is nowhere better articulated than in the work of women writers themselves. In at least some of Jean Rhys's fiction, sensibility is privileged, intensely valued as an ethical mode of attending to the world, valued above other such modes. And yet, at the same time, it is articulated through discursive practices which put into question the particularity of its cultural construction, of its place in a given web of social relations, in other words, its specific *positions*. The Rhys heroine, for example, in *Good Morning, Midnight* and *After Leaving Mr Mackenzie*, might be thought of as a heroine of sensibility. In both cases, the protagonist lives primarily as sensibility, subject to 'the winds of emotion and impulse', as Rhys's Julia has it.[14] In Rhys, sensibility is precisely valued in contrast to a kind of closure within the cognitive endeavour that characterises the men in her world, in particular, and that easily breeds calculation and mean prudence. 'He had more than once allowed himself to be drawn into affairs which he had regretted bitterly afterwards', thinks Mackenzie to himself, at one point, 'though when it came to getting out of these affairs his business instinct came to his help'

(*After Leaving Mr Mackenzie*, p. 19). Julia, by contrast, like Sasha in *Good Morning, Midnight*, is above all susceptible, open to affect, in ways that may seem sudden and surprising and are sometimes obscure: 'But much too strong – the room, the street, the thing in myself, oh, much too strong.'[15] Rhys's heroines are characterised by their power of constant involvement, of gratuitous disinterest (in Levinas's sense), their disposition for self-expenditure, a giving away of self. It is precisely this that – banally enough – Mackenzie cannot credit in Julia:

> Almost he was forced to believe that she was a female without the instinct of self-preservation. And it was against Mr Mackenzie's code to believe that any female existed without a sense of self-preservation. (p. 20)

What we have in Rhys's heroines, in fact, is expenditure without reserve. This is not to be confused with compassion, though these heroines are susceptible enough to others' pain, as when Julia suddenly and reasonlessly cries 'for the old woman with the bald head, for all the sadness of this damned world, for all the fools and all defeated' (p. 25). Compassion implies both deliberation and distance, whereas the women in question are given up to an unwilled and unrelenting exposure. Actually, this is less effectively registered in Julia's tears than in all the tiny, incidental vignettes of women's pain, grief, anger, drudgery and difficulty with which *After Leaving Mr Mackenzie* is strewn. Sasha simply registers all these little moments 'on the surface of her skin', as it were, and the point would seem to be precisely that the moments in question are not given any peculiar emphasis or worked up into any sort of particular significance. For Rhys to do so would be for her to opt for a kind of static focus which would at once betray the movement of sensibility itself.

Here, too, the power of sensibility is intimately tied to a non-coincidence in subjectivity, a dissolution of anything that might be grasped as identity. 'I have no pride', says Sasha, 'no pride, no name, no face, no country' (*Good Morning Midnight*, p. 48). The corollary, however, is a raw, acute vulnerability, where exposure to affect is also constant exposure to the sheer random violence of suffering. In Rhys's fiction, of course, supremely, the exemplary woman of sensibility is also exemplary victim, constantly prey to casual cruelties and wanton injustices. Here, surely, we appear to trace the limit to Rhys's ethics of sensibility: under patriarchy, the drive to self-exposure that might constitute a given woman's power inexorably leads her to degradation, defeat and tragedy. Indeed, in such circumstances, it is never clear that the will to self-exposure is not in fact inverted power, power proclaiming its own hopelessness and therefore issuing in or inseparable from a will to self-destruction. Rhys, however, does not need critics to trace the limits to an ethics of sensibility in her work. She traces those limits herself. Whilst sustaining a commitment to sensibility as ethical value, she also refuses to grant it any finality, at least, in its particular manifestations in these two texts. in other words, sensibility is put into play as part of what Irigaray means by 'masquerade'. Here, I am taking my cue from Nancy Harrison's brilliantly suggestive study *Jean Rhys and the Novel as Women's Text*. Harrison notes passivity, openness, susceptibility as characteristic of Rhys's heroines. But she also argues that Rhys's texts are characterised by a particular practice shared with other modern women writers and which Harrison calls 'staging'. The formal strategies in novels by modern women writers, she suggests, are often gender specific. They are distinct from those in similar works by their male counterparts or, at least, have distinct effects. 'Staging' is the most important aspect of these strategies. In the hands of the modern woman novelist the novel becomes a performance, a 'gestural presentation' in which the novelist consciously 'stages' the lives of her characters, in which discourse is perceived as shaping those lives on the page. It is precisely 'staging' that makes for what is distinctively 'feminine' in modern women's writing. Rhys's novels are best thought of as 'spectacular'. In Harrison's terms, in Rhys, there is a gestural significance to the way in which the text displays itself.

It might not seem, however, as though, on Harrison's account of it, 'staging' is fully distinct from the more familiar forms of self-reflexivity in modern and postmodern fiction. In Rhys's case, too, we do not seem very far away from an account of the formal strategies in women's writing as activating a reflexive critical intelligence taking sensibility as its object. This in its turn would return us to that 'play of the critical mind' that Leavis takes to be the most crucial ethical activity in the novel. In other words, it may seem as though we have returned precisely to the relegation of sensibility to secondary status which I suggested earlier has been characteristic of the Anglo-American critical tradition. But Harrison argues that the 'self-consciousness of the woman writer *is* different from the self-consciousness associated with male novelists in this century':

> The performative aspect of the woman's novel, the feminine gesture that distances for perspective and *at the same time* invites the reader to personal participation, allows the drama of women's writing to surface in form as well as content. For the woman reader, the woman's novel invokes an audience whose response is communal, though private – 'communal' because it is perceived by each reader as private and personal; as we say, 'the personal is political.'[16]

Harrison is right about the formal specificity of Rhys's narrative practices. Equally, she is surely right to suggest that such practices in the modern woman's novel are not just means by which cognition and critique are privileged all over again. And yet, at the same time, the first part of the passage I have quoted seems altogether more compelling than the second. The concept of performative strategy in the woman's novel as paradoxically both invitation and distanciation seems appropriate enough to Rhys's distinctive narrative mode. In this mode, narrative contradictorily draws us into the world of a story that it also tells us is not whole, or not the whole story. But the claim that Rhys's novels also generate a communal response is less convincing. How could we ever know this? How can a novel evoke a communal response *because* it evokes a personal one – unless, that is, we still believe in the universal truths of the human (or female) heart? Indeed, does this assertion of the communal within the private not merely resort to a familiar metaphysics that always sees the general 'within' the particular? Here, Harrison would seem to be open to the kind of feminist critique that Drucilla Cornell directs at Rorty and Gadamer: like them, Harrison fails to take account of the play of difference across identity, and can therefore continue to believe in a 'we' who share a tradition or a conversation.[17] In fact, there is relatively little to distinguish Harrison's confident faith in the shared experience of a readership from that of a thoroughly traditional, humanist critic like Wayne Booth. It is worth recalling, here, that, as Cornell points out, for Levinas, the basis of ethics cannot be '*identification with* those whom we recognise as like ourselves' (*Philosophy of the Limit*, p. 66). On this point, Harrison does indeed seem curiously resistant to the thought of difference – not least, of the differences internal to Rhys's texts. For Harrison, in the end, the Rhys text is fundamentally self-identical, and summons the reader herself to an act of identification.

But textual or narrative self-difference is surely crucial, not only to the strategy of 'staging' in the modern woman's novel, but to the place or, better, the articulation of sensibility within that novel, and its treatment of the suffering that so often appears to be the consequence of sensibility itself. Certainly, for example, the constant slippages in narrative focus, angle or point of view in *After Leaving Mr Mackenzie* are not mere instances of reflexive distancing whereby Rhys informs us that sensibility is only one attitude towards the world. In that respect, sensibility simply *is* Rhys's commitment. Rather, in breaking up the narrative, in converting narrative into a series of 'gestural presentations', the shifts and slippages in the novel break up the flow of sensibility itself, displacing it, even deconstructing it, making it 'episodic'. As Julia herself refers to her life as made up of 'disconnected episodes' (p. 129), so, too, in a slightly different manner, is the narrative in which she appears:

> The central heating was not working properly and she felt cold. She dressed herself and then went and stood by the window to make up her face and to put kohl on her eyes, which were beautiful – long and dark, very candid, almost childish in expression.
>
> Her eyes gave her away. By her eyes and the deep circles under them you saw that she was a dreamer, that she was vulnerable – too vulnerable ever to make a success of a career of chance. (p. 11)

There is a check in or revision of the narrative, here, that is the result of the shift from third to second person narration, the transition from free indirect discourse to an exterior point of view and the abrupt effect of 'deepening' that is ushered in with the second paragraph. Narrative breaks of this kind occur throughout the novel, ensuring that sensibility manifests itself insistently, but also unpredictably and often fleetingly. In *After Leaving Mr Mackenzie*, sensibility has no consistency – precisely, 'no identity' – and is brought to no completion. In that respect, paradoxically, the disruptions of the flow of sensibility ensure its continuing mobility, its free passage, its openness to alterity. By the same token, in Rhys's rendering of it, *pace* my earlier quotation from Harrison, suffering is intensely particular. But it is also always likely to enter into composition with other possibilities and is never final:

> Julia had abandoned herself. She was kneeling and sobbing and wishing she had brought another handkerchief. She was crying now because she remembered that her life had been a long succession of humiliations and mistakes and ridiculous efforts. Everybody's life was like that. At the same time, in a miraculous manner, some essence of her was shooting upwards like a flame. She was great. She was a defiant flame shooting upwards not to plead but to threaten. Then the flame sank down again, useless, having reached nothing. (pp. 94–5)

Of course, we can scarcely read this as a unique revelation of 'the essential Julia'. Julia's assertion of her 'essence' is precisely a defiant 'gesture', in Harrison's specific sense. But it is nonetheless compelling for that, and as gesture, it underlines the conditional character of Julia's suffering while not in the slightest denying its force. Elsewhere in her book – specifically, in her own account of *After Leaving Mr Mackenzie* – Harrison herself is aware of the mutability of suffering in Rhys's work:

> *Writing* is the end of all communication – the logical attempt to communicate that erases all the talk and certainly any communication that went before. Just as Rhys has told us: 'I found when I was a child that if I could put the hurt into words it would go.... I would write to forget, to get rid of sad moments. Once they were written down, they were gone'. (*Jean Rhys*, p. 121)

In Rhys, then, narrative serves both as an insistent record of and an insistent escape or movement on from suffering. Conversely, suffering itself has both a drearily repetitive and yet also a provisional aspect. What I have said about the shifts in point of view in *After Leaving Mr Mackenzie* also holds for the divisions in the narrative voice or the shifts in narrative mode in *Good Morning, Midnight*:

> 'Now, where shall we go?' He puts his arm through mine and says, in French: 'Now, where?'
>
> Well, what harm can he do to me? He is out for money and I haven't got any. I am invulnerable.
>
> There we are, arm in arm, outside the Closerie des Lilas and

> when I think of my life it seems to me so comical that I have to laugh. It has taken me a long time to see how comical it has been, but I see it now, I do.
>
> 'You must tell me where to go,' he says, 'because I don't know Paris'. (pp. 64–5)

Once again, the separation of the different paragraphs and the distinct tones is characteristic. It constitutes a refusal to 'put everything on the same plane', to quote the novel itself (p. 12). But if the experience of the heroine of sensibility is presented on different planes, the effect is to render it both searingly vivid and ghostly and unreal. Ghostliness recurs in Rhys's novels as both theme and metaphor. Her heroines repeatedly meditate on their own 'ghostliness', the ghostliness, the dream-like unreality of their lives, the arbitrary strangeness of the courses their lives have happened to take. Rhys's narrative practices emphasise this. They shift constantly from one mode of representation to another. As they do so, representation itself is increasingly traversed by a principle of instability. But that principle is of cardinal importance. 'If I could get to the end of what I was feeling', says Julia, at one point, 'it would be the truth about myself and about the world and about everything that one puzzles and pains about all the time' (*After Leaving Mr Mackenzie*, p. 41). But representation in Rhys starts out from the premise that there is no such truth and no such end, no end to the life of sensibility. It is to the sense of unreality as much as of reality that the novels bear witness. In doing so, they obstinately sustain a conviction of the need for ethics and for justice. In other words, if only in the negative, behind all the suffering that is so evident in Rhys's novels, there always glimmers a sense of what Sasha calls 'a world that could be so different' (*Good Morning Midnight*, p. 89).

11.3 CORNELL, NIN AND 'FISSURES IN REALITY'

'Staging', then, has finally to be understood as more than mere self-consciousness. It can rather be glossed in the terms of Drucilla Cornell's ethical feminism: it constitutes a response to the need for new articulations of the material suffering of women; and it does so in a kind of writing that is adequate to women's difference, disrupts the tyranny of 'established reality' and continually affirms the possibility of a different version of a given story. In my last quotation from Rhys, it is worth noting that Sasha's word is 'could' and not 'might'. That in itself is an index of Rhys's concern with what Cornell has repeatedly referred to as 'the unerasable moment of utopianism' (and has also understood as inherent in Levinas's work, *Philosophy of the Limit*, p. 8). For Cornell, it is in deconstructive and other postmodern ethics, or ethics that can be read in postmodern terms – Levinas, Adorno – but, above all, in her conception of her own 'ethical feminism' that the 'unerasable moment of utopianism' is chiefly guarded. This is vital to Cornell's principal concern, the possibility of a feminist jurisprudence. But she also intermittently identifies it with certain women writers and novels by women. Indeed, it is surely the case that certain aspects of the specific practice of writing that Cornell associates with Derridean deconstruction (or 'the philosophy of the limit', as she prefers to call it) and ethical feminism are evident in the work of modern women writers, not least Jean Rhys. For Cornell, if the practice of such a writing is ethical, it is so not least in its engagement with the question of women's sufferings. But in Rhys, as we have seen, such a practice is also peculiarly well-suited to the problematics of sensibility in literature. At the very least, we might understand Rhys as keeping alive a version of the woman's story in which sensibility, vulnerability, expenditure without reserve might no longer mean humiliation, exploitation and victimisation. If sensibility is ethical, then, in Rhys, an ethics of sensibility is not sufficient in itself. In effect, an adequate ethics of sensibility must have a proleptic dimension. This is still more evidently the point to the more extravagant, flamboyant, even ecstatic mode of 'staging' to be found in Anaïs Nin's fiction, which will now serve as my chief example. Since my argument about Nin will be heavily reliant on Cornell's terms, however, I shall turn to Cornell first.

For Cornell, it is crucial that women's reality be recognised for what it is: a hinterland or middle ground between fiction and fact, representation and materiality, writing and 'the fundamental empirical reality of *actual* women'.[18] This 'reality of actual women' is quite distinct from what Cornell calls 'reality' (in inverted commas), the real as it has thus far been constructed under patriarchy. Women and their lives and sufferings require a certain mode of writing. On the one hand, Cornell calls for an 'elaboration of the suffering of women as unique to women'. There can be no 'indifference' to its specificity (*Beyond Accommodation*, pp. 4, 6). On the other hand, there is the constant danger, in the very production of narratives of women's lives and sufferings – in the expression of women's difference – of lapsing back into the terms of the masculine imaginary or the masculine symbolic, into 'the law of the replication of existing gender identity' (p. 9). Most crucially of all, perhaps, a historicising, backward look, whilst crucially important, also risks remaining imprisoned within ontology and foundationalism and their foreclosure on possibility. It is precisely this concern, for example, that underlies Cornell's critique of Catharine MacKinnon and MacKinnon's 'politics of revenge' (*Beyond Accommodation*, p. 11). For Cornell, the problem with MacKinnon's adversarial feminism is that it reverses the established gender hierarchy without displacing its terms. While seeking to institute women in positions that have previously been occupied by men, it fails to interrogate those positions themselves insofar as they have been constructed by men and are themselves an effect of patriarchy. Even in the act of identifying with and articulating a response to women's sufferings, MacKinnon runs the risk of confirming at least certain structures that made such sufferings possible. For what MacKinnon cannot see is that 'the feminine is precisely what is denied the specificity of a "nature" or a "being" within the masculine symbolic', that 'the Other to the gender hierarchy *is not now a reality*'.[19] Cornell's point about MacKinnon's feminist ethics is also that it is insufficiently attentive to the ethical significance of questions of representation and discourse. It lacks both the subtlety and the engagement with 'the full disruptive power of the imagination' that are necessary to ethics (p. 35). MacKinnon fails to understand that the challenge to patriarchy must also be a challenge to established modes of representation and writing insofar as these have always evolved under and therefore been contaminated by patriarchy.

For Cornell, by contrast, ethics is 'beyond accommodation' with the masculine symbolic (p. 64). Ethical feminism will therefore look to the Good as the latter might lie beyond the deconstruction of foundationalist philosophy. In that respect, ethical feminism deals in a utopianism that opens up with postmodernism and is particular to it (*Beyond Accommodation*, p. 18). But ethics itself will *always* be concerned as much with what is to come as with what has been. Since 'the Good is beyond any of its current justifications', when we appeal '"back" to what has been established', we must also 'look forward to what might be' (*Philosophy of the Limit*, p. 110). It is precisely thus that Cornell reads Levinas:

> The call of the Good in Levinas's sense commits us to the not yet of what has never been present, cannot be fully recalled, and therefore cannot be adequately projected in an all-encompassing *positive* description of the Good or of Justice. (p. 94)

The insistence on the limits to positive description is crucial. Ethics cannot be confined to the description of values deemed to exist prior to any account of them. In Cornell's work, this argument has two principal consequences. On the one hand, in jurisprudence as in literature, representation that is both feminist and ethical will seek to give a name to hitherto unnamed and unnoticed 'harms', of which 'date rape' would be a simple instance (p. 21). In that respect, in literature and law alike, ethical feminism recognises the performative nature of language and adduces new metaphors, providing terms where none existed before. Secondly, however, and even more importantly, in Cornell's account of it, ethical feminism insistently thinks the possible. It is intrinsically concerned with 'the imagined ethical expression of another mode of being with the Other' which is 'given play as the embodiment of an explicitly utopian longing' (p. 8). Since an ethical feminism is vitally concerned with goodness and justice, it cannot confine or chiefly limit its gaze to the past. Of course, it is crucially important to 'break the silence' that has kept the history of women, 'in all its variations, from being heard'. But 'we also need to recognise explicitly the "should be" inherent in accounts of feminine sexual difference' (*Transformations*, p. 59). The goodness and justice that ethical feminism ardently desires are not to be found in the past and can only be imagined, as, at the present time, the right and rational society – the society that is just to women – seems astonishingly remote. It is here, in part, that ethical feminism resembles and draws on deconstruction and even shares its temporality: we are prisoners of the most dismaying and extraordinary irrationalities beyond which there is no immediate and decisive progress. Yet ethical feminism and deconstruction alike must continue to invite us to 'new worlds' – however far off these latter may seem – as part of the very commitment to reason (*Philosophy of the Limit*, p. 107). At the same time, both enjoin an obligation to patient labour which nonetheless preserves the unerasable, utopian moment.

In this respect, Cornell's case interestingly resembles some of

Christopher Norris's recent arguments, but is ultimately far more compelling than Norris can be, caught as he is in the discursive traps of an English moralism. Both deconstruction and ethical feminism do not so much break with as radically reformulate the Enlightenment project. They express a desire for what lies, not beyond the Enlightenment itself, but beyond 'the *current definition* of Enlightenment ideals' (*Philosophy of the Limit*, p. 11, italics mine). Thus ethical feminism produces a challenge to the containment of women which also keeps open the future of sexual difference. Like deconstruction, it is as much future-oriented as it is backward-looking, oscillating between retrospection and prolepsis, holding a consciousness of suffering in tension with creativity and hope. Yet if ethics is anticipatory, utopian, even millennarian, for Cornell, as indeed for Levinas, it is so because that is the very condition of ethics. Ethics is a function of imperfection or – in Cornell's terms – 'inadequation'. It is precisely their insistence on 'inadequation' with reality – on the fact that no description can encompass the real – that makes ethical feminism and deconstruction utopian (*Beyond Accommodation*, p. 107). For the insistence on inadequation is also an insistence on the emergence of future constructions, and therefore on creativity and the possibility of radical transformation.[20] This is crucial both to Cornell and to the women novelists who have attracted her attention. In Cornell's terms, for example, in Marguerite Duras's women, we get the measure of a suffering 'that Kristeva fears tracks women down in a masculine-dominated society. Mourning becomes an all encompassing despair or grief because there can be no location of feminine identity' (p. 57). Yet, at the same time, for Duras, ethically, the absence of such a location is also an opening or opportunity. Duras turns aside as, say, MacKinnon does not from the search for female identity itself, and looks 'to the subversive power of the holes in discourse' that point beyond the order of the masculine symbolic to a feminine that is shut out of it except as represented in male fantasy; to a feminine that therefore has still to be articulated or created (*Transformations*, p. 79). Likewise, in *Cassandra*, Christa Wolf articulates a female past that is not exactly an expression of 'the truth of woman as she is or was'. It is rather a mythical past and, as such, a celebration 'of the utopian potential of the feminine' (pp. 109–10). Myth is one instance of a mode of narrative that is suited to the ethical feminist in that it inhabits a hinterland between actuality and possibility: the 'reality' presented in myth cannot be separated from the metaphoric power of language (p. 109). Fantasy is another such narrative mode in that it affirms 'the feminine as performance' and evokes 'a different way of being altogether that challenges gender hierarchy' (*Beyond Accommodation*, p. 19). Cornell also takes up a Kristevan position on modes of narrative that disrupt 'the linear narrative of masculine discourse' and its orientation 'towards the coherent expression' of a pre-ordained message (pp. 43, 47). The point about such narrative modes is precisely the extent to which they can be deployed in elaboration of 'a utopian ethical moment from within women's actual experience' (p. 45).

As I have tried to indicate, the effort to preserve that 'utopian moment' runs like a thread through the work of Jean Rhys. As such, however, it surely functions chiefly as a refusal to let the utopian horizon disappear utterly. It is a way of insistently breaking up the threnody, of refusing to let grief have the last word. The fiction of Anaïs Nin, however, effects a much more sustained balance or oscillation between 'actual experience' and the ethical moment. Nin herself has been amply clear about the extent to which writing for her was always inseparable from the utopian drive, the need 'to create a world in which one can live'.[21] Indeed, that balance or oscillation is arguably the *raison d'être* of Nin's fiction, and is crucial to what is made of sensibility within it. I want to stress from the start that it is Nin's fiction that is under discussion. As Philip Jason has recently pointed out, in the eighties and nineties, most criticism of Nin has been centred on the *Diary*.[22] That preoccupation, however – certainly in England – is surely a reflection of a continuing critical disposition in favour of positive description, the backward look; of documentary, reportage or narrative that can be read as in some sense aspiring to the status of either. But the corollary of such a preoccupation is deafness to the kind of narrative mode exemplified in the fiction. For it seems to me that the mode of the fiction – notably the five novels that make up *Cities of the Interior* – is distinguished precisely by the extent to which it holds 'actual experience' in tension with utopian possibility. In Nin's fiction, too, sensibility and suffering are elaborated precisely in the terms of that tension. The emphasis on an art which looks towards the future – an art in which representation is drastically modified by the proleptic impulse – is recurrent throughout Nin's essays and her theoretical work. It is intrinsic to her commitment to the avant-garde. The emphasis is well brought out in Patricia Deduck's helpful little book on Nin's (and Robbe-

Grillet's) theories of the novel.[23] On the one hand, as Deduck suggests, the essays insistently stress the construction of 'the world of tomorrow' as opposed to what Cornell would call 'reality' and to what Nin conceives of as decadence, 'the systematic repetition of forms' (Deduck, p. 33). On the other hand, there is the repudiation of mimesis in the neo-Aristotelean rather than the Irigarayan sense, in the form of what Nin calls 'photographic realism'. For that realism 'discounts all possibility of change, of transformations, and therefore does not show the way out of situations which trap human beings'.[24] Where *The Novel of the Future* presents the diary form as 'exposing constantly the relation between the past and the present' (p. 159), the fifth volume of the *Diary* presents the novel as a mobile construct in which 'the lens of the camera eye ... each time catches new aspects, new territories of experience' or what Nin calls new 'elements', on which the reader is therefore 'forced to concentrate'.[25] This is not to say that the novel should deal in unreality or dispense with experience, that it can cut itself off from 'the chamber of horrors we call history' (*In Favour of the Sensitive Man*, p. 17). But it nonetheless inflects the genre forwards, returning the novel to its 'original intent' as 'derived from the italian *novella* – the never-before-experienced' (*Novel of the Future*, p. 90), but also allowing it to become 'a dynamic form serving as a catalyst for future transformation' (Deduck, p. 90).

Such a 'dynamic form' tends to open up 'fissures in reality', in the words of the narrator of *House of Incest*, 'fissures', that is, not just in 'reality' in Cornell's sense, but in the 'reality' to which the novel in some sense remains tied.[26] In the order of this 'reality', one of the 'situations' which 'trap' Nin's women is precisely what I referred to earlier as the problematics of sensibility. The protagonist in *House of Incest*, for example, lives primarily as sensibility, being given to 'loving without knowingness', in Nin's terms, possessed of a power of 'secret soft yielding' (pp. 178, 182). *House of Incest*, indeed, might be thought of as really a prose poem on sensibility as an intensity, even a superfluity of ethical consciousness, on 'hearing far too much and seeing more than is humanly bearable', as the protagonist puts it (p. 188). Yet here, once more, openness to affect is also constant exposure to violent and arbitrary pain. 'Night is the collaborator of torturers', says Nin's protagonist. 'Day is the light on harrowing discoveries' (ibid.). In general, Nin's women might appropriately be described as prodigies of sensibility. The erotica are not perhaps the best example of this. After all, they were written to order – as Nin understood matters – for a male 'collector', and Nin herself seems to have agreed to republish them only at the instigation of badgering males.[27] Yet Nin's own preface to *Delta of Venus* precisely stresses its distinctiveness as a 'feminine treatment of sexual experience' where 'masculine language' – in Cornell's terms, the masculine symbolic – has proved 'inadequate'.[28] Not that it was possible to produce a fully 'feminised' version of erotic art, given her client's demands. But her own voice 'was not completely suppressed. In numerous passages I was intuitively using a woman's language' (ibid.). Indeed, where such a transformation of erotic discourse is discernible in *Delta of Venus* and *Little Birds*, it is so inasmuch as the writing takes on a utopian dimension. Nin was well aware that the world of pornography is essentially rarefied: the exclusive focus on 'the sexual life', she wrote, 'is not natural'.[29] Having recognised that fact, however, what she does is to take the unnaturalness of the pornographic mode and both feminise and transform it precisely by shifting it decisively in a utopian direction. In effect, the erotica produce a world in which women can risk all without pain, in which the only lasting flaw is likely to be the limits to men's responsiveness. The minutely detailed elaboration of erotic feeling, the rush and profusion of passionate and erotic precisions, the luxuriant dwelling on the modes of openness and responsiveness might be thought of as one kind of version of the movements of sensibility. But the very condition of pornography – certainly in Nin's version of it – is that sensibility can be sheltered from eventual devastation.

This is what separates the pornography from the serious fiction and means that, while the former illuminates the latter, it does so only in a minor mode. Sensibility is arguably the most distinctive feature of the women who dominate the novels of *Cities of the Interior*. A 'power of absorption' and 'receptivity' – a 'principle of great love, as a hunger of the eyes, skin, of the whole body' – go hand in hand with an acute 'vulnerability and sentience' and the capacity of experiencing 'the pain of the whole world'.[30] In the world of *Cities of the Interior*, sensibility does indeed take on extraordinary dimensions, becoming 'mythical', in Cornell's sense:

> You are like a person who consumes herself in love and giving and does not know the miracles that are born of this .... The burning of your eyes, of your gestures, a bonfire of faith and dissolution .... What the soul so often cannot say through the

> body because the body is not subtle enough, you can say. (p. 434)

The words are Donald's to Sabina, in *A Spy in the House of Love*. On the one hand, sensibility is given a Levinasian priority over the cognitive endeavour to which patriarchy commits itself ('in the drunkenness of caresses history is made, and science, and philosophy' [*Cities of the Interior*, p. 277]). On the other hand, sensibility is necessarily and profoundly ethical: 'No hurt will come from me', thinks Lillian to herself. 'No judgment. No woman ever judged the life stirring within her womb' (p. 53). In a discussion of Levinas and Derrida, Cornell argues against the myth of impenetrability, of the self-enclosure involved in 'the relegation of the Other to pure externality' (*Philosophy of the Limit*, p. 54). The denial of 'the "trace" of the Other' in oneself involves a 'hubris of the myth of safety' and a choice of certainty as opposed to generosity. Nin's women, however, have no truck with such a denial. Indeed, if the option is available to them at all, it is so only transiently. In Nin's world, the denial of self-difference, of the principle of alterity within the self is principally masculine and equally manifests itself as a denial of sensibility and its ethical power. Nin's most sustained account of the collision of masculine and feminine principles, in this respect, surely emerges in *Winter of Artifice*, particularly in the treatment of the relationship between father and daughter in the middle section of that novel. Here, what troubles Stella, perhaps above all, is precisely her father's self-enclosure, a self-enclosure which refuses to recognise her, to 'take her in'. That self-enclosure is matched by the systemic self-enclosure of the masculine symbolic, the 'man-made world' which offers Stella no place other than on its own terms.[31] Both are forms of 'a cramp due to ... false positions too long sustained' (*Winter of Artifice*, p. 81). The father is condemned to fixture:

> It was something like pain for him to move about easily in the realm of impulse. He was now as incapable of an impulse as his body was incapable of moving, incapable of abandoning himself to the great uneven flow of life with its necessary disorder and ugliness. (ibid.)

The daughter, by contrast, is associated with a principle of fluidity which insistently takes her out elsewhere, towards the other, and indeed towards her father:

> To leap out freely beyond the self, love must flow out and beyond this wall of confused identities. Now she is all confused in her boundaries. She doesn't know where her father begins, where she begins, where it is he ends, what is the difference between them. (p. 91)

It is precisely on this conflict or contrast – a contrast that never lapses back into essentialism or becomes an opposition, since one of its terms is never stable – that *Winter of Artifice* hinges its critique of patriarchy, and the defeat of sensibility that is the inseparable accompaniment of patriarchal authority.

If *Winter of Artifice* is Nin's most sustained analysis of the predicament of woman under patriarchy, however, it is also for that reason a strikingly programmatic work. Most of the leading men in Nin's fiction are much less negatively portrayed. In this respect, again, there is no clear-cut division between genders. What the men suffer from is rather what we might term the Vronsky syndrome: beyond a certain point or at a critical juncture, they fail to keep pace, a failure given metaphorical expression by Tolstoy in the detail of Vronsky's fall in the horse race. As, at the key point in *Anna Karenina*, Vronsky falls back in the saddle, so, too, in *Cities of the Interior*, at a certain point or beyond a certain limit, Nin's men recoil into detachment, return to a principle of self (or self-sameness). This movement may effectively be involuntary. But it nonetheless represents a failure in sensibility relative to the heroines. This is the case with Jay, for instance, in *Ladders to Fire*, and the eventual collapse of his relationship with Lillian:

> No noise, no care, no work undone, no love scene unresumed, no problem unsolved, ever kept him awake. He could roll over and forget .... He just rolled over and extinguished everything. (*Cities of the Interior*, p. 54)

Nin's men are hardly the less loveable for this failure, either to the author herself or her heroines. And yet, for all their closeness to Nin's women, they remain infected by a patriarchal principle that itself invariably infects their relationships and limits their power to give. Furthermore, if we extrapolate from that infection to its larger social context, we arrive at the 'bigger world full of cruelties, dangers and corruptions' that Djuna senses just outside her room (*Cities of the Interior*, p. 168). This latter is Jean Rhys's world, the world of 'the father, authority, men of power, men of wealth', where 'one sells one's charms, one's playfulness, and enters a rigid world of discipline, duty, contracts, accountings' (ibid.). Out there, with an exact and remorseless logic, suffering lies in wait. But equally, the rarefied world of the room, the private space, the 'city of the interior' cannot ultimately remain immune. For the possibility of suffering at once invades with the Other towards whom sensibility is ineluctably turned. The fate of sensibility in this respect, its parallel consequences in both public and private worlds, is nowhere better demonstrated than in *The Four-Chambered Heart*. Djuna is finally driven desperate by giving unstintingly, first to her lover Rango, then to him and his wife. She flees to England for rest, only to be awoken on the boat by the fearfully needy *grand blessé de guerre*, who immediately and instinctively feels that she is the very 'woman I can talk to' (*Cities of the Interior*, pp. 316–17), and drains her of the little she has left to give.

Faced with the seeming inextricability of sensibility and suffering in the world she evokes, Nin responds with a variety of differing narrative and aesthetic strategies. For all their variety, however, the effect is broadly the same. Rather than 'fleshing out' her fictional world and lending it 'authenticity', Nin works to strip it of 'reality' and 'conviction', to open up those 'fissures in reality' I referred to earlier. She thereby attempts to preserve a sense both of utopian possibility within the world she evokes, and of its contingency. Thus for example with the abandonment of linear development. In her introduction to *Cities of the Interior*, Nin herself points out, for example, that the separate books are interchangeable in position, like the parts of a mobile, and can be read in any order (p. xii). The effect, as, we saw earlier, Kristeva would have it, is precisely to deny that sense of a preordained fixity (to the text, in this instance) which always requires the backward look and is apparently well-nigh intrinsic to the masculine imaginary. The abrupt breaks and lateral shifts likewise introduce a principle of irreducible self-difference to the narrative which means that neither the narrative present nor the narrative future is likely to be entirely comprehensible in terms of the narrative past. So, too, with characterisation: Nin's women are not altogether separate, fully 'individualised' figures. As Nin herself tirelessly emphasises, they are always becoming, never petrified into being. (Indeed, it is precisely because they are always becoming that they exist primarily as sensibility). The heroines thus continually cross boundaries and threaten to resemble each other more than they do themselves. The shifts and transformations in narrative mode are similar indications of a principle of self-difference at work. But digressions and narrative excursions can have another consequence, too, as with the account of the sirocco in *Ladders to Fire* (*Cities of the Interior*, p. 36). Since it is Djuna's feelings that are really at issue in this passage, what the latter makes possible is a more or less covert remetaphorisation of the woman's experience which – again – effectively becomes at least an exploration of the boundaries of the masculine symbolic. The struggle to reconceptualise and remetaphorise is surely evident everywhere in *Cities of the Interior*. In that respect, the novels look forward, not just to a qualitatively different world, but to a new expressive repertoire that it will call forth. It is perhaps the dominant style and discursive mode in *Cities of the Interior* that are most crucial to the novels' effect. There is an extraordinary prevalence of abstraction and generality over empirical documentation, of the symbolic over the literal and, in Genette's terms, of 'iterative' over 'singulative' and 'summary' over 'scene'. Taken together, they reflect Nin's commitment to 'mythological' as opposed to 'factual' discourse. 'You never ask the kind of question I hate', says Sabina to Lillian in *Ladders to Fire*, 'What city? What man? What year? What time? Facts. I despise them' (*Cities of the Interior*, p. 97). The novels very largely neglect questions of 'factuality' and empirical precision. We might tentatively categorise them as peculiarly strenuous instances of feminist anti-positivism which drastically reduce the status of positive knowledge so that 'only the important dates of deep feeling may recur again and again each time anew through the wells, fountains and rivers of music' (ibid., p. 238). In other words, Nin's novels offer us the life of sensibility as the significant life. At one point in *The Four-Chambered Heart*, Djuna rails against

> novels promising experience and then remaining on the periphery, reporting only the semblance, the illusions, the costumes, and the falsities, opening no wells .... Teaching nothing, revealing nothing, cheating us of truth, of immediacy, of reality. (*Cities of the Interior*, p. 272)

The 'reality' in question, here, might seem to be a visionary or, at least, an envisioned one. But in fact the word does double duty, and also has a sense that is close to Cornell's. What all the novels referred to in the quotation have also avoided is the reality of 'the crises, the pitfalls, the wars, and the traps of human life', 'the naked knowledge of the cruelties that take place between men and women in the pit of solitary nights' (ibid.). No passage more clearly gives us, on the one hand, an account of the problematics of sensibility in Nin's work, and, on the other, an indication of the connection between it and the aesthetic strategies she adopts. But the strategies in question do not merely serve to register or display the problem. Rather, they set to work on it, deconstruct it, explore its limits along with its possibilities. In that sense, like Cornell's, like that of other women writers in Cornell's accounts of them, like Rhys's, though in a less ambivalent mode, Nin's work constantly reaches towards a future in which the fate of sensibility – like that of women themselves – will be constitutively different.

Notes

1. Henry Mackenzie, *The Man of Feeling* (Oxford University Press, 1970) 116.
2. T. S. Eliot, 'The Metaphysical Poets', in *Selected Essays* (London: Faber and Faber, 1941) 281–91; 288.
3. Eliot, 'Philip Massinger', op. cit., 205–20; 209–10.
4. See Remy de Gourmont, *Le Problème du Style: Questions d'Art, de Litterature et de Grammaire*, (3rd edn, Paris: Société de Mercure de France, 1902) 70. For the influence of de Gourmont on Eliot, in this respect, see F. W. Bateson, 'Contributions to a Dictionary of Critical Terms II: Dissociation of Sensibility', *Essays in Criticism*, 1, 3 (July, 1951) 302–12; 305–8.
5. F. R. Leavis, 'The Line of Wit', in *Revaluation* (Harmondsworth: Peregrine, 1978) 17–45, esp. 37–8.
6. Leavis, 'Shelley', op. cit., 191–224; 200–1.
7. Emmanuel Levinas, *Otherwise than Being, or Beyond Essence*, trans. Alphonso Lingis (The Hague: Martinus Nijhoff, 1981) 78.
8. Levinas, *Totality and Infinity*, trans. Alphonso Lingis (Pittsburgh, PA: Duquesne University Press, 1994) 135.
9. Emmanuel Levinas, *Existence and Existents*, trans. Alphonso Lingis (Dordrecht: Kluwer, 1988) 19.
10. Emmanuel Levinas, *Collected Philosophical Papers*, trans. Alphonso Lingis (Dordrecht: Kluwer, 1995), 146–7.
11. See my 'Postmodern Ethics and *Sense and Sensibility*', forthcoming.
12. Tina Chanter, 'Feminism and the Other', in Robert Bernasconi and David Wood, eds, *The Provocation of Levinas* (London: Routledge, 1986) 32–56; 36.

13. On the female masquerade, see for instance Margaret Whitford, ed., *The Irigaray Reader* (Oxford: Blackwell, 1991) 135–6.
14. Jean Rhys, *After Leaving Mr Mackenzie* (Harmondsworth: Penguin, 1982) 18.
15. Jean Rhys, *Good Morning, Midnight*, (Harmondsworth: Penguin, 1984) 108.
16. Nancy R. Harrison, *Jean Rhys and the Novel as Women's Text* (Chapel Hill: University of North Carolina Press, 1988) 4.
17. Drucilla Cornell, *The Philosophy of the Limit* (London: Routledge, 1992) 35.
18. Drucilla Cornell, *Beyond Accommodation: Ethical Feminism, Deconstruction and the Law* (London: Routledge, 1991) 3.
19. Drucilla Cornell, *Transformations: Recollective Imagination and Sexual Difference* (London: Routledge, 1993) 6.
20. At the same time, for Cornell, there is also no escape from inadequation. That means that the utopianism in question in her work is precisely 'a structural *moment*', 'endlessly there', and not 'a chronological *moment* to be surpassed' (ibid.). In that respect, in Cornell as in Levinas, ethics is always in the instant itself (*Beyond Accommodation*, p. 107).
21. Anaïs Nin, 'The New Woman', in *In Favour of the Sensitive Man and Other Essays* (New York: Harcourt Brace Jovanovich, 1976) 12–19; 12. Nin goes on:
    'I could not live in any of the worlds offered me – the world of my parents, the world of war, the world of politics. I had to create a world of my own, like a climate, a country, an atmosphere in which I could breathe, reign, and recreate myself when destroyed by living.'
22. Philip K. Jason, 'Introduction', *The Critical Response to Anaïs Nin* (Westport, CT: Greenwood, 1996) 1–7; 3.
23. Patricia A. Deduck, *Realism, Reality and the Fictional Theory of Alain Robbe-Grillet and Anaïs Nin* (Washington, DC: University Press of America, 1982).
24. Anaïs Nin, *The Novel of the Future* (New York: Macmillan, 1968) 199.
25. Anaïs Nin, *Diary*, Vol. 5 (London: Peter Owen, 1974) 55–6.
26. Anaïs Nin, *House of Incest* (London: Peter Owen, 1974) 191.
27. John Ferrone makes it clear that the 'collector' was in fact a myth. Though Nin herself was unaware of it, 'he' was in fact an underground business located in New York. It is also clear from Ferrone – clearer, perhaps, than he would wish – that he and her husband pressurised a reluctant Nin into agreeing to reprint the erotica when she was ageing and in ill health. See John Ferrone, 'The Making of *Delta of Venus*', in Sharon Spencer, ed., *Anaïs, Art and Artists: A Collection of Essays* (Greenwood, FL: Penkevill, 1986) 35–43.
28. Anaïs Nin, *Delta of Venus* (London: W.H. Allen, 1978) xvi. The emphasis on the development of a distinct feminine as opposed to established masculine modes and perspectives is also recurrent in Nin's essays, as is an emphasis on the need for women not to seek freedom simply by reversing male roles. See for instance the discussion of women writers and female sexuality in 'Eroticism and

Women' in *In Favour of the Sensitive Man*, 3–11; 10. Both emphases appear to place Nin on Cornell's (and Irigaray's) side as opposed to MacKinnon's. As in both Cornell and Irigaray, too, the emphasis on the distinctiveness of the feminine imaginary is also inseparable from Nin's utopianism. See for instance ibid., 29.

29. Anaïs Nin, *Little Birds* (Harmondsworth: Penguin, 1990) 70.
30. Anaïs Nin, *Cities of the Interior*, introd. Sharon Spencer, with a preface by Gunther Stahlmann (London: Peter Owen, 1978) 28, 12–13. All references to the five novels are to this composite edition.
31. Anaïs Nin, *Winter of Artifice* (London: Peter Owen, 1974) 71.

12
Moral Capacities and Other Constraints

Cristina Mejía

> Copernicus displaced us from the centre of the universe. Darwin closed Eden, showing that we are apes with shrews for ancestors and cabbages for cousins. Freud pointed out that we are not our own masters even in our own heads. This is the familiar litany of our dispossession, the story of how we began to acquire a sense of proportion.
>
> Galen Strawson[1]

If the loss of Eden is indeed signalled by the shedding of certain naive and self-important illusions about the nature and place of humanity, then it is surely odd that it has come to serve, in the Western literary tradition, as a metaphor not for virtue, but for a fatal moral lapse. Evidently, however, intellectual virtue is its own reward, for the prospect of losing the last of the old comforting certainties about our species has not dissuaded today's literary theorists from completing the task of deconstructing 'the moral subject' that was in a sense begun by the last century's men of science. Our possession of a moral sense, once widely held to be a uniquely human trait, has become a dubious distinction, not so much because other creatures have turned out to possess something like it, as because the idea of moral truth, and the idea that moral knowledge is possible, have gone the way of other ideas of reason, and fallen into critical disfavour.

Certainly, there are good arguments to be made for approaching the notion of a moral nature with a measure of scepticism – the notion is inadequate, for instance, in the face of overwhelming evidence that we tend as much to cruelty as to kindness. Yet literary theorists may have less disinterested reasons for maintaining such historicist scepticism, for literary theory has had much to gain from the discarding of moral self-knowledge as the necessary end to our intellectual and artistic exercises. The tradition of Western literary criticism, after all, started with an intellectually disciplined desire, in Aristotle's *Poetics*, to free art from the cruder didactic and utilitarian demands of ethics, with a view to elucidating a more refined conception of ethics and art's relation to such ends as the good or worthy life and the just society. That is, from a certain degree of moral scepticism, literary theory has stood to gain not only freedom from crude evaluative frameworks, but also the opportunity to refashion ethics after its own critical habits.

The subsequent history of modern literary theory may be said to have fulfilled the ethical promise of the Greeks' critical discipline, insofar as liberalism in the matter of art has today come to serve as a touchstone for the higher moral authority that attaches to political liberalism. In particular, Romanticism provided the moral impetus for liberal defences of art by insisting that the relation between art and the good or worthy life is far subtler than the language of public morality can capture, and by appealing instead to the notion of a shared humanity construed not so much as a scientific or natural fact as a common capacity for rich (rather than righteous) experience or an overarching moral purpose intrinsic to the concept of a perfectible humanity. That is, Romanticism succeeded at defending artistic works and practices from the attacks of public morality in part by offering a metaphysical account of moral personhood that depicted human beings as creatures defined not by the need to regulate their public and political interactions but by a normative relation to an idealised and *a priori* conception of themselves.

Within the framework of more recent theory, however, the relation between such accounts of the human (and therefore moral) subject and the good or worthy life has become attenuated. Liberal theory in art, ethics, or politics has fastened on the permanent suspension of critical judgement as its guiding principle, and discarded the notion of a shared humanity as naive, spurious, and worse: totalising, oppressive, and offensive to the liberal commitment to personal and aesthetic autonomy – the final obstacle to a sort of gentle invasion of the ethical field by aesthetics, a scenario in which the good or worthy life will no longer be held hostage to truth-seeking, reasoning, and judgement about human relations, but require only that we take a properly aesthetic attitude towards others.

Whether or not such a replacement of ethics by aesthetics is philosophically justifiable should surely depend on how assimilable aesthetic and ethical attitudes are. In what do these attitudes consist, and can it be meaningful to speak of them without reference to a shared human nature and a non-arbitrary standard of moral personhood? In what follows, I argue that while the properly aesthetic response (to a work) and the properly ethical one (to a human situation) may be perfectly analogous in requiring of 'the subject' an other-regarding attitude, both also necessarily involve a range of critical or evaluative acts that are not always so interchangeable. Nor are they always so crude and cruel: to refrain from making moral and critical judgements, I shall suggest, is to lose sight of liberalism's proper aim, which is surely not to flatten the ethical experience of value, but to enrich it by refining our faculties of judgement. What is more, I shall cleave to an account of human nature that constrains – though it does not determine – our moral agency.

This is not to suggest that liberal aversion to moral and critical judgement is entirely a matter of intellectual faddishness. Richard Rorty, who has acted as philosophical underlabourer to postmodernist literary theory, has reasoned that scepticism about normative accounts of human nature is consistent with modern science's insight that human existence is not defined by some necessary moral *telos* but takes shape randomly against an indifferent natural world; and insofar as this is an informed and accurate premise, we should examine his argument not so much for the validity of his scepticism as for the accuracy with which he draws the limits of moral knowledge.

In his well-known prefatory remarks to *Contingency, Irony, and Solidarity*, Rorty sums up the case for the historicism that has gained orthodoxy in literary studies today: 'socialization, and thus historical circumstance, go all the way down ... there is nothing "beneath" socialization or prior to history which is definatory of the human'.[2] Assuming that Rorty cannot possibly be refuting biological facts which distinguish humans from other higher primates, let us examine his claim as it relates first to the problem of a moral rather than a biological nature; secondly to the aims of moral philosophy; and finally to the problem of moral and critical evaluations of what he calls our 'describing activities'.

An immediate implication of the historicist claim, Rorty writes, is that we are left with no firm ground to stand upon when we try to answer

> Plato's ... question, 'Why is it in one's interest to be just?' and Christianity's claim that perfect self-realization can be attained through service to others. Such metaphysical or theological attempts to unite a striving for perfection with a sense of community require us to acknowledge a common human nature. They ask us to believe that what is most important to each of us is what we have in common with others – that the springs of private fulfilment and of human solidarity are the same. (p. xiii)

This is not, Rorty insists, to be sceptical of morals: like Nietzsche he believes that such 'metaphysics and theology are transparent attempts to make altruism more reasonable than it is' (p. xiii), but unlike Nietzsche he does not believe that there are more pernicious human impulses – say, the 'will to power' – that militate against the possibility of a genuine sense of human solidarity. Rather, this is to be uncompromisingly historicist: if there is no human nature in which a sense of an authentic self can be rooted, neither is there a common moral nature of which we need be sceptical. So far as he is concerned, both of these crucial moral ideas – a deeply private self and a human community – are merely 'forms which history has thrown up so far' (p. 60), to which we have formed passionate commitments for purely historically contingent reasons – say, the rise of free-market economics and the attendant discourse of individual rights in the West. These commitments he believes we should continue to hold, not because they are recommended by reason and demonstrably 'better' than other commitments, but because they have brought us such ethical goods as the freedom to pursue individual conceptions of perfection and social institutions that are more just and less cruel. That the demands of each frequently fail to mesh, he believes, should come as no surprise at all, since there is nothing naturally or conceptually binding them.

What Rorty *is* sceptical of, then, is not the possibility of genuinely moral behaviour, but the authority of moral philosophy in guiding our discovery of moral truths. He does not believe it is possible to reason from general principles through our stock of moral knowledge to a greater stock of moral knowledge, for there is simply no 'order beyond time and change which both determines the point of human existence and establishes a hierarchy of responsibilities' (p. xv). Accordingly there can be no 'well-grounded theoretical answers' (p. xv) to moral questions.

For Rorty, moral philosophy, rational inquiry and truth-seeking are essentially pointless and irrelevant, because truth is 'made rather than found …. Truth cannot be out there. The world is out there, but descriptions of the world are not. Only descriptions of the world can be true or false. The world on its own – unaided by the describing activities of human beings – cannot' (pp. 3-7). That is, there is no order that lies outside our social and linguistic constructions to underwrite our beliefs. For Rorty, truth is no more than 'a property of linguistic entities, of sentences' (p. 7), descriptions that are unconstrained by any necessary relations either to an indifferent physical reality or to other descriptions; they are simply true by virtue of being expressed in a private vocabulary, to which, on this view, all experience of value reduces. And this is particularly true of moral statements, or descriptions of 'human flourishing', 'the good life' and 'the just society'. We arbitrarily create, rather than discover, the truth of our moral purposes; hence Rorty's view that moral philosophy should 'take the form of historical narration and utopian speculation, rather than a search for general principles' (p. 60). In his utopia, Rorty writes, 'human solidarity would be seen not as a fact to be recognized by clearing away "prejudice" or burrowing down to previously hidden depths,' but rather as a goal

> to be achieved not by inquiry but by imagination, the imaginative ability to see strange people as fellow sufferers. Solidarity is not discovered by reflection but created. It is created by increasing our sensitivity to the particular details of the pain and humiliation of other, unfamiliar sorts of people …. This process of coming to see other human beings as 'one of us' rather than as 'them' is a matter of detailed description of what unfamiliar sorts of people are like and of the redescription of what we ourselves are like. This is a task not for theory but for genres such as ethnography, the journalist's report, the comic book, the docudrama, and, especially, the novel. (p. xvi)

This sounds much like a defence of criticism as a form of truth-seeking, but Rorty – and this is what identifies him as both a political liberal and a radical aesthete – is anxious to remove such private descriptions from the reach of public scrutiny and rational debate about ethics and critical standards in literary theory. Because any deep, irreducible sense of self is no more than a certain description, within a certain vocabulary, he likens our moral self-creation to poetry – unconstrained, indeterminate, and eminently linguistic in character – and any attempt to evaluate their truth is simply unjustifiable: a form, effectively, of social and critical violence. For to subject another's self-description to the evaluations of public, prosaic reason is no more decisive than any other instance of redescription; and according to Rorty, '*redescription often humiliates*' (p. 91; emphasis mine). For, he writes,

> most people do not want to be redescribed. They want to be taken on their own terms – taken seriously just as they are and just as they talk ... the best way to cause people long-lasting pain is to humiliate them by making the things that seemed most important to them look futile, obsolete, and powerless. Consider what happens when a child's precious possessions – the little things around which he weaves fantasies that make him a little different from all other children – are described as 'trash', and are thrown away. Or consider what happens when these possessions are made to look ridiculous alongside the possessions of another, richer, child. Something like that presumably happens to a primitive culture when it is conquered by a more advanced one. (pp. 89–90)

It is thus no exaggeration to say that Rorty seeks to replace ethics with aesthetics, or, in his own words, 'a general turn against theory and toward narrative' (p. xvi). The project is intriguing, riddled with paradoxes, not the least of which is that in turning against ethics, its overarching aims are unmistakably and admirably ethical: to cultivate the just and liberal society, to spare hapless citizens the humiliation of evaluative redescription, to minimise cruelty in public life, and to promote instead a sort of aesthetic appreciation of each other's lives. On the desirability of such ends there can be no disagreement. But whether they are self-sufficient, whether the ethical project of liberalism can be sustained exclusively by the desirability of its ideals, as Rorty envisions, with no buttressing by practical activities – reasoning and truth-seeking, say, or literary criticism – is a matter that invites serious quibbling. For Rorty's is a 'thin' account of moral life, one which rightly aligns goodness with other-regarding behaviour, including (or especially) attitudes of sympathy and solidarity, but which would be adequate only if good, other-regarding intentions are indeed sufficient for moral success, and if moral goods could not be differentiated as more important and less, more meaningful and less, more enduring and less, given the particular circumstances in which we try to live rich moral lives.

In fact, some of Rorty's own premises require a 'thicker' conception of morality, one which takes into account the natural springs, as well as the limits, of altruistic behaviour. And these must include the practical, evaluative activities required for moral discernment, no less in a 'post-metaphysical' and historicist age in which notions of a human essence or distinction have been largely discredited than in the theological and metaphysical past. Indeed, it is paradoxical that talk of human nature should be seen within the historicist tradition as inconsistent with post-metaphysical commitments, for it was historically the scientific vindication of naturalism – the claim, proved by Darwin's theory of natural selection, that the universe holds together without purposiveness – which required the philosophical invalidation of a great deal of metaphysical talk – of Romantic notions of intrinsic human dignity and authentic human selves. Rorty appears to believe that, having solved the puzzle of 'the human condition', and having found it to be no more than the outcome of a random evolutionary process, we can now dismiss the question of human nature as non-necessary, radically mutable, and therefore theoretically non-binding; human nature, on Rorty's account, can determine nothing regarding the moral purposes so meaningful within our self-descriptions, or moral vocabularies.

But this is to overlook the fact that the much-vaunted variability of moral purposes is directly a function of biological traits peculiar to (or partly 'definatory of') human beings: namely, the large size of our brains, without which we could not have the rich languages of moral life – the ability not just to have imaginative and empathetic inner states (the rudiments of which, cognitive research has shown, are instinctual), but also to then make higher-order statements about them. Rorty is right to resist the (sociobiological) suggestion that morality is *determined* by our biological nature, but his intuition is right not because we have no nature and are therefore radically mutable, but because our biological nature happens to be characterised partly by a highly sophisticated level of cognitive capacities that allow us to experience value. So there may be no 'deepest level of the self', but there is a much more obvious level of the human being which allows us to experience value – and experience value *richly*, with an unexpected 'value added' component, so to speak, which strict determinism cannot explain. E.M. Forster in *Howards*

End captures this difference between biologically determined behaviour and 'biologically afforded' moral experience with the observation that 'far more mysterious than the call of sex to sex is the tenderness we throw into that call'[3] – which, it should be noted, is not specifically required by the biological functions it helps to serve. The ensemble of our cognitive abilities involves varying degrees, standards and objects of evaluation, so that we can appreciate multiple facets of a situation and experience both conflicting inner states and extraordinarily harmonious ones. Forster illustrates this earlier on in the novel with the inadequacy of the cynical Helen Schlegel's attempt to give an account of the brief infatuation between Paul Wilcox and herself:

> Deep down in him something whispered: 'This girl would let you kiss her; you might not have such a chance again' .... That was 'how it happened,' or, rather, how Helen described it to her sister, using words even more unsympathetic than my own. But the poetry of that kiss, the wonder of it, the magic that there was in life for hours after it – who can describe that? It is so easy for an Englishman to sneer at these chance collisions of human beings .... It is so easy to talk of 'passing emotion', and how to forget how vivid the emotion was ere it passed. (p. 25)

Of course, richness of cognitive experience constitutes neither moral refinement nor aesthetic refinement, but Forster suggests it is a condition-of-possibility for both; Helen's failure to realise the possibility of true sympathy latent in the scene is apparently crucial to her characterisation as the novel's tragically flawed moral agent:

> Our impulse to sneer, to forget, is at root a good one. We recognize that emotion is not enough, and that men and women are capable of sustained relations, not mere opportunities for an electrical discharge. Yet we rate the impulse too highly. We do not admit that by collisions of this trivial sort the doors of heaven may be shaken open. To Helen, at all events, her life was to bring nothing more intense than the embrace of this boy who played no part in it. He had drawn her out of the house, where there was danger of surprise and light; he had led her by a path he knew, until they stood under the column of the vast wych-elm. A man in the darkness, he had whispered, 'I love you' when she was desiring love. In time his slender personality faded, the scene

> that he had evoked endured. In all the variable years that followed she never saw the like of it again. (pp. 25–6)

Helen's shortcoming – tragic, but not morally damning – is apparently a temperamental disinclination to reason and reflect on her more instinctive or compulsive responses. And it is suggested in the novel that her 'poor judgement', or lack of restraint, is morally problematic because reason – the reflective, non-instrumental intellect – is thought in the rich, literate, liberal Schlegels' moral universe to be part of the good or just person's native equipment, naturally connected with sympathy and the imagination as a single set of inner resources, and to be nurtured with 'years of self-scrutiny, conducted for no ulterior motive' (p. 204), lest it develop rampant instrumentality or 'the vice of the vulgar mind' (p. 30).

In contrast, the Schlegels' idea of good judgement or restraint is not to be confused with caution – 'only prigs do that' (p. 76) – but what Margaret describes as the use of proportion 'as a last resource, when the better things have failed', the better things being a range of virtuous dispositions: kindness, sympathy, generosity, and so forth. Extending these to others, she realises, entails risks, but also rich possibilities: 'she felt that those who prepare for all the emergencies of life beforehand may equip themselves at the expense of joy. It is necessary to prepare for an examination, or a possible fall in the price of stock: those who attempt human relations must adopt another method, or fail …. Margaret hoped that for the future she would be less cautious, not more ….' (pp. 62, 111)

The faith the Schlegels place in reason, or the intellect, as a unique faculty that might rein in the other mental faculties and place them at the service of the good is clearly a Romantic one: naively, 'in their own fashion they cared deeply about politics, though not as politicians would have us care; they desired that public life should mirror whatever is good in the life within' (p. 28). But the Schlegel account of the intellect, if one may call it that, is not necessarily spurious. In fact, it resembles some current theories of mind, according to which the distinctive level of animal consciousness or intentionality that humans possess is polymorphous, residing not in a single faculty but in the combination of mental faculties human morphology has enabled. If these theories are right, then the Schlegels' reliance on reason as the natural ally of sympathy and the imagination as an instrument of moral cognition is not entirely wrong-headed.

This should come as no surprise – the idea that moral reason is *the* human distinction is a Hellenic one – and perhaps for Rorty the biological account of human nature, like mathematical statements, is simply too obvious to have any bearing on interesting problems. But in dismissing the biological account from the purview, he deprives himself of the only possible explanatory mechanism by which aesthetics can possibly refashion ethics after itself. Rorty's 'liberal utopia' hinges on the possibility of individuals' extending sympathy to each other, but without referring to a common capacity for empathy and without recourse to an equally natural (as opposed to socially or linguistically constructed) ability to reason in order to guide our empathetic responses, the occurrence of such sympathy would have to be contingent on preposterous scenarios – the extraordinary coincidence of simultaneous firings in two or more brains, say, or a theological order in which humans have no free will – to say nothing of how such random sympathy is supposed to be sustained. To be sure, the natural capacity for empathy is not one which we possess exclusively or uniformly as a species – dogs have it, and chimps have it, while humans certainly possess it in very uneven amounts – and it is not a capacity that can underwrite all our moral beliefs. Still, as a response or behaviour that can be evaluated for appropriateness, it is so fundamental a condition-of-possibility for moral life that we are inclined to be suspicious of, say, acts of charity that do not appear to be motivated by genuine compassion, sympathy and related attitudes, and we are horrified at the mother who, in the interests of justice and impartiality, will save someone else's child as readily as her own when both are drowning.

That our ability to reason is as natural as our ability to experience affect should begin to vindicate the opposing view (to Rorty's) that reason has an important, if complicated, role to play in moral experience. Certainly, some foundationalist moral philosophy is wrong to imply that reason will point to a single universal hierarchy of goods and responsibilities, but Rorty's scepticism about the uses of moral philosophy leads him to overlook the fact that empathy requires a fair bit of reflection, rather than what he calls arbitrary 'creation', if it is to be extended to persons beyond kith or kin to constitute a fully moral act, involving an attitude that is both voluntary and other-regarding.

This is by no means to suggest that ethics is so logical and exhaustive a series of true statements that there is no ethical problem which moral theorising could not solve. The natural and conceptual constraints on moral experience – sympathy, judgements of appropriateness, necessary relations among other-regarding attitudes and paradigmatic moral principles – can say decisively that some actions can be classed as genuinely good or genuinely wicked, but cannot decisively rank them from best to worst. Highly specific circumstances may show clearly that some actions are better than others, but circumstances are not always so deterministic. It is not too difficult to think of instances in which the contingent world proves to be perfectly indifferent to our moral aims; moral experience involves areas of real ambiguity. Should one neglect one's marriage for the sake of urgent social and political work? What are we to make of monastic lives characterised by the repudiation of personal relations but also by the certain absence of the risk of harming others? Or of people who provide unconditional support to self-destructive and emotionally troubled lovers and friends?

Decidedly, no amount of reasoning about ethics will yield straightforward answers to such troubling questions. But this is hardly reason enough to abandon moral philosophy. Rorty's claims about the uselessness of moral philosophy in a world with no overarching moral *telos* are greatly exaggerated. They present us with a set of false choices, between moral judgement and moral understanding, between moral nihilism and moral high-handedness, between a full-blown theology or metaphysics and utter moral indeterminacy. But it is unclear exactly where the inescapable connection lies between theorising about the human experience of right and wrong and some pathological ambition to draw up what Rorty calls 'one true lading-list, one true description of the human situation, one universal context of human lives' (p. 28) that will reconcile public and private conceptions of the good. His only reason for urging us to abandon moral philosophy appears to be its failure to yield such a list, but such a definition of moral philosophy's aims is purely stipulative, and his judgement inappropriate. To claim that reasoning about moral situations is possible, and bound by such facts about human nature as we can point to, need not entail an indefensible theology or metaphysics. Realist or foundationalist moral philosophy can take the quite modest form of a search for the appropriate constraints on moral action and inquiry, rather than the grandiose imposition of a hierarchy of responsibilities where there is clearly no good reason for it; or rather, where there are good reasons to suppose that there is room for a variety of moral descriptions – irrational and poetic, if need be. In Philippa Foot's words, 'there could be both fixed starting-points and an element of play in the system, allowing different and irreconcileable points of view about certain things'.[4]

Thus far, finally, we might justifiably agree to disagree. If historicists acknowledge that our nature as rational creatures can draw the real boundaries of the ethical field, then realists can admit that within the parameters the playing-field is level, so to speak, that there can be no argument against the liberal plurality of private purposes, and no justifiable attempt to evaluate private descriptions. This should suit the liberal political theorist; the liberal aesthete and the liberal moral philosopher, if they are worth their salt, should sue for more, reserving the right to keep the field of people's self-descriptions open to critical scrutiny. Indeed, the field of value lies open; it is marked off only from the larger landscape of fact and instrumental relations; within it, no line has been drawn separating public from private goods.

Such a line will remain elusive, for as Rorty well knows, moral value does not reside in a 'deepest level of the self' but in the activities of the other-regarding, social self. Certainly, a subject may be more reticent or less with respect to the social world, and as Margaret realises, exposure to human relations brings the risk of evaluation and redescription; but severed from the context of human relations, there can be no possibility of that rich value which leads to moral knowledge. So the problem with Rorty's overscrupulous relegation of individual self-descriptons to a purely private and poetic domain, on which prosaic moral reason cannot encroach, is not so much the assumption that all moral descriptions are equally fictional, irrational and irreconcilable with public ethical objectives, as the failure of such a rigid distinction between public and private to do justice to the aims of those self-descriptions. If one's self-descriptions have a strongly ethical thrust, addressing how one should live in relation to others and to the world, then it is somewhat galling to have one's self-descriptions regarded as interchangeable with works of art, which are beautiful but which stand in no necessary or relevant relation to the social world. This is not to suggest that our self-descriptions are reducible to ethical projects; but they are not reducible to poems either. To so reduce them is to dilute or impoverish our conception of moral agency, as though to acknowledge that we each have a hidden poetic life, and then to tip-toe round each other's self-descriptions, is morally exemplary.

Admittedly, within a modest moral realist scheme, this would be morally sufficient. Does the scheme then restrict us to what Iris Murdoch has called moral mediocrity, since one would only have to fulfil a modicum of obligations – the most obvious ones – to achieve goodness. This minimal realism seems to leave out of the purview a great many of those experiences which we intuitively count as moral goods: nurturing relationships, actions and attitudes of concern for others, even certain exercises in self-creation. But precisely because they exceed a modicum of demands, they can be counted as instances of genuine supererogation. And this is arguably the proper ethical domain of literature and aesthetics: the forms of attention we learn from engaging with works of art cannot really replace the methods of moral philosophy, but they do help us to recognise the distinction – or originality or poignancy – of moral claims which reason cannot decisively rank.

Minimal realism also allows for a much thicker conception of moral knowledge than does Rorty, who assumes that moral knowledge will necessarily take the form of suspect moral judgements. But genuine moral understanding, of the kind he believes 'narrative', rather than theory, can offer, surely cannot obtain without an element of moral judgement. Consider the example of the lover who unconditionally supports a self-destructive beloved. Presumably, the moral distinction of such an act flows from the profound sympathy that motivates it; and surely genuine sympathy requires a deep appreciation of the difficulties of the beloved's position, including the correct judgement that he or she has become entangled in a set of moral failings and misfortunes, rather than a readiness to overlook those difficulties, which is what tip-toeing round each other's self-descriptions amounts to.

That moral life is difficult because it is rich, that it is full of risks because it is full of possibilities, is the insight that the moral disappointments of *Howards End* illustrate so intricately. That the attempt to be better rather than worse moral subjects (we cannot know, in an ateleological universe, what the best moral agents might be like) requires realism about the moral risks of human relations is particularly evident in the relations between Margaret Schlegel and Leonard Bast, the young office clerk who comes to grief partly through Margaret and her sister's sincere meddling (they want to help him 'connect', but it is in connecting with him herself that Helen's moral life is deepened) and at the hands of the Wilcoxes, Margaret's husband's family of philistines. Leonard aspires to distinguish himself from the rest of his class, not graspingly, but because he senses that life might be less humiliating than his circumstances insist. He wants to get 'upsides with life', and imagines he will manage this by acquiring culture of the kind the cosmopolitan Schlegels have. The sisters admire the spirit of his ambitions, yet their attitudes towards him could not be more disparate. Helen romanticises him thoroughly, and at the first major crisis in the novel dismisses his objections that he can no longer aspire to her elevated life, refusing to acknowledge crucial differences in their circumstances:

> 'I don't trouble after books as I used. I can imagine that with regular work we should settle down again. It stops one thinking.'
>
> 'Settle down to what?'
>
> 'Oh, just settle down.'
>
> 'And that's to be life!' said Helen with a catch in her throat. 'How can you, with all the beautiful things to see and do – with music – with walking at night –'
>
> 'Walking's well enough when a man's in work,' he answered. 'Oh, I did talk a lot of nonsense once, but there's nothing like a bailiff in the house to drive it out of you .... My books are back again thanks to you, but they'll never be the same again, and I shan't ever again think night in the woods is wonderful.'
>
> 'Why not?' asked Helen, throwing up the window.
>
> 'Because I see one must have money.'
>
> 'Well, you're wrong .... Death and Money are the eternal foes, not Death and Life. Never mind what lies behind Death, Mr Bast, but be sure that the poet and the musician and the tramp will be happier in it than the man who has never learnt to say *I am I*.' (pp. 248–9)

By contrast, Margaret is far more careful in her dealings with Leonard, sizing up his character and tastes, and taking note of the difference between themselves. While taking a kindly interest in him, her assessment is almost scathing:

> Hints of robustness survived in him, more than a hint of primitive good looks, and Margaret, noting the spine that might have been straight, and the chest that might have broadened, wondered whether it paid to give up the glory of the animal for a tail-coat and a couple of ideas. Culture had worked in her own

> case, but during the last few weeks she had doubted whether it humanized the majority, so wide and widening is the gulf that stretches between the natural and the philosophic man, so many the good chaps who are wrecked in trying to cross it. She knew this type very well – the vague aspirations, the mental dishonesty, the familiarity with the outsides of books. She knew the very tones in which he would address her. (pp. 120–1)

As it happens, Leonard *is* wrecked in trying to cross the gulf between himself and the Schlegels, and there are good reasons to suppose that Margaret bears a greater responsibility for his tragedy than she seems to acknowledge. It is partly at her behest that the Schlegels abandon him after ruining him with bad advice, when arguably she might do more to find him employment in Henry Wilcox's firm. That she decides against this is all the more galling because she apparently does so in order to save her engagement to Henry despite the final proof of his moral degradation (he had taken Leonard's wife as his mistress when his late wife was still living) and despite her usual principled solidarity with the wronged:

> Was he worth all this bother?... Henry's inner life had long laid open to her – his intellectual confusion, his obtuseness to personal influence, his strong but furtive passions. Should she refuse him because his outer life corresponded? Perhaps. Perhaps, if the dishonour had been done to her, but it was done long before her day. She struggled against the feeling. She told herself that Mrs Wilcox's wrong was her own. But she was not a barren theorist. As she undressed, her anger, her regard for the dead, her desire for a scene all grew weak. Henry must have it as he liked, for she loved him ... Henry must be forgiven, and made better by love; nothing else mattered. Mrs Wilcox, that unquiet yet kindly ghost must be left to her own wrong .... (p. 254)

Margaret's musings about Mrs Wilcox's ghost explain a little of the attitude she has taken towards Leonard: throughout the Schlegels' association with him, she is conscious of the need to let him, in Shakespeare's words, 'reckon for his own soul', just as she reckons for her own; this is why she refuses to patronize him when they first meet. And if she refuses to obscure the differences between him and themselves, it is because she realises that they are a function of the difference in their economic circumstances – a difference that cannot be reduced without 'pauperizing' him. Whereas 'most ladies would have laughed' when he suspected her sister of stealing his umbrella, 'Margaret really minded, for it gave her a glimpse into squalor. To trust people is a luxury in which only the wealthy can indulge; the poor cannot afford it' (p. 36).

Of course, it is easy to respect others' ability to reckon for themselves when one has nothing to gain and everything to lose from reckoning for them, but in Margaret's case acting in her own interest happens to mean acting out of love for Henry – surely an other-regarding emotion, and one which holds the promise of other ethical goods: his moral redemption (which the final crisis bears out, when he is forced to take responsibility for his past actions), as well as her own growth from a 'barren theorist' to a lucid and forgiving human being, sensitive to the failings of others, and under no illusions about her own strength of principle.

Margaret's uneasy dealings with Leonard, in other words, are not a reflection of moral complacency or insincerity, but of the competing claims on her moral agency – a conflict her moral reason helps her not to dissolve but to discern and to address as best she can. She can deliberate her way through the conflict to a combination of reasoned beliefs – that proper respect for Leonard as a moral agent requires that she and Helen stop patronising him, and that the demands of her love for Henry override the demands of her altruistic interest in Leonard Bast – and she can act on the basis of these beliefs to bring about more of what by her lights is good, rather than more harm. But it is significant that she is uneasy about her course of action – 'her conscience pricked her a little about the Basts' (p. 273) – for she has come up against the limits of ethical reasoning. Particularly where her engagement is concerned, she is made to realise that at some points, ethical demands are irreconcilable.

Finally, it is telling that despite her critical discernment, or rather *because* of it, Margaret alone, in the cast of the tragicomedy, emerges from the downward spiral of the action with her faith in 'moral subjects', as creatures whose lives do not reduce to the instrumentality of their actions, intact. At the end of the novel, when Leonard is killed, it is she and not Helen and not even Leonard himself who sees that Leonard's self-description, ludicrous as it is and fatal, remains irreducible and worthy: 'In this jangle of causes and effects', she wonders,

> what had become of their true selves? Here Leonard lay dead in the garden, from natural causes; yet life was a deep, deep river, death a blue sky, life was a house, death a wisp of hay, a flower, a tower, life and death were anything and everything, except this ordered insanity, where the king takes the queen, and the ace the king. Ah, no; there was beauty and adventure behind, such as the man at her feet had yearned for; there was hope this side of the grave; there were truer relationships beyond the limits that fetter us now. (p. 345)

Thus *Howards End* ends, somewhat unsatisfactorily, for Margaret's reasonableness has not saved Leonard's life, and has not even helped her to make prudent decisions. Yet it has brought her deeper moral understanding, a clearer picture of what ethical agency involves: a great deal of reflection and risk, of weighing an uneven mix of self-interest and altruism, of cold judgement and emotional involvement. This does not point to a liberal utopia in which moral agreement is achieved adventitiously; it points to the real world, which is morally chaotic, but not altogether beyond our understanding.

Notes

1. Galen Strawson, 'In Deepest Sympathy', *Times Literary Supplement*, 29 November 1996, 3–4.
2. Richard Rorty, *Contingency, Irony, and Solidarity* (Cambridge University Press, 1989) xiii. Subsequent references to this work appear in parentheses, in the main text.
3. E.M. Forster, *Howards End* (1910; New York: Knopf, 1991) 252. Subsequent references are given in parentheses.
4. Philippa Foot, 'Morality and Art', *Proceedings of the British Academy*, 56 (1970) 131–44; 132–3.

Part V
Public Morality

13

'Sweet Dreams, Monstered Nothings': Catachresis in Kant and *Coriolanus*

Ortwin de Graef

In *The Contest of Faculties*, Kant warns us that we should not be overly optimistic in our hopes for the improvement of mankind, lest these hopes be ridiculed as 'the daydream of an overexcited head [*Träumerei eines überspannten Kopfs*]' – yet somehow, a footnote adds, the dream must go on:

> The hope that a political product [*Staatsprodukt*] as it is conceived of here will one day, no matter how far away, come to fulfilment [*Vollendung*] is a sweet dream [*süßer Traum*]; yet to approach it is not only *thinkable* but also, insofar as it can coexist with the moral law, a *duty* [...][1]

The obvious obstacle for this approach in Kant's critical system is that the state he has in mind is pre-eminently a state of freedom, that freedom is preeminently an idea, and that ideas cannot, strictly speaking, be produced as objective reality. Yet what strictly cannot, positively must; and in the monument erected to commemorate that indispensable error, *The Critique of Judgement*, Kant teaches us how to go about articulating this impossible but imperative dream. First, we must project the idea onto a sensible object, then we must map our reflection upon our intuition of that object onto the idea, of which the object is only a symbolic hypotyposis. To further facilitate this hypotypotic double-dealing, Kant gives a significant example:

> In this way a monarchical state is represented as a living body when it is governed by constitutional laws [*innern Volksgesetzen*],

> but as a mere machine (like a hand-mill) when it is governed by an individual absolute will; but in both cases the representation is merely *symbolic*. For there is certainly no likeness between a despotic state and a hand-mill, whereas there surely is between the rules of reflection upon both and their causality. Hitherto this function has been but little analysed, worthy as it is of a deeper study. Still this is not the place to dwell upon it.[2]

… *so sehr es auch eine tiefere Untersuchung verdient*: a famous proto-Derridean moment[3] rightly singled out by Paul de Man as an instance of Kant's 'mental cruelty' in leaving undeveloped tantalising suggestions in the *Third Critique*.[4] Yet de Man's own failure to further flesh out the detail of Kant's figures is no less frustrating, particularly since the Body Politic and the Handmill Despotic are just the kind of tropes one would have expected him to turn to in his critique of aesthetic ideology as, specifically, a poor reading of Kant. We should think here, for instance, of the relation between the non-despotic State as *beseeltes Körper* and Schiller's vision of the Aesthetic State as an English dance – a vision de Man sees deconstructed in the dead souls of Kleist's marionettes.[5] We could also think, more brutally, of the relation between Kant's symbolic hypotyposis of the state as a vision of bodily beauty and Goebbels's vision of the state as a transformation of the people produced by politics as a plastic art.[6] Yet de Man never quite explores this particular connection between Kant's political hypotyposes and the fate of his aesthetics as ideology, even though he does (mis)quote them:

> For example, an enlightened state will be symbolized by an organic body in which part and whole relate in a free and harmonious way, whereas a tyranny will be properly symbolized by a machine such as a treadmill. Everyone understands that the state *is* not a body or a machine, but that it functions like one, and that this function is conveyed more economically by the symbol than by lengthy abstract explanations. We seem at last to have come closer to controlling the tropes.[7]

We have, of course, done no such thing – as de Man then indeed goes on to demonstrate, without, however, returning to Kant's political figures and thus without asking whether everyone indeed *does* understand that the state 'is' not a body or machine, but instead 'functions like one'. Which one? In what way is a monarchical state governed by a single absolute will like a hand-mill? Or is it a tread-mill? And in what way is a monarchical state governed by 'inner laws of the people' like a *beseeltes Körper*? Unlike de Man, Kant does not tell us what precisely the ground for the latter comparison is, and while de Man's identification of the operative principle as the free and harmonious relation of part and whole is eminently sensible, the problem remains that this principle is itself super-sensible. For what does it mean to say that a body and its parts are in free harmony? Is there anything there to *be* free? Free from what, what for? How is a body like the state of freedom, the 'ideal' state?

At a later stage in the *Third Critique*, in the course of a disquisition on purposiveness in nature, Kant once again turns to the body as the proper symbol of the political ideal. Although 'strictly speaking' the causally self-contained 'organisation of nature' is in no way analogous to the mediated causality of human practice, Kant notes that we may nonetheless conversely use the idea of natural purposiveness in order to elucidate a notion of human harmony 'to be found more often in idea than in fact':

> Thus in the case of a complete transformation, recently undertaken, of a great people into a state, the word *organisation* has frequently, and with much propriety, been used for the constitution of the legal authorities and even of the entire body politic [*Staatskörpers*]. For in a whole of this kind certainly no member should be a mere means, but should also be an end [*nicht bloß Mittel, sondern zugleich auch Zweck*], and, seeing that he contributes to the possibility of the entire body, should have his position and function in turn defined by the idea of the whole.[8]

A first, impertinently simple question here would be what in fact Kant is talking about. What is the 'neuerlich unternommen gänzlichen Umbildung eines großen Volks zu einem Staat'? Is it, as Hannah Arendt believes, the American Revolution?[9] Or is it, as Alexis Philonenko has it, the French Revolution?[10] Does it matter whether we can name Kant's referent or not? But how could it not matter, when the point is precisely that the union in question is 'to be found more often in idea than in fact' and when it is precisely the task of symbolic analogic to reliably effect the passage from bodiless idea to nameable *Wirklichkeit* against all the odds and across all the obstacles so painstakingly registered by Kant? And after all, unless we can actually name this transformation, this

Umbildung, as a historical event, we have merely repeated what we set out to make real – the very idea of ideas in the realm of freedom: the coincidence of end and means in the categorical imperative.

Something more definite is required to give body to Kant's 'sweet dream' of the ideal state produced in accordance with the imperatives of reason as the reality of an effective constitution, a *Staatsverfassung*. For one thing, the dream needs a subject whose duty it is to approach it – a task, Kant candidly specifies, 'not for the citizens of the state [*Staatsbürger*], but for the head of the state [*Staatsoberhaupts*]'.[11] But what can this head dream other than itself as head? And why should it even dream this dream, seeing that it already is what it is supposed to dutifully dream – the head of the body politic? What deserves further reflection here – and here *is* the place to dwell upon it – is not the question whether Kant was or was not a democrat (though that, too, remains a duty) but rather, say, whether a head is ever a member of its body and whether the performance of a body (headless or no) ever figures forth what we call freedom. In what follows I propose to rehearse that question in a reading of what is arguably one of its most intensely critical representations, Shakespeare's *Coriolanus*.

***

There was a time when meadow, grove and stream, the earth and every common sight – in the face of crisis – told a tale. Here is Menenius Agrippa's famous attempt to fabulate the rioting Roman plebs into renewed submission to the public thing (*Coriolanus*, I, i, 95–152):[12]

> There was a time, when all the body's members,
> Rebell'd against the belly, thus accus'd it:
> That only like a gulf it did remain
> I'th'midst o'th'body, idle and unactive,
> Still cupboarding the viand, never bearing
> Like labour with the rest, where th'other instruments
> Did see, and hear, devise, instruct, walk, feel,
> And, mutually participate, did minister
> Unto the appetite and affection common
> Of the whole body. The belly answered [...]
> 'True is it, my incorporate friends,' [...]
> 'That I receive the general food at first

Which you do live upon; and fit it is,
Because I am the storehouse and the shop
Of the whole body. But, if you do remember,
I send it through the rivers of your blood
Even to the court, the heart, to th'seat o'th'brain;
And through the cranks and offices of man
The strongest nerves and small inferior veins
From me receive that natural competency
Whereby they live. [...]'
The senators of Rome are this good belly,
And you the mutinous members.

What Menenius offers the mob here is an eminently commonsensical justification of privilege and authority as necessary conditions for the proper functioning of the polis. To the members' objection that the belly is guilty of a breach of social contract in that it fails to observe the 'mutually participate' ministration of the body, the belly replies, entirely consistently, that it is nothing other than the very figure of such reciprocal exchange. The tables are turned, and in the same turn we receive the type of reflection on causality Kant failed to explicitate in his hypotyposis of the beautiful body politic. It may not quite be what Kant had in mind – the mind, after all, is just about squeezed out of the picture – but it will do. That is: it spells out just in what way the polis is like a body and in doing so it sets out a plot for historico-ideological investigation.

Such an investigation would first have to consider the history of this fable prior to Shakespeare's recycling, inserting whatever internal modulation of the archetype Shakespeare effected into the puzzle of his politics.[13] This would minimally require a resurrection of as much material as possible from both the specific political universe of discourse in which Shakespeare composed the play and the specific practical political constellation in which it was produced. Such historico-ideological research is not, however, my primary interest here – not just because most of this material has been fairly exhaustively recovered already,[14] but because prior to covering all this, we must emphasise that the tale as quoted above is not Shakespeare's version but a doctored reduction to the frame his thought feeds on. For Shakespeare's actual rendering of the fable as a piece of political oratory constantly interrupted by its audience requires that we suspend our critical investigation of the viability of this particular fable and instead ask ourselves the question what on earth is happening here, what is taking place not just *in* this conflict but as its very possibility condition. As Stanley Cavell has put it, 'This is not a play about politics, [but] about the formation of the political',[15] and precisely because it monitors the untenable yet inevitable ethical distinction between politics and the political[16] – this is a *critical* tragedy, a tragedy facing a crisis of the political as what such a crisis can only ever be: a crisis of representation.

A first index of this critical sensitivity to the issue of political representation is the fact that prior to taking up the Fable of the Belly, Menenius had already run through a whole gamut of hypotyposes with which he tries to preserve the citizens from what he accurately diagnoses as a self-undoing. In rioting, the citizens undo themselves as citizens and as the First Citizen indicates, this damage may well have already been done (I, i, 61–3):

Men. Why masters, my good friends, my honest neighbours,
Will you undo yourselves?
First Cit. We cannot, sir, we are already undone.

Menenius tries to undo the damage by representing 'the Roman state' (I, i, 68) first as an implacable heaven, then as an unstoppable moving thing on course to crush the insurgents, then – translating conflict into recuperation – as the ship of state of which the patricians are the helmsmen, and finally as a happy family (I, i, 75–7); but the First Citizen will have nothing of this and redirects the conflict to its actual origin in hunger, accusing the rich 'fathers' of feeding on the poor: 'If the wars eat us not up, they will; and there's all the love they bear us' (I, i, 84–5).

Importantly, then, it is only when the otherwise extremely powerful figure of the Political Family has been rejected that Menenius cunningly relays the insurgents' intent on food in order to redo them after their own image (I, i, 88–94):

Men. I shall tell you
A pretty tale; it may be you have heard it,
But since it serves my purpose, I will venture
To stale't a little more.
First Cit. Well, I'll hear it, sir; yet you must not think to fob off our disgrace with a tale; but and't please you, deliver.

The most salient feature of this curious little exchange (I shall – may be – but – I will – Well, I will – yet – but) is its combination of critical awareness and a sense of boredom: both parties know already what is going to be said, and both parties are fully aware why it is about to be said, yet they still join in the communicative contract. Menenius duly bores his listeners and further wears out the fable's fabric; and the listeners will listen and indeed be moved to persuasion even though they know they are about to be conned, and by a tale they already know by heart to boot. That the citizens in fact do know the tale is suggested by the First Citizen's interruption of Menenius's rendering just as he is about to reveal the belly's apology (I, i, 112–17):

> Your belly's answer – what?
> The kingly crown'd head, the vigilant eye,
> The counsellor heart, the arm our soldier,
> Our steed the leg, the tongue our trumpeter,
> With other muniments and petty helps
> In this our fabric […]

Rather than an index of impatient confusion in the plebs,[17] dying to hear the point of the tale, the very cataloguing of these clichés bespeaks the Citizen's boredom. After all, once this tropological mechanism has been assimilated – as clearly it has been by the Citizen – one would have to be unthinkably stupid, strictly and radically inarticulate, not to know that the belly will be the storehouse and shop of the body – the site of its overhead. The plebs may be dumb, but surely they are not that dumb? The First Citizen, at any rate, is not: his is the voice that opens the play, and from the first he is profiled as linguistically sensitive. Indeed, one of his first interventions is a brief rhetorical remark on the meaning (or lack of it) of the adjective 'good' which he immediately develops towards the alimentary isotopy later picked up in the fable (I, i, 14–24). Once this plebeian orator has assigned the various members of the body the specific function of participants in a coherent project, only a sudden stroke of aphasia could have prevented him from ventriloquising the tropological programme to its conclusion.

We shall return to this inexorable dynamic of the tragedy in due course – for now, the point of this farcical exchange between the bored boor and the punning patrician – an exchange in which the fable of the Body Politic is quite literally dismembered – is that its emphatic staging prevents us from taking the tale as read. This is not just to say that Shakespeare thereby highlights the strategic, purposive, ideological nature of the fable: the text does not just invite us to be on our guards when politicians resort to allegorical narrative (which of course we must be, but that is hardly exciting news). Rather (yet perhaps equally predictably), what we are facing is the enactment of the very possibility condition and the sheer inevitability of such strategic artifice: a communicative contract itself constitutive of community as such – an exchange fabricating the social fabric as constitutive exchange.

Perhaps the most intense instance of this compelling constitutive contract can be read in Menenius's belly's pun on membership and memory: 'But, if you do remember, / I send [the food] through the rivers of your blood [...]' (I, i, 133–4). That is: if you remember that you are a member, you will realise that yours is not to reason why, yours is just to live the lie. Or, more accurately, remember the membership-myth by which we live and thereby become the member you always already are. Thus, what we have here is an ironical reflection on a political allegory itself constitutive of the political: the scene reveals the condition of political community in a communicative project and thereby registers the precarious predicament of community itself.[18] In this light, it is hardly surprising that *Coriolanus* should be the tragedy of political representation as a crisis of voice as much as of body: it is a play tracing the people's vote as well as its image. This too, of course, is a little dull: once again, it all boils down to language, to the social fabric and its reraveling in *Coriolanus* as a text ready to be staled a little more. Yet stale it we must.

The re-membering of the body politic urged by Menenius is powered by a radical version of the central figure of linguistic abuse: catachresis, in this case, and in Kantian terms, the imposition of a symbolic hypotyposis with which to make sense of what is not available as objective reality – only, if at all, as an idea.[19] The catachresis is radical insofar as it is declarative (or performative): it is not so much that there is a stable political constitution made accessible for ideological understanding by means of a convenient figure; rather, the political constitution is itself declared into existence by means of the figure. In the strictest sense, the Fable of the Belly remembers nothing: it remembers a tale known to all participants as the fiction that makes them participants in the first place and in this remembrance it institutes a particular political situation obscuring the unthought condition of its constitution in the political. The

Fable remembers nothing, that nothing that makes possible a political community but disappears the moment it is translated as a convenient catachresis. In other words, the Fable repeats only its auto-fabulation and the disturbing power of this repetition is that it erases its originary catachrestic imposition precisely by repeating it: contrary to etymological usage, catachresis here *is* usage itself – it is what constitutes the community as a sensible reality, the common place of common sense.[20] As in Plato's *Republic*, the fabulous power of this cynical mechanism is that it grows more convincing the further it reaches back – first through imposition, then through repetition – in the narrative memory of the polis (III, 415 c–d). Yet as the tragedy creeps to its conclusion, the crisis of representation the fable seeks to conjure is recognised as the monstrosity we cannot but call it.

***

Coriolanus, freshly returned from the victory over the Volsces that won him his name, is to ask the citizens of Rome for their support in his half-hearted bid for consulship. Here are the Citizens debating the issue (II, iii, 1–13):

> *First Cit.* Once, if he do require our voices, we ought not to deny him.
> *Second Cit.* We may, sir, if we will.
> *Third Cit.* We have power in ourselves to do it, but it is a power that we have no power to do. For if he show us his wounds and tell us his deeds, we are to put our tongues into those wounds and speak for them. So if he tell us his noble deeds, we must also tell him our noble acceptance of them. Ingratitude is monstrous, and for the multitude to be ingrateful, were to make a monster of the multitude; of the which we being members, should bring ourselves to be monstrous members.

Such is the monstrously consistent logic of political representation: Coriolanus can only become a representative of the people when the people represent him as the representative he already is in his representation of the Roman body as its arms ('the arm our soldier' [I, i, 115], as the First Citizen reminded us – as if we needed reminding). The form of this predicament is a maddening tautology: not Kant's ethical *non sequitur* 'we cannot, therefore we must', but simply 'we can only, therefore we must' – or, more accurately (for nothing is simple here), 'we cannot not so cannot have to since we will even as we must', or something in that vein. Coriolanus must be *declared* – not just recognised but quite literally *made* – a representative of the people *because* he already is just that. Not just 'Rome claims the body that it names',[21] but the body claims to be already named Rome's long before Rome even considered claiming it. Thus, the impact of the people's voice is precisely nothing, yet unless this nothing is performed, the body politic is revealed as a monstrosity. Which is not to say that the eventual performance of this nothing is therefore any the less monstrous – such is the strictly unnegotiable double bind of representation here.[22] For is it not monstrous to declare something into existence that already exists, to read out the print of the Volscian swords and translate it into the print of the swords of Rome's enemies, to make a representative a representative? Is it not monstrous to remember the body politic in a metaleptic catachresis that has the people's tongues stuck in the stutter of a bloody tautology?

The force of Shakespeare's concise delirium on gratitude, monstrosity, naming and necessity is that it lifts the baseless fabric of political representation and reveals, precisely, nothing. When Cominius, a little earlier in the play, is about to sing Coriolanus's praises, the hero walks off saying that he is loath '[t]o hear [his] nothings monstered' (II, ii, 77). The standard reading of this line as 'a sardonic comment on the processes of fame' (Brockbank's annotation) certainly chimes with the common perception of Coriolanus as a figure suspended between arrogance and modesty, unwilling to be put on display for the doubting Thomases whose judgement means nothing to him. Yet the phrase has a more disturbing ring to it: it suggests that what is about to take place is indeed the monstrous transformation of something inaccessible to the conceptual language of ideology into the commonplace of exemplary representative behaviour – a transformation that monsters nothing into solid evidence. But it also suggests that recognising and resisting this catachrestic recuperation monsters nothing into pure disaster: the disastrous totalisation of uncompromising purity, whether it be Coriolanus's or Cordelia's.

That Coriolanus's resistance to representation is 'in the same class with Cordelia's fatal inability to flatter Lear'[23] has frequently been pointed out, but what must particularly exercise us here is that *Lear*, too, begins with a disastrous attempt to represent nothing, to give voice to the nothing that cannot be represented in any model for human community. The bond of the family and the bond of the polis are both conceptual impositions on something that is not previously available for communal representation: this is why both Cordelia and Coriolanus say in so many words that their participation in their respective communal contexts is a matter of 'nothing'. Both also abandon this terribly pure nothing and begin to compromise precisely by returning to the starkest forms of communal representation: 'According to my bond, nor more nor less' (*Lear*, I, i, 85); 'Kindly, sir, I pray let me ha't' (*Coriolanus*, II, iii, 76) – a minimal and possibly hypocritical concession, but a concession nonetheless. Not, perhaps, too little; but certainly too late.

Coriolanus's resistance to representation does not ultimately take shape as silence but as a committed intent on pure representation. Throughout the play, he figures as a discursive disciplinarian, disgusted with the communal repetitions of proverbs (I, i, 204), determined to 'coin words' (III, i, 82) against impure abusage and to police the felicity conditions for performatives. Typically, his interventions as a prescriptive grammarian start off with a trigger response[24] that echoes his interlocutor's speech in order to disclaim it, as if such repetition could purify the words of the tribe, or the Tribunes. Thus, when Sicinius Velutus declares that Coriolanus's outrage 'shall remain a poison where it is / Not poison any further' (III, i, 86–7), Coriolanus raps an instant sample:

> Shall remain!
> Hear you this Triton of the minnows? Mark you
> His absolute 'shall'?
>
> (III, i, 87–8)

The coloured future, it would appear, must be reserved for the lords of language, and protected against the 'popular' (III, i, 105) abuse of magistrates. Yet it is these Tribunes who declare the felicity conditions and thereby drive Coriolanus to absurdity. Towards the end of Act III, when Coriolanus's feeble attempts at pretending to sollicit the citizens's favour have misfired (as how could they not), Sicinius once again resorts to the absolute shall, ordering Coriolanus's banishment: 'I'th'people's name / I say it shall be so!' (III, iii, 104–5) And in their own name, the people countersign the decision: 'It shall be so! Let him away! / He's banished and it shall be so' (III, iii, 106–7). Upon which Cominius desperately tries to reverse the verdict by doing a Regan for Rome, expressing respect for his country 'more holy and profound' (III, iii, 113) than the love he bears himself, his wife and children. But unlike Lear, Rome has no more time for such niceties and Brutus repeats the rabble's repetition of his colleague's verdict. 'There's no more to be said but he is banished, / An enemy to the people and his country. / It shall be so.' – '*All Pleb.* It shall be so, it shall be so!' (III, iii, 116–20). To which Coriolanus, finally, outraged by such ungrammatical behaviour, famously responds by redefining the very concept of banishment, turning the tables, in a very precise double figure, on the *voice* of the people: 'You common cry of curs [...] I banish you!' (III, iii, 120–3).

As Stanley Fish has observed in his splendid though far too cheerful essay on *Coriolanus*, this astonishing illocutionary act harbours the moral that 'institutions are no more than the (temporary) effects of speech act agreements'.[25] Yet if this were indeed the bottom line of *Coriolanus*'s ethics, the play would not be a tragedy but a theatrical exercise in linguistic stoicism – which to some extent, of course, it also is, and Fish is right to point out that the characters often act 'as if they were early practitioners of Oxford or ordinary language philosophy'.[26] Neither would *Coriolanus* be a tragedy if, after having banished the Romans, Coriolanus had actually succeeded in sacking the city – in which case, as Kenneth Burke has observed,[27] he would be the true Romanus, no longer the 'kind of nothing, titleless' (V, i, 13) drifting between names as the tragedy stammers on. If Coriolanus had forged himself a new name, the play would have been an uncritical revenge performance intent on communally cancelling the abyssal logic of monstrous repetition.

But Coriolanus's efforts at self-creation are aborted precisely by the reappearance of an unnegotiable representation of community: his declarative purism is reduced to naught the moment he is remembered by the woman that gave him a name and a place outside her body in a body founded on the nothing that is both more and less than the bond of human community. By 'unnatural[ly]' (V, iii, 184) kneeling for her son, Volumnia reincorporates him for Rome and the bonds of family and body politic seem to merge in the happy sacrificial participation she has celebrated throughout.[28] Yet *Coriolanus* is not a comedy and the return of the nothing we catachrestically call family only serves to trigger a final switch set in the very first scene.

***

When Coriolanus furiously dismisses Sicinius's first absolute shall, Cominius makes a curious remark: 'Twas from the canon' (III, i, 89). Philip Brockbank notes that this can either mean that Sicinius's speech was 'contrary to the established rule' or that, on the contrary, it was 'according to the rule', in accordance with the Tribunes' veto. Context and metre favour the first reading, but the liminal ambiguity remains arresting because it so clearly rehearses the play's central concern not so much with the question whether human beings abide by the conventions they live by or no (as Fish would have it), but more radically with the question as to what these conventions that constitute human community ultimately cover and keep in check: not the dull certainty of somebody's self-interest, not the real possibility of somebody's psychotic (or bourgeois) self-constitution, but precisely nothing. The point of the phrase would then reside in the very notion of the canon as the linguistic imposition of a rule of repetition – irrespective of what, exactly, the rule rules for repetition, as long as it is repeated, conjuring nothing, as if our sole vocation were endless imitation. Such is indeed the rule of the play's first scene.

Dr Johnson, who interestingly considered *Coriolanus* one of Shakespeare's 'most amusing performances' ('Come and see the violence inherent in the system!'), observed that 'the various revolutions of the hero's fortunes fill the mind with anxious curiosity', but added, on a slightly more critical note, that there was 'perhaps too much bustle in the first act, and too little in the last'.[29] The reason for this imbalance may well be that the first scene already contains the last in that our anxious curiosity involves something we did not quite hear, though we were expecting it, and have known all along, like the bored citizens listening to their belly, that it must eventually come to pass.

'*Enter a company of mutinous Citizens, with staves, clubs, and other weapons*' (I, i). That the play should open on a scene spelling public violence makes it unique for its period, yet the true power of this opening lies in the suspension of that violence. In fact, the play does not strictly speaking begin with an insurrection – it opens on an interruption (*Coriolanus*, I, i, 1–12):

First Cit. Before we proceed any further, hear me speak.
All Speak, speak.

First Cit. You are all resolved rather to die than to famish?
All Resolved, resolved.
First Cit. First, you know Caius Martius is chief enemy to the people.
All We know't, we know't.
First Cit. Let us kill him, and we'll have corn at our own price. Is't a verdict?
All No more talking on't; let it be done. Away, away!

The play has hardly begun, and already the game is up. But not quite. The Second Citizen begs to be heard first: 'One word, good citizens' (I,i,13). The First Citizen begs to differ and questions the appropriateness of the one word 'good': the tragedy is on course. 'One word': at several critical junctures, the performance stumbles on the interjection of 'one word, [...] but a word' (III, i, 213–14), 'a word or two' (III, i, 280), 'one word more, one word' (III, i, 308), so many words that ultimately come to name the one word that cannot be held in check, the one word in the First Citizen's opening interruption that was not echoed by all. For after *speak speak*, *resolved resolved*, and *we know't we know't*, something should have followed, something coming from as far back as the madness of King Lear[30] should have been echoed. As indeed it finally is, in the final scene, five times: '*All Con.* Kill, kill, kill, kill, kill him' (V, vi, 130). Upon which Aufidius can finally and without fear of further interruption claim the absolute shall to re-member Martius's body (V, vi, 153–4):

Yet he shall have a noble memory.
Assist.

Assist: remember nothing. Consign nothing to memory in a labour of mourning erasing the monstrous imposition of a name for human community and erecting a catachrestic monument to that name. Dream on.

Notes

1. Immanuel Kant, *Der Streit der Fakultäten*, in *Schrifte zur Anthropologie, Geschichtsphilosophie, Politik and Pädagogik, Erster Teil*, Vol. 9 of *Werke in Zehn Bänden* ed. Wilhelm Weischedel (Darmstadt: Wissenschaftliche Buchgesellschaft, 1970) Section 2, Para. 9.
2. Immanuel Kant, *The Critique of Judgement*, trans. James Creed Meredith (Oxford: Clarendon Press, 1969) 59.
3. Indeed quoted by Derrida in his classical acceptance of Kant's challenge – see *Marges de la philosophie* (Paris: Minuit, 1972) 267 n. 16. Cf. also Derrida, *La vérité en peinture* (Paris: Flammarion, 1978) 47, 131.
4. Paul de Man, *Aesthetic Ideology*, ed. Andrzej Warminski (Minneapolis: University of Minnesota Press, 1996) 120.
5. Paul de Man, *The Rhetoric of Romanticism* (New York: Columbia University Press, 1984) 263–90.
6. That a *beseeltes*, and hence human body is indeed by definition and exemplarily beautiful is an essential tenet in the Kantian aesthetic (see e.g. *Critique of Judgement*, Para. 17). For de Man's somewhat sketchy jump from Kant over Schiller to Goebbels, see *Aesthetic Ideology*, 155.
7. de Man, *Aesthetic Ideology*, 46–7.
8. Kant, *Critique of Judgement*, Para. 65.
9. Hannah Arendt, *Lectures on Kant's Political Philosophy*, ed. Ronald Beiner (University of Chicago Press, 1982) 16.
10. Immanuel Kant, *Critique de la faculté de juger*, trans. (into French) Alexis Philoneko (Paris: Vrin, 1993) 299 n. 3.
11. Kant, *Der Streit*, Section 2, Para. 9.
12. All references are to the Arden Edition, ed. Philip Brockbank (London: Routledge, 1990, rpt. of 1976).
13. For perspectives on Shakespeare's politics in connection with *Coriolanus*, see e.g. Margot Heinemann, 'How Brecht Read Shakespeare', in Jonathan Dollimore and Alan Sinfield, eds, *Political Shakespeare: New Essays in Cultural Materialism* (Manchester University Press, 1985) 202–30; Martin Scofield, 'Drama, Politics and the Hero: *Coriolanus*, Brecht and Grass', *Comparative Drama* 24:4 (1990) 322–41; Terence Hawkes, *Meaning by Shakespeare* (London: Routledge, 1992).
14. For a recent rhetorically sensitive survey of this matter see Arthur Riss, 'The Belly Politic: *Coriolanus* and the Revolt of Language', *English Literary History* 59 (1992) 53–75.
15. Stanley Cavell, 'Who Does the Wolf Love? *Coriolanus* and the Interpretation of Politics', in Patricia Parker and Geoffrey Hartman, eds, *Shakespeare and the Question of Theory* (New York: Methuen, 1985) 245–72; 262.
16. See, for example, Simon Critchley, *The Ethics of Deconstruction: Derrida and Levinas* (Oxford: Blackwell, 1992) 200–19.
17. *Pace* Riss, 'Belly Politic', 61. For yet another account of the First Citizen's interventions in the Fable, see Tetsuya Motohashi, 'Body Politic and Political Body in *Coriolanus*', *Forum for Modern Language Studies*, 30, 2 (1994) 97–112; 100–1.

18. For a reflection on the notion of 'predicament' congenial to my purpose here, see Dirk De Schutter, 'Till life do us part: Nicholas Moseley's *Hopeful Monsters*', in Ortwin de Graef, *et al*, eds, *Acknowledged Legislators: Essays on English Literature in Honour of Herman Servotte* (Kapellen: Pelckmans, 1994) 292–308.
19. I take the term catachresis here in its strict rhetorical sense as the name for the figure that names the nameless – classical examples being the legs of the table, the arms of the chair, the face of the mountain and indeed, perhaps, the head of state. See Heinrich Lausberg, *Elemente der literarischen Rhetorik* (München: Max Hueber Verlag, 1963) 65 (Para. 178). In its wider acceptance, catachresis is unfortunately read etymologically and, I would submit, misused as merely meaning 'a word misused (e.g. *anachronism* for *anomaly, to subject* for *to subordinate*)'. Eric Partridge, under the entry containing this definition, says of the book that contains it, *Usage and Abusage: A Guide to Good English* (London: Hamish Hamilton, 1947), that 'it deals with the commonest catachreses of the English language; to write at length on the nature of catachresis is therefore unnecessary' – thereby adding a *non sequitur* to a mistake.
20. That catachresis is in fact usage itself is also suggested in Lausberg's definition of the figure as a substitute for a non-existent proper word in the deficient *consuetudo*.
21. Hawkes, *Meaning by Shakespeare*, 105.
22. That is, strictly speaking unnegotiable – negotiation itself being, of course, the relaxation of strictures on speech. See also Motohashi, 'Body Politic', 105, where the Third Citizen's discourse is more sanguinely read as the representation of 'an idea of democracy which can only be sustained through negotiation'. For another reading of this scene as a saving moment of 'radical theatricality', see John Plotz, '*Coriolanus* and the Failure of Performatives', *English Literary History*, 63 (1996) 809–32; 824–6.
23. Kenneth Burke, *Language as Symbolic Action: Essays in Life, Literature, and Method* (Berkeley: University of California Press, 1968) 84.
24. Joyce Van Dyke, 'Making a Scene: Language and Gesture in *Coriolanus*', *Shakespeare Survey*, 30 (1977) 135–46; 138.
25. Stanley E. Fish, 'How to Do Things with Austin and Searle: Speech Act Theory and Literary Criticism', *Modern Language Notes*, 91 (1976) 983–1025; 997.
26. Fish, 'How to Do Things', 1002. Fish specifies that he does not claim that his reading of *Coriolanus* is 'exhaustive' or 'wholly new', but he insists that 'it doesn't cheat' (p. 1001). While indeed he omits possibilities (such as the 'absolute shall') and repeats previously made points (some of them repeated here), he does, perhaps, cheat a little in his happy embrace of the human 'speech act community' as a principle of saving irony that can in the end 'reclaim [Coriolanus] as inescapably its own' (p. 1001). See also Plotz, '*Coriolanus* and the Failure of Performatives', 812. I shall return to the play's finale below. One further index of Fish's cheerfulness is his decision to delete the Third Citizen's remarks on monstrosity when he discusses the

passage on political representation (p. 985): the point is not that these remarks substantially alter the reasoning but rather that they charge the argument with a tragic pathos Fish seeks to ward off. For a very different quarrel with Fish's cheating *Coriolanus* out of its genre, see James Marlow, 'Fish Doing Things with Austin and Searle', *Modern Language Notes*, 91 (1976) 1603–12.

27. Kenneth Burke, *Language as Symbolic Action*, p. 91.
28. For the politics of the family here, see also Scofield, 'Drama, Politics, and the Hero', 336 and esp. Motohashi, 'Body Politic', 102, 108.
29. Samuel Johnson, *Jonson on Shakepeare*, ed. Walter Raleigh (London: Oxford University Press, 1959) 179.
30. See Burke, *Language as Symbolic Action*, 91.

14
Literature and Existentialist Ethics in Simone de Beauvoir's 'Moral Period'

Terry Keefe

In one corner of the large territory covered by issues concerning the relations between literature and ethics, there are questions concerning the positions of particular practising authors on this matter. Few would claim that Simone de Beauvoir has unique insights in this area, but her case as such is an outstandingly rich and fascinating one. Within the relatively short period of her career under examination, she wrote – among other things – one play, two novels, a number of ethical works, and an essay on the theory of literature, all of which items are intricately interrelated in a variety of ways. Together they provide an intriguing body of material from which certain questions and certain points about literature and ethics emerge very strongly. One important factor is that we are dealing with a set of formally stated moral views on the one hand, and what we might begin by calling a 'corresponding' group of literary works on the other. This is already quite rare, since most ethical theorists do not write novels, and novelists, whatever their personal moral views, do not usually write essays about ethics.

A useful starting-point in Beauvoir's case is a passage – one of a number late on in the second volume of her memoirs, *The Prime of Life*, in which she explains how the outbreak of World War Two had a drastic impact upon her:

> Before the war I had followed my own bent, learning about the world and constructing a private pattern of happiness. Morality became identified in my mind with this process; it was a Golden Age. My experience was limited, but I stuck to it body and soul, and never dreamed of discussing it. I was just sufficiently

> detached from it to want to make other people conscious of it: this is what I tried to do in *She Came to Stay*. But from 1939 onwards, everything changed. The world became chaotic, and my work of construction stopped altogether. My one recourse was the verbal exorcism implicit in abstract moral judgements: I looked for reasons or formulas that would justify undergoing the things that were imposed upon me. I found one or two in which I still have faith; I discovered human solidarity and my personal responsibilities, and the fact that it was possible to accept death in order that life might keep its meaning. But I learned these truths, in a way, against my natural inclinations. I used words to talk myself into accepting them. I explained them to myself, tried to persuade myself, and taught myself a regular lesson. It was this lesson that I strove to pass on, ignoring the fact that it might not come as freshly to the reader as it had come to me.
>
> Thus I embarked upon what I might term the 'moral period' of my literary career, which lasted for a number of years. I no longer took my natural spontaneity as a guide; I was drawn to question myself concerning my principles and aims, and, after some hesitation, I even went to the length of composing an essay on the problem.[1]

One interesting question is why and how such a period ever comes to an end, but for present purposes it is sufficient to suggest its broad shape. If the period concerned began in 1939, when Sartre was mobilised, it was certainly marked by a crucial development when he returned to Paris from his prisoner-of-war camp in spring 1941 determined to abandon his individualistic, a-political pre-war stance and to *commit* himself. And the period probably drew to an end at a less clearly defined point in the late 1940s, when he and Beauvoir, like many other French people and Europeans generally, came to see the super-powers of the USA and USSR as so dominant that the whole *moral* as well as political map needed to be redrawn. Beauvoir's novel *The Mandarins* of 1954[2] looks back on part of that period and ends with the two main male characters, after the dramatic experiences of the story, concluding that it is as impossible to act morally in an unjust society as it is to draw a straight line in curved space.

The Prime of Life was, of course, published later still, in 1960 (and followed by a volume with the balancing title *The Force of*

Circumstance),[3] and it is interesting from the present viewpoint that Beauvoir comes to use the notion of her 'moral period' in the context of a discussion of the extent to which her second novel *The Blood of Others*, of 1945,[4] is over-didactic, monologic, a 'roman à thèse'. Having described and analysed her book as she habitually does in her memoirs, she quotes Blanchot as saying that, while it is absurd to reproach a novel for having a meaning, there is a big difference between meaning something and *demonstrating* something. Existence always has significance but it never proves anything, and the writer's goal is to *display* existence by recreating it in words. He or she betrays and impoverishes existence in failing to respect its ambiguity. Beauvoir agrees, then, that *She Came to Stay* is not a 'roman à thèse', because it has an open ending, whereas the ending of *The Blood of Others* is unambiguous and reducible to maxims or concepts. She even goes further than Blanchot and claims that this is a flaw inherent in the book as a whole, not just its final pages. It is not clear that this further point is entirely justified, but the judgement on the ending of *The Blood of Others* as such – where a whole variety of characters previously shown as in sharp conflict come together in the unity of the Resistance – will be shared by many readers. It is worth noting, nevertheless, that, in suggesting that *The Blood of Others* is undesirably unambiguous, Beauvoir simultaneously claims – consistently or not – that, in at least one major respect, readers took her novel to be something that it was never intended to be. In fact, this last point was important enough to cause her to recreate the experience in *The Mandarins*, where Henri Perron's first novel after the Liberation is also taken to be a story essentially about the Resistance, which he claims he never intended it to be.

In any case, Beauvoir's critical view of *The Blood of Others* involves the belief that her characters are defined by moral attitudes whose living roots she fails to establish, and she makes a similar criticism of her one and only play, *Who Shall Die?*, which she wrote in about three months in the middle of 1945.[5] Again, it is worth quoting Beauvoir, in order to show what kind of moral themes were preoccupying her, how she thinks they should and should not be treated, and how she compares the treatment in her different writings (Jean Blomart is the central male figure of *The Blood of Others*):

> I made the same mistake as in *The Blood of Others*, from which I also took up many themes: my characters are reducible to ethical

> attitudes. The leading male character, Jean-Pierre, is another version of Jean Blomart. Being incapable of finding actions that do justice to all men, he opts for abstention, asking: 'How can one measure the weight of a tear against the weight of one drop of blood?' Then he realises that his abstention involves collusion in crimes that are committed without his participation, and, like Blomart, he becomes involved in action.[6]

Beauvoir goes on to say that she deplores the didacticism of her play, and that *Who Shall Die?* is a work in the same vein as *The Blood of Others* and her moral essay *Pyrrhus and Cinéas*,[7] but that their common faults – which in 1960 she summarises as a kind of idealism – are even harder to tolerate in the theatre than elsewhere. She also has, in connection with the quotation concerning the relative weight of tears and bloodshed, a notable footnote, connecting these earlier works with *The Mandarins*, but also differentiating them from the later novel:

> I notice that, ten years later, I put this question, almost word for word, into the mouth of the heroine of *The Mandarins*, Anne Dubreuilh. But there is a great difference: Anne's attitude, which is closely bound up with her character as a whole, represents neither truth nor error; it is challenged by that of Dubreuilh and Henri Perron; and the novel shows no preference for one attitude rather than the other. On the contrary, in the case of Jean-Pierre, as with Blomart, abstention as such is one moment in a moral evolution, and they both finally go beyond it. An unambiguous, edifying conclusion is reached, whereas in *The Mandarins* no decision is arrived at; we do not know who is right and who is wrong; ambiguity is respected.[8]

Already by now, enough has been said to give more than a flavour of what Beauvoir designates as her own 'moral' period, her later notion being that she was somehow going against the grain in looking for moral principles and formulas. Two direct products of this search were the essay on ethics already referred to, *Pyrrhus and Cinéas*, published in 1944, and in 1947 a much longer moral treatise, *The Ethics of Ambiguity*,[9] and the parallels between the moral positions in the two essays on the one hand, and situations and attitudes depicted in her novels and her play on the other are enormous and obvious to all. There may be some criss-crossing in the parallels to be drawn: perhaps, for instance, the first of the two novels relates more closely to the second of the moral essays, and vice versa. Furthermore, one can detect a certain change and development in Beauvoir's positions even in the brief period of time involved. But the change involved is slight in relation to the homogeneity of the philosophy in this group of works, which form a genuine *block*. It is not appropriate to illustrate in great detail here how the fiction illustrates the moral thinking. The most fruitful way of seeing the matter is possibly in terms of an overlap in preoccupations and perspectives, rather than one of specific moral prescriptions,[10] but, in any case, it is probably sufficient for present purposes to leave aside the play, *Who Shall Die?*, and to make a few brief comments about the relationship between the moral essays and Beauvoir's two novels, *The Blood of Others* and *All Men are Mortal*.[11]

The first thing to say is that, at a very broad level of interpretation, the 'messages' conveyed by the novels conform very obviously indeed to the philosophical and moral stance of the essays. Such messages, furthermore, might be said to be both moral and ethical; that is, to relate both to questions of what morality *is* – what sort of experience it is to be a moral agent – and to substantive, prescriptive moral judgements and stances. Indeed, it is arguable that a major aspect of what Beauvoir is saying during this period, as is the case with Sartre, is that the two kinds of question are entirely inseparable.

Looking first, then, at the essay *Pyrrhus and Cinéas*, we see that it is clearly structured around the debate between the two historical figures:

> Plutarch relates that one day Pyrrhus was planning military conquests. 'First we will conquer the whole of Greece', he said. 'And after that?', Cinéas asked. 'We shall reach Africa'. 'After Africa?' 'We shall move on to Asia, conquer Asia Minor, Arabia.' 'And after that?' 'We'll go right on to India.' 'And after India?' 'Oh, I'll rest', said Pyrrhus. 'Then why not rest now?' asked Cinéas.
>
> Cinéas seems wise. What is the point of setting out, if the object is to come back home again? What is the point of starting if you know that you will have to stop? ... From the reflective point of view, every human project seems absurd, since it exists only by

> setting its own limits, and these limits can always be surpassed: one can always ask oneself critically: 'Why only as far as that? Why no further? What is the point?'[12]

The dialogue between Pyrrhus and Cinéas goes on, says Beauvoir, but Pyrrhus has to make a decision: does he go or does he stay? If he goes, *where* does he go? Candide's 'We must cultivate our own garden' is no answer, she says: What *is* my garden? Who *is* my neighbour? She takes these in a very general way to be the central moral questions that humans face: 'What is the measure of a man? What goals can he set himself? And what hopes are legitimate?' These are the questions that she sets out to address in her essay.

It will be no surprise to many to learn that the answers she gives are imprecise, tentative, perhaps even self-contradictory. But Beauvoir's broad argument is unmistakably that human life and human beings are essentially limited, finite; and that, far from deploring this, we should actually welcome it and take strength from it. This is, of course, a very abstract thesis and what is rather remarkable is that Beauvoir should have found such a striking way of 'illustrating' it in the most concrete fashion in her third novel, with its pointed titled, *All Men are Mortal*. The core of the novel is the long story of one Raymond Fosca, who drinks an immortality potion in early 14th-century Italy and comes to enjoy enormous power of various kinds in the course of some 600 years. But over that time he also comes to see every victory turn into defeat, as well as defeat turn into victory; he repeatedly finds that once he has achieved a certain goal, it is insufficient, disappointing, just another starting-point for something else. By the end of the novel he is an appallingly, uniquely sad, pathetic figure – alone because of his immortality, utterly purposeless because of his immortality.

Beauvoir had the further inspiration of setting Fosca's story within the frame of part of the life of an ambitious young actress, Régine, who believes that her own salvation lies in Fosca's immortality but is gradually persuaded, as he tells his story, that immortality is or would be a curse. This is a most dreadful discovery for her, and the very last sentence of the book proper indicates that the agony of living on without hope is about to begin for her:

> she was beaten; in a state of horror, of terror, she accepted the metamorphosis: no more than a gnat, an ant, dross till the end of her days. 'It's only the beginning' .... It was when the clock in the

church tower began chiming the hour that she uttered her first scream.

Yet Fosca's story as such ends on a very different note, with the revolutionary figure of Armand in mid-nineteenth-century France entirely willing to accept all of the limitations of the human situation, equally content to be a 'man among men' at moments of victory and defeat; and showing that the brief period between birth and death is enough – even for those humans who know that everything done is undone in the end – to find things worth living and dying for. In short, it is difficult to imagine a better note than that on which Fosca's story ends with which to counter Régine's sense of hopelessness, or to illustrate more directly or more clearly the central moral thesis of *Pyrrhus and Cinéas*, even if the interpretation of *All Men are Mortal* as a whole is complicated by the fact that it is Régine who, as it were, has the last word.

Equally, still at the broadest level of interpretation, *The Blood of Others* unmistakably embodies many of the key ideas of both *Pyrrhus and Cinéas* and *The Ethics of Ambiguity*. This latter moral essay of 1947 picks up many of the themes of the earlier one, but dwells at much more length on questions of action, human relations and freedom. The last of these concepts, of course, is above all the one associated with French existentialism and with existentialist ethics, and the essay repeatedly comes back to the point that human freedom is the ultimate and only goal to which men should devote themselves. It also argues – and it is here that there are differences, at least differences of emphasis and timing, between the writings of Sartre and Beauvoir – that we need others to be free, in order that they may give our lives a kind of justification by continuing our projects. Yet Beauvoir is clear, as she was in *Pyrrhus and Cinéas*, that the notion of solidarity with *all* of one's fellow human beings is a notion with no coherence or application: we can only act on behalf of some by acting against others – a point graphically illustrated, of course, by the case of the Resistance movements in occupied France.

After an early experience of feeling responsible for someone's death, Jean Blomart, one of the two central figures of *The Blood of Others* – once more there is one male and one female protagonist, who act as narrative focalisers at different stages of the text: a technique that was to be used on a further occasion by Beauvoir in *The Mandarins* – goes through a long period when he tries to abstain from any action that will harm anyone. But he eventually engages in action that involves spilling the blood of others, not because all means to a particular end are good, but, on the contrary, because all means are equally bad. As Beauvoir stresses in *The Ethics of Ambiguity*, in the end we have no alternative but to act in a situation of risk and uncertainty. And just as freedom is the supreme goal in the essay, so freedom is the ideal that finally brings everyone together at the end of the novel: political freedom, of course, but also the freedom that we must recognise at the individual level in the way in which others react to us. Blomart has felt guilty over the harmful consequences that he sees himself as having brought about in the life of his lover Hélène, but is convinced and consoled in the end by her insistence on her deathbed that she has *freely chosen* her involvement with him.

There can scarcely be a novel that deals more explicitly, more extensively, or more intensively with moral issues than *The Blood of Others*: from the issues involved in relations between parents and their increasingly independent adolescent children, through those involved in one-sided love relationships, to questions of the possibility of moral abstention, questions of means and ends, the significance of art, the dilemmas of violence, and so on. It is not in the least difficult to see why Beauvoir or anyone else should come to regard it as *over*-stuffed with moral matter, but we should not allow this to cause us to forget that some specific situations and sequences in the novel provide outstandingly graphic and memorable fictional embodiments of particular moral problems and dilemmas. To the extent that we see literature as a source of situations for moral examination and analysis, then the illustrations of the impossibility of abstention, of the ways in which we intrude into the lives of others whether we wish to or not, of the moral anguish of the leader – these are almost as good as we could wish such illustrations to be in a work of fiction.

To what extent literature, or just fiction, *should* be seen in this way is, of course, controversial and debatable. But in this sense, too, Beauvoir's case is a particularly useful one, since even in her 'moral' period she herself was also engaged in *theorising* the relations between philosophy and literature, first in an interview and then in an essay called 'Literature and Metaphysics', published first in April 1946 and then as part of a collection of broadly moral essays called *Existentialism and the Wisdom of Nations*.[13]

In general, Beauvoir's views are close to Sartre's, which are more familiar, because of the publication of *What is Literature?* in 1948.[14] It may be felt, however, that they are somewhat less sophisticated than those of Sartre, who is rather less obviously open to attack from those who have taken the theory of literature so far in recent decades. Without developing Beauvoir's arguments in any detail, it is possible to pick up some points implicit in comments already quoted. In this period of her career, as well as later, she was very anxious to deny that literature – or, as always, one has to say that she really means *good* literature – simply illustrates philosophical positions already arrived at. Her key idea here is that writing a novel is a kind of search or inquiry. At least at some points she takes this to mean that an author does not know what he/she intends when setting out to write a novel. But she is really saying is that it must *show* in the final product that the author was *seeking* in the course of writing. This is linked – though less insistently by Beauvoir than by Sartre – with the need for the author, like the reader, to be *free* in the writing and reading process. As far as the reader is concerned, he/she, too, has a part of the bargain to fulfil. Just as the novel must be a living discovery for the writer, so it must be for the reader. But often readers do not read in the way in which they are being called upon to read; they are afraid of taking risks, of being adventurous, and seek to translate the experience into their own, known terms; they fail to respond to the appeal to their freedom which is the essence of literature. (Sartre talks of a 'generosity pact', within which both author and reader assume the other to be free.) Honestly written, honestly read, says Beauvoir, the metaphysical novel reveals or 'unveils' existence in a way that no other form of expression can.

She records that from early on she always thought it was a waste of time reading novels after she had been reading Spinoza or Kant, but equally considered it a waste of time constructing systems after she had been following the imaginary fortunes of Julien Sorel or Tess of the D'Urbervilles. Her view in 'Literature and Metaphysics' is that the novel is only justified if it is a means of communication irreducible to other means. The philosopher or essay writer gives readers an intellectual reconstruction of his/her experience: the novel gives the experience itself reconstituted on the imaginary level, but before it is elucidated. (This, of course, is the kind of unsophisticated comment that is rather troublesome, especially as at other points Beauvoir says that literature takes us *beyond* the over-narrow limits of real experience.) Readers are hence able to keep their freedom of thought: the opacity and ambiguity of life are conveyed by literature, and readers react in the way that they do when faced with real life. They question themselves, have doubts, adopt positions, and this hesitant development of their thought brings an enrichment that no doctrinal teaching could possibly bring. The true novel cannot be reduced to formulas; its meaning cannot be detached from it any more than a smile can be detached from a face. Characters must not be created on the basis of theories, formulas, labels. The plot must not unfold in a mechanically contrived way. The novelist must believe strongly enough in what he/she is creating for ideas and meanings to spring from the original conception, suggesting problems, unexpected developments – it will seem to the reader like the recreation of a genuine spiritual adventure. A novel simply giving fictional form to an ideological core should be condemned. It is difficult to see how an imaginary story could helpfully illustrate a philosophical theory already properly formulated: it could only *impoverish* it, by reducing the general to the particular.

As the title of her essay suggests, Beauvoir is focusing on metaphysics, but it will be clear how this is relevant to ethics as such. Metaphysics, she argues, is not first and foremost a system; the essence is a metaphysical *attitude*, with the whole human being confronting the whole world. It is not possible to imagine an Aristotelian novel, a Spinozist novel, a Leibnizian novel, since neither subjectivity nor temporality has a significant place in their metaphysics. But existentialism, as an attempt to reconcile the objective and the subjective, the absolute and the relative, the a-temporal and the historical is just the philosophy to be expressed in both essays and fiction. In fiction the existentialist is trying to express an aspect of metaphysical experience that cannot be expressed in any other way: its subjective, singular, dramatic side, and also its ambiguity. Good and evil are not abstract notions: they can only be grasped in the good and bad actions performed by men.

Although some of these comments have been significantly overtaken by insights in literary theory since the 1940s, others open up lines of approach to the relationship between literature and ethics that are especially fruitful. These lines might be thought to travel in two major directions. Firstly, there is a whole cluster of questions concerning the purposes, functions and profound nature of literature itself. Beauvoir's stance on this involves ascribing an unmistakably moral purpose to literature. This is already clear in 'Literature and Metaphysics', but comes out even more strongly in a contribution that she made to a symposium on the nature of literature in 1964,[15] when she explicitly argued that authentic literature is a way of taking account of human separation, but in a sense surmounting it: and that it talks of failure, scandal, death not to make readers despair, but in order to save them from despair. This is a view that has not been a fashionable one for some time, while markedly different, contrasting perceptions have been much more to the fore. It has never been clear, however, that it is a view of literature that can coherently be abandoned entirely, and it may be time to revisit that debate.

Secondly, in much or even conceivably all of what we have seen Beauvoir as arguing, 'ethics' could be substituted for metaphysics without any change – either for better or worse – in the plausibility of her points. Just as she wants to talk of a metaphysical 'attitude' rather than some definitively constituted metaphysics, so it may be much more helpful to talk about a moral attitude rather than a formed body of moral prescriptions or prohibitions. In any case, this is how things stand within an existentialist framework. Beauvoir is surely right to suggest that, because of its emphasis on the singular and the subjective, existentialism lends itself so much better than many another philosophy to expression in literature. Or the point can be put negatively, since any philosophy that stresses freedom as its central value necessarily has great difficulty in specifying any particular rules that humans should follow.

And this in turn brings us back to something touched on earlier: that we are dealing here as much with ethics as with morality; that is, with the most fundamental questions about what morality, or moral sensitivity, or moral awareness *is*. For those seeking a morality that takes the form of something like the Ten Commandments, existentialism has left very little by way of a legacy. But if one is seeking insights into exactly what *kind* of human activity morality is, it may be said to have made a major contribution to twentieth-century thought; and Beauvoir has played a significant part in this. It is not easy to formulate with any great precision her positive position on the kind of enterprise that morality is, but it certainly involves seeing it as permeating virtually all areas of human enquiry and human thought. Hence her view tends to elide the distinction between metaphysics and ethics *and* to urge that literature, like the other arts, is a major area in which human beings engage with, interact with, and investigate the world. The stance of Beauvoir and Sartre on literature has itself been very influential; on some French intellectuals who subsequently came to see literature in a very different way, but also on British figures like Iris Murdoch, whose book *Metaphysics as a Guide to Morals*,[16] which is greatly occupied with literature in a way that the title does not indicate, appears to be one of the latest major developments of such a position.

If we finally come back to the two novels, *The Blood of Others* and *All Men are Mortal*, it is possible this time not to show how they illustrate Beauvoir's ethical views, but to indicate briefly ways in which they put into practice her ideal that novels should be open-ended and enquiring rather than dogmatic and doctrinal. The criticism that the ending of *The Blood of Others* fails to live up to this ideal has already been accepted, and it also undoubtedly true that earlier in the novel quite diverse strands are artificially made to run in parallel; for instance, the private and public dimensions of Blomart's life, or his own development and that of his artist friend Marcel. But the other side of the coin is that the moral issues, conflicts and dilemmas associated with these different strands are themselves exceptionally well realised in the fiction – that is to say, they are well brought out as *problems* lending themselves to no easy answers. Indeed, it is because they are *so* well brought out that the alleged 'solution' to everything at the end of the book seems over-neat and inadequate. We could go even further and say that, in Blomart's case, there is effectively a double layer to his problems. The very way in which he sees living in the world with others as problematic – he talks of the original 'curse' of existence and of the 'scandal' of otherness – this *in itself* is to some extent problematised in the novel, by other characters and possibly the structure of the book as a whole. It is difficult to accept Beauvoir's account of the difference between Anne's difficulty in weighing bloodshed against tears in *The Mandarins* and Blomart's difficulty; in both cases we are sufficiently detached from the character concerned to be able to raise certain questions about seeing things in this way at all. Similarly, it can very easily be argued that, *in spite of* the ending of *The Blood of Others* some of the issues concerning different conceptions of love and their link with gender – among many other issues – emerge powerfully from the book as open, unresolved issues.

And two things are very striking about *All Men are Mortal* in this connection. Firstly, in spite of the general thesis about mortality, the novel ends in almost exactly the opposite way to *The Blood of*

Others, with various elements visibly diverging rather than all coming together. The reader or critic can make very different things indeed out of *All Men are Mortal*, depending upon which of *three* characters is given most weight at the end. If it is Armand, then there is a message of optimism; if it is Régine, then a deep pessimism prevails; and, as for Fosca, he only compounds the problem, since, precisely because he is not human but immortal, it is possible to draw sharply contrasting conclusions from the sad state that he is shown as being in at the end. Should we, as mortals, draw indirect encouragement from his unhappy state? Or should we see him as quasi-human and therefore constituting a dire warning to us? The other point about the novel is the paradoxical one that there are aspects of human relations that are more memorably embodied through the character of an immortal here than anywhere else in Beauvoir's novels. The treatment of the emotions of fatherhood is unique in her fiction, as is the depth of her portrayal of relations between men, be they relations of hatred or friendship. In short, it is the unexpected, unexpectedly moving elements in *All Men are Mortal* that cause the texture of the novel to break out of any broad doctrinal structure that might be thought to hold it together; these are the equivalents of the moral uncertainties and questionings that, equally, make *The Blood of Others* so much more than a lesson in the importance of freedom.

Beauvoir is right to say that books must be 'honestly' read as well as honestly written. Part of the reader's honesty in this case must consist in not being determined at all costs to find illustrations of particular positions in her novels. We have been concerned with the moral positions set out in her essays of the mid-forties, but later what will need to be resisted is the determination, at all costs, to see certain specific feminist arguments in her fiction, just because she wrote *The Second Sex*. That is quite another story, of course, but it does seem that what we have here is a third, or possibly a fourth dimension to the question of literature and ethics. Fiction may *illustrate* moral views; literature may have a moral *function* and that may entail that the writer must avoid being *didactic* in any direct way; and now we are reminded again that *readers and critics* may have certain moral responsibilities in engaging with works of fiction. It is because questions at all of these levels arise quite naturally out of consideration of the writings of Simone de Beauvoir's 'moral period' that her case is such a fertile one for examination in the context of any discussion of the relations between literature and ethics.

Notes

1. *La Force de l'âge* (Paris: Gallimard, 1960); translated by P. Green as *The Prime of Life* (Harmondsworth: Penguin, 1965). References will be given firstly to the French 'Folio' edition of the text (FA) and then to the English translation (PL). The reference here is: FA, 625–6; PL, 547. (In this case as in others, I have modified the translation where this seemed to me to be required.)
   She Came to Stay, trans. Y. Moyse and R. Senhouse (London: Fontana, 1984) is the translation title of Beauvoir's first novel, *L'Invitée* (Paris: Gallimard, 1943). For each French text I give details of an English translation, where one is available. But because there are different translations on the market, only for *The Prime of Life* do I give page-references to an English as well as the French version of Beauvoir's text.
2. *Les Mandarins* (Paris: Gallimard, 1954), translated by L.M. Friedman as *The Mandarins* (London: Fontana, 1982).
3. *La Force des choses* (Paris: Gallimard, 1963), translated by R. Howard as *Force of Circumstance* (Harmondsworth: Penguin, 1985).
4. *Le Sang des autres* (Paris: Gallimard, 1945), translated by Y. Moyse and R. Senhouse as *The Blood of Others* (Harmondsworth: Penguin, 1978).
5. *Les Bouches inutiles* (Paris: Gallimard, 1945), translated by C. Francis and F. Gontier as *Who Shall Die?* (Florissant, MO: River Press, 1983).
6. FA, 673–4; PL, 588–9.
7. *Pyrrhus et Cinéas* (Paris: Gallimard, 1944) ('Idées').
8. FA, 673; PL, 589.
9. *Pour une morale de l'ambiguïté* (Paris: Gallimard, 1947); translated by B. Frechtman as *The Ethics of Ambiguity* (New York: Philosophical Library, 1948) (a better translation title would have been *Towards an Ethics of Ambiguity*).
10. See my *French Existentialist Fiction: Changing Moral Perspectives* (London: Croom Helm, 1986).
11. *Tous les hommes sont mortels* (Paris: Gallimard, 1946); translated by E. Cameron as *All Men are Mortal* (London: Virago, 1996).
12. 233–4; my own translation.
13. 'Littérature et métaphysique', in *L'Existentialisme et la sagesse des nations* (Paris: Nagel, 1948) 89–107.
14. *Qu'est-ce que la littérature?* was first published in book-form, together with other writings on literature, in Sartre's *Situations II* (Paris: Gallimard, 1948); translated by Bernard Frechtman as *What is Literature?* (London: Methuen, 1951).
15. In Y. Buin, ed., *Que peut la littérature?* (Paris: Union Générale d'Editions, 1965) (collection '10/18'); Beauvoir's contribution is on 73–92.
16. Iris Murdoch, *Metaphysics as a Guide to Morals* (London: Chatto and Windus, 1992; Penguin, 1993).

15
Sympathy and Science in *Frankenstein*

Janis McLarren Caldwell

Over the last two decades, the field of biomedical ethics has claimed *Frankenstein* as its classic narrative, a cautionary tale warning that science divorced from ethics will produce monsters. But *Frankenstein* is a critique, not so much of an amoral science, as of a conflation of scientific and moral theory – in the theory of physiologic sympathy. In *Frankenstein*'s strange world, both scientifically modern and gothically melodramatic, everybody is searching for sympathy, which functions as both a natural, material principle and the highest ideal of social interaction. The theory of physiologic sympathy, however, posits fragile bodies, susceptible to contagion and collapse. Under this model, social sympathy is safe only for people of nearly identical psychological and somatic constitutions. Shelley critiques the Romantic attempt to resolve science and ethics into a theory of physiologic sympathy, which she depicts as a narcissistic reduction, impatiently and prematurely synthetic, and therefore brittle in its demand for universal similitude, harmony, and unity.

Sympathy, judging from the word's frequency and weight in the text of *Frankenstein*, is the major theme and recurrent problem of the novel. Each narrator yearns for or mourns the loss of sympathetic relationship. Walton desires 'the company of a man who could sympathize with me', and hopes he has found such a man when, with Frankenstein's arrival, the stranger's 'constant and deep grief fills me with sympathy and compassion'.[1] Walton's sympathy, however, is repulsed: 'I thank you,' Frankenstein replies, 'for your sympathy, but it is useless' (p. 24). Frankenstein has already had such a friend in Clerval, whose 'true sympathy' is now destroyed (p. 69). As for the Monster, who claims he 'was fashioned to be susceptible of love and sympathy', he 'sympathizes' with the

DeLaceys as he witnesses how they 'sympathized with one another' (pp. 217, 108, 127). After his unsuccessful self-exposure to the DeLaceys, the failure of hoped-for sympathy tortures him: 'Finding myself unsympathized with, [I] wished to tear up the trees, spread havoc and destruction around me, and then to have sat down and enjoyed the ruin' (p. 132). The Monster then pursues Frankenstein with the demand that he create a female monster, thinking he cannot live without the 'interchange of those sympathies necessary for my being' (p. 140). Frankenstein, although finally coerced into agreement, flatly states 'I could not sympathize with him' (p. 143). And after Frankenstein's death, the Monster concludes: 'No sympathy may I ever find ... I am quite alone' (pp. 218–19). The search for sympathy amounts to an obsession for each narrator in this novel, and Shelley seems to be repeating that sympathy is impossible – or at least that it is a good deal more fragile than many Romantics assumed.

For the Romantics, sympathy meant primarily 'fellow feeling', but the word carried with it two other important historical connotations, of magical correspondence and of 'modern' mechanical communication. Before the scientific revolution, sympathy implied powerful magical correspondence that could occur on a variety of levels: celestial, between heavenly bodies; social, especially between friends, lovers and relatives; physiological, between one's parts or organs, especially between mind and body; and elemental, between inanimate particles. For instance, in its oldest usage, sympathy was said to exist between the moon and the ocean, two lovers even at extreme distance, the liver and the mind, iron and a lodestone, and so on (*OED*). It seems that when correspondences were noted but unaccounted for – that is, there was no clearly detailed or adequately understood mode of communication – sympathy became the explanatory concept.

In the eighteenth century, as physical science gained authority, mechanical explanations were offered for sympathy, and a crude materialism began to stand in for the previously occult attributes of sympathy. Following John Locke's empiricism, David Hume in moral philosophy and David Hartley in psychology used the rhetoric of 'vibrations' and 'impressions' to describe accurate communication of physical units of feeling. Tiny packets of information 'impressed' themselves on the senses, and set up vibrations in the 'aether', a supposedly airy substance flowing through the nerves. In his *Observations on Man*, David Hartley writes: 'The

Vibrations ... are excited, propagated, and kept up, partly by the Aether, i.e. by a very subtle and elastic fluid, and partly by the Uniformity, Continuity, Softness ... of the medullary substance of the Brain, Spinal Marrow, and Nerves.'[2] Of course, Hartley is not really explaining the physiology of the association of ideas – he is merely assigning physical substance to ideas, 'confirming' their plausibility by constructing an ostensibly 'scientific' account of how associations might imprint themselves on the body. In this attempt, however, he makes a significant move: the 'free propagation of vibrations' requires 'sufficiently uniform' substance. Repeatedly, Hartley invokes the 'softness', 'uniformity', and 'continuity' – basically the passivity and the similarity of the substances necessary to provide for connection and communication of discrete impressions.

The softest, most responsive and resonant nerves, according to eighteenth-century moral philosophy and physiology, belonged to persons of 'sensibility', or finely tuned physiologic sympathy. According to physician George Cheyne, 'those *who govern*' were 'mark'd out by Nature' from 'those who *are governed*' by their 'delicate and *elastic Organs* of *Thinking* and *Sensibility*'. Thus, aristocrats were perfected in their 'Heads, Faculties and Spiritual Nature' whereas the lower classes were designed for the 'Exercise and Use of their Bodies, Limbs and Material Organs'.[3] Erecting a physical basis for social difference, theories of sensibility operated to justify the privileges of nobility. The supposedly exquisite delicacy of the person of sensibility, however, was thought to put him or her at risk for physical and mental derangement – such as melancholia, the vapours, hysteria or hypochondria – and the rapid communication of illness between one's own mind and body.

Theorists of physiologic sympathy typically subscribed as well to a belief in social sympathy, or the literal transmission of sympathy from body to body. Hume wrote in *A Treatise of Human Nature* that there is 'a transition of passion' in any act of social sympathy, in which we not only imagine the experience of the other, but feel it on our nerves: 'As in strings equally wound up, the motion of one communicates itself to the rest; so all the affections readily pass from one person to another, and beget correspondent movements in every human creature.'[4] Hume posited a direct, 'instantaneous' transformation of the imagined idea into a neural 'impression', reproducing 'the very passion itself' in the onlooker through a rapid, unmediated transfer of identical information.

Although Hume proposed this immediacy as a foundation for

moral behaviour, fears of social contamination inevitably arose. The Earl of Shaftesbury, for instance, extolled sympathy within gentlemanly fellowship, but mistrusted sympathetic contact with the mob, whose 'very looks' could be 'infectious'; passion and panic might spread 'from face to face'.[5] Medical texts, such as the following by eighteenth-century physician Robert Whytt, regarded sympathy ambivalently, both as normal physiology and as susceptibility to disease:

> [T]here is a remarkable sympathy, by means of the nerves, between the various parts of the body; and now it appears that there is a still more wonderful sympathy between the nervous systems of different persons whence various motions and morbid symptoms are often transferred, from one to another, without any corporeal contact or infection.[6]

Whytt's sentence quickly moves from admiration for the 'remarkable' intra-body sympathy and the 'still more wonderful' interpersonal sympathy, to anxiety about the consequences of sympathy, betrayed by his reference to 'morbid symptoms' that leap from person to person with more efficacy even than an 'infection'.

Romantic thinkers altered very little of these eighteenth-century ideas about sympathy. Wordsworth shifted the privilege of extraordinary sensibility (or finely tuned sympathy between body parts) from the eighteenth-century well-bred aristocrat to the Romantic poet, and yet maintained the idea of physically grounded sensibility. In the *Preface* to *Lyrical Ballads*, a poet is 'a man speaking to men', but he distinguishes himself from his rustic brothers by possessing 'more than usual organic sensibility'. Poetic imagination was a capacious enough concept to serve as a bridge between the eighteenth-century mechanism and Romantic idealism. Thus, William Hazlitt, the premier Romantic theorist of social sympathy, rejects an explicitly mechanical or 'secret sympathy' between people, but offers 'imagination' as the 'faculty' to which the projections of sensations 'make the same direct appeal ... whether they relate to ourselves, or others, as the eye receives with equal directness the impression of our own external form, or that of others'.[7] True to Coleridge's definition of the imagination as a 'blending, fusing power', Hazlitt's sympathetic imagination, through which he 'can go out of [himself] entirely and enter into the minds and feeling of others', overleaps the differences between self and other.[8]

The variety of ideas about sympathy, then, for Mary Shelley's culture, all relied on the insistent resemblance or identification, magically wrought, materially necessary, or powerfully imagined, between sympathetic participants. The problem with this kind of sympathy, according to Mary Shelley's critique, was that it presupposed sameness or at least extraordinary similarity as the necessary medium for such communication, and, as a corollary, an easy permeability between bodies and minds, and between people.

In good Gothic form, Shelley uses repetition of structure, doubling of characters and suggestions of incest to evoke the fear of excessive similitude. The symmetries of *Frankenstein* contribute to a suffocating sensation of enclosure in the novel. The famous 'frame' or 'box-within-a box' structure of the novel, with Walton's letters to Mrs Saville surrounding Frankenstein's narration, surrounding the monster's autobiography, gives this novel about monstrosity a perverse neatness. Of course, there is the well-known *doppelgänger* effect of Frankenstein and his creature, pursuing and pursued by one another, exchanging the roles of master and servant. Similarly, if less overtly, Walton is included in this brotherhood, as each man's rhetoric resembles the others'. Each recounts his story in the same vocabulary and lofty, oratorical style so that, as Beth Newman writes, each narration is less a contrasting point of view than an echoic parallel.[9]

The theme of excessive similitude recurs in the incestuous suggestions regarding the Frankenstein family. Caroline Beaufort is the ward of Victor's father for two years before he marries her. Elizabeth and Victor in the 1818 edition are cousins, and to Victor, she is his 'more than sister'. When Victor seems reluctant to marry Elizabeth, Victor's father suspects that he views her as a sister, and Elizabeth asks, 'But as brother and sister often entertain a lively affection towards each other, without desiring a more intimate union, may not such also be our case?' As a whole, the Frankenstein family is itself a 'circle' with all undesirable things 'banished' from its enclosure:

> Such was our domestic circle, from which care and pain seemed for ever banished. My father directed our studies, and my mother partook of our enjoyments. Neither of us possessed the slightest pre-eminence over the other; the voice of command was never heard amongst us; but mutual affection engaged us all to comply with and obey the slightest desire of each other. (p. 37)

The family's peace and equality are overshadowed by the perfection that prescribes a stultifying harmony, in which each member must 'comply' and 'obey'.

Outside of the family circle, each character searches for a reflection of himself, or the engulfment or ownership of another. Walton desires a friend 'whose eyes would reply to mine', wishes to 'possess' the stranger Frankenstein 'as the brother of my heart', and turns in his failure to seeking the sympathy of his sister, Mrs Saville (pp. 13, 22). Frankenstein's desire to create his own species stems from a desire for relationship even closer, less diluted, than fatherhood: 'A new species would bless me as its creator and source; many happy and excellent natures would owe their being to me. No father could claim the gratitude of his child so completely as I should deserve theirs' (p. 49). And, of course, the monster wants a partner just like himself, created by the same 'father': 'My companion must be of the same species,' he warns Frankenstein, 'and have the same defects' (p. 140).

Frankenstein incorporates this harmonic ideal into his search for knowledge. Shelley carefully details young Victor's early education, that 'train of ideas' imparting 'the fatal impulse that led to my ruin' (p. 33). Onto his occult reading of Cornelius Agrippa, Paracelsus and Albertus Magnus, Victor's father superimposes corrective instruction in 'modern' science. But modern science does not completely supplant alchemical pseudoscience, despite his father's practical lessons in electricity. Significantly, 'by some fatality' (which Frankenstein alternately explains as resistance to paternal authority, disinclination for modern studies, and the 'accident' of missing a lecture series), Victor arrives at the university well-versed only in the ancients. There, Victor's attraction to metaphysics continues to threaten his modern education. M. Krempe insists that Victor break with alchemy and embrace 'modern natural philosophy'. Krempe, product of an 'enlightened and scientific age', appears to be a thorough-going empiricist, and Victor rejects with 'contempt' his study of dingy 'realities' unadorned by metaphysical speculation (p. 41).

In pursuit of harmony, Victor finds his intellectual model in M. Waldman, the Romantic scientist who unifies ancient and modern knowledge for Victor. Waldman, as Anne Mellor demonstrates, resembles Humphry Davy, the British chemist whom Shelley had read just prior to writing *Frankenstein*.[10] According to historian of science D.M. Knight, Davy typifies the Romantic movement in science; especially its grand unifying schemes and resemblance to alchemy:

> The widespread belief in the unity of matter, the view of chemical synthesis as a union of opposites, and the idea, implicit in Davy's *Consolations*, that the researches of the chemist can somehow cast light on the problems of the existence of God, freedom and immortality, all show an affinity with the alchemical scheme of things.[11]

Waldman wins Victor's confidence by affirming Victor's favourite alchemists: '[T]hese were men to whose indefatigable zeal modern philosophers were indebted for most of the foundations of their knowledge' (pp. 42–3). In describing Frankenstein's 'fatal' education as a reconciliation of chemistry and alchemy, Shelley reflects negatively on the natural supernaturalism of her Romantic peers – especially on the sort of conversation, mixing Gothic German ghost stories and modern galvanic experiments, that engendered her own dream of horror – the dream which, as she recounts in her 1831 preface, inspired *Frankenstein*.

The Krempe-Waldman contrast furnishes another form of haunting similitude. Frankenstein examines each man's 'physiognomy', or physical appearance. The pseudoscience of physiognomy held that the body, especially the face and posture, revealed, or was sympathetic to, the moral and emotional constitution. Thus, M. Krempe, the materialist, is 'a little squat man, with a gruff voice and repulsive countenance' whereas Waldman presents 'an aspect expressive of the greatest benevolence', and a 'voice the sweetest I had ever heard' (p. 41). Frankenstein makes harmony of body a criterion for the assessment of ideas: of Krempe he says, 'the teacher did not prepossess me in favor of the doctrine'. By his own admission, Frankenstein is highly prejudiced by his 'secluded' childhood, full of 'old familiar faces,' which 'had given me invincible repugnance to new countenances' (p. 40). We are prepared then to expect Frankenstein – if he is 'repulsed' by the realistic disharmony of Krempe's ideas and appearance – to be incapable of tolerating the disjunctions of his creature.

When the assumptions of physiognomy were coupled with the notion that the person of sensibility should be highly impressionable, the result was a belief that the sensible body would be soft and susceptible, and extraordinarily responsive to the mind.

Throughout *Frankenstein*, characters sicken from mental depression. Beaufort dies of grief, with no other apparent illness, and Frankenstein's father's stroke is precipitated by Elizabeth's death. But Frankenstein himself is the prime exemplar of this model. He palpitates and trembles as he plans his monster, falls into a nervous fever after creating him, nearly dies after he is accused of Clerval's murder.

A similar physical fragility ruins the DeLacey family after they see the monster. Agatha faints, Safie flees, and Felix is overwhelmed by his terror. When the monster returns to the cottage he overhears Felix report that 'the life of my father is in the greatest danger, owing to the dreadful circumstance that I have related. My wife and my sister will never recover [from] their horror' (p. 134). The very beauty and tender sensitivity that attracted Felix and Safie to one another, promising a sympathy that overleaps racial and linguistic differences, renders them both susceptible to crippling illness.

Sympathy of mind and body can also, however, operate to Frankenstein's advantage. Although Frankenstein's body predictably collapses when he is overwrought, his mind is also capable of directing his body to do its will. When he is accused of Clerval's murder, for instance, he is sinking with distress and fatigue, but thinks 'it politic to rouse all my strength, that no physical debility might be construed into apprehension or conscious guilt' (p. 171). Later, on his deathbed, Frankenstein re-animates when his spirit soars to admonish Walton's mutineers. Walton writes: 'Frankenstein, who had at first been silent, and indeed, appeared hardly to have force enough to attend, now roused himself; his eye sparkled, and his cheeks flushed with momentary vigour' (p. 212). Frankenstein's sparkling eyes and volitional reanimation contrast with the monster's dull skin and eyes at the time of his creation, in which he is coerced into a life which he will regret.

The monster's mind and body have a strangely tangled relation. The monster's mind arises from his material body, but matter does not in turn accurately express his mind. Miserable as he is, he continues to be excessively healthy, easily withstanding extreme cold and hunger, able to cross oceans and scale mountains with incredible speed and dexterity. Psychologically sensitive but somatically impervious, the monster violates the assumptions of sensibility theory.

For men of sensibility who must confront the monster's physical body, it is this lack of correspondence between mind and materiality that is most horrifying; in fact, there is some suggestion that the beholder projects bestiality onto the monster only because he cannot tolerate this disjunction. Frankenstein labours to create a 'beautiful' creature, and does not consider the 'lifeless form' ugly; it is only after the creature opens his eyes that Frankenstein is repelled. Note the 'contrast' between the 'luxuriances' of the monster's body and the 'watery' eye, the organ of speculation or consciousness:

> How can I describe my emotions at this catastrophe, or how delineate the wretch whom with such infinite pains and care I had endeavoured to form? His limbs were in proportion, and I had selected his features as beautiful. Beautiful! – Great God! His yellow skin scarcely covered the work of muscles and arteries beneath; his hair was of a lustrous black, and flowing; his teeth of a pearly whiteness; but these luxuriances only formed a more horrid contrast with his watery eyes, that seemed almost of the same colour as the dun white sockets in which they were set, his shrivelled complexion, and straight black lips. (p. 52)

This 'horrid contrast' is repeated whenever Frankenstein or Walton observes the monster's facial expression. Walton is also most horrified by the mismatch of the monster's partly decayed flesh and the vitality apparent in his face. Approaching the monster from behind, Walton notes the 'mummy'-like texture of the monster's hand. But he is calm until the monster turns and Walton sees his face: 'Never did I behold a vision so horrible as his face, of such loathsome, yet appalling hideousness' (p. 216). The men of sensibility in the novel cannot fathom a mismatch of mind and body, or cannot tolerate the disjunction between a body which calls attention to its materiality and a mind which attempts nonetheless to reveal itself though the opacity of that medium.

The plot of *Frankenstein*, then, repeatedly dramatises failure of a social sympathy. However, *Frankenstein*'s readers, from the Romantic period to the present, have quite predictably sympathised with the monster. Is reading *Frankenstein* a heuristic exercise, teaching a different kind of sympathy than that posited by Victor Frankenstein and company? I think Shelley may be redefining sympathy as an active reception of difference, rather than passive transmission necessitating similarity, particularly whenever she emphasises listening to language, as she does in every near-sympathetic encounter permitted in the novel. Unlike the automatic uniformity of contagious physiologic sympathy, sympathetic listening, or straining to hear what one cannot see, does not happen naturally, but only through attentive exertion. It does not demand identification, but rather accommodates difference.

Shelley is working against a Romantic tradition in which the auditory was used to signify a transcendence of difference. Thomas Frosch points out that the Romantic poets frequently choose 'anti-visual images', especially auditory images, in order to stimulate a reformulation of perception. Wordsworth uses mist and light to break down 'the eye's hunger for boundaries'; and in the Snowdon episode of *The Prelude*, the mist-covered mountain is translated into a roaring sea, visual images dissolving into an aural symphony. Coleridge figures imagination as the Eolian harp, receiving an unmediated message from Nature. Blake and Shelley 'are fond of images that are so complex visually that the eye is unable to follow them securely'.[12] Their shifting metaphoricity still appeals to the senses, according to Frosch, but the fluidity of images requires a 'synaesthesia', an undifferentiated perception that leaks out of neat perceptual categories.

In celebrating the auditory, Romantic poets were undoubtedly building on eighteenth-century sensibility theory, which often used musical analogies to explain the sympathetic transmission of feeling. G. J. Barker-Benfield notes that George Cheyne repeatedly compares the 'sensorium' to a '*Musician*' and the nerves to '*Keys*', and that Newton's vibrations in the ether of the nerves became popularized as 'thrills' along 'heartstrings'.[13] Shelley initially borrows this analogy in describing the development of her monster's consciousness, but later portrays a mature state in which the monster's sensorium must accommodate conflictual rather than harmonious reception.

In his immature state, the newly created monster experiences fresh, 'indistinct' sensorial acuity: 'A strange multiplicity of sensations seized me, and I saw, felt, heard, and smelt, at the same time; and it was, indeed a long time before I learned to distinguish between the operations of my various senses' (p. 97). Synaesthesia here is a developmental stage from which one must learn to 'distinguish' differing sensations. One of the first distinctions the monster makes is between the fluid beauty of a bird's song, and the 'uncouth and inarticulate sounds' in which he tries 'to express [his] sensations' (p. 99). Later, he notes the contrast between the DeLacey's music, so 'divine' as to 'enchant' him, and Felix's speech, 'sounds that were monotonous, and neither resembling the harmony of the old man's instrument or the songs of the birds' (p. 105). Language, though heard, is not analogous to music, but impure, discordant, and mundane – and ultimately, as the monster learns, more effectual.

Of course, it is not only the difference between language and music, but the more dramatic difference between language and vision that convinces the monster that the evidences of the senses frequently conflict with one another. As Peter Brooks writes, the novel rehearses 'the opposition of sight and language, of the hideous body and the persuasive tongue'.[14] The eloquent monster presents himself to blind DeLacey, who responds to the monster's verbal overtures with 'I am blind, and cannot judge of your countenance, but there is *something in your words* which persuades me that you are sincere' (p. 130, italics added). With the intrusion of the sighted characters, vision interrupts the beginnings of a sympathy based on listening to the persuasive words of the monster.

In fact, listening to language is instrumental in every near-sympathetic encounter with the monster. The monster begs Frankenstein to 'hear' him tell his tale; within the space of two pages, I count nine pleas of 'Listen to me' or 'Hear my tale' (pp. 96–7). But, lest we (or Frankenstein) miss the message, the monster touchingly mimes it. Frankenstein narrates his monster's cry for sympathy: '"Thus I relieve thee, my creator", he said, and placed his hated hands before my eyes, which I flung from me with violence: "thus I take from thee a *sight* which you abhor. Still thou canst *listen to me*, and grant me thy compassion"' (p. 96, italics added). Frankenstein is persuaded 'at least to listen', and, after the tale admits: 'His words had a strange effect upon me. I compassionated him, and sometimes felt a wish to console him; but when I looked upon him, when I saw the filthy mass that moved and talked, my heart sickened, and my feelings were altered to those of horror and hatred' (p. 143). When Frankenstein hears, he 'compassionates', but when he 'looks' he is horrified.

Shelley repeats the motif of a hand placed before the eyes in the monster's encounter with William: 'As soon as [the child] beheld my form, he placed his hands before his eyes.' The monster, intending to 'educate' the child, 'drew his hand forcibly from his face, and said, "Child, what is the meaning of this? I do not intend to hurt you; listen to me"' (p. 139). But William, predictably, cannot sort out the difference between the monster's appearance and his verbal appeal – cannot be suddenly 'educated' into compartmentalising his visual and verbal sensations – and the encounter ends fatally for him.

Walton must also shield his vision in order to feel for the monster. 'I shut my eyes', writes Walton, and wisely 'dared not again raise my looks upon his face, there was something so scaring and unearthly in his ugliness'. As the one sighted person who voluntarily averts his gaze, Walton hears the monster's 'voice [which] seemed suffocated'. Now Walton's 'duty of obeying the dying request of my friend' is 'suspended by a mixture of curiosity and compassion' (p. 217). Listening interrupts the automatic horror of the man of sensibility, the man looking for harmony in the face of the like-minded. He 'suspends' his former associations, tolerating the 'mixture' of his uneven response. In this state of active reception, Walton listens to the monster's final speech, which Walton deems a 'final and wonderful catastrophe' without which his tale would not be complete. In keeping with the rule of fragile sympathy in the novel, however, Walton 'again cast[s] his eyes on the lifeless form of my friend' and 'indignation' is 'kindled within' him (p. 218).

The reader is finally more successful in sympathising with the monster than is Walton. Might blind DeLacey or self-blinded Walton, both temporarily capable of sympathetic listening, be analogues for the reader, demonstrating the active reception involved in construing a text from words alone? If so, then Shelley has more completely articulated a reception theory than has Keats in his more famous theory of 'negative capability'. Keats's incomplete if fascinating definition of negative capability – 'when man is capable of being in uncertainties, Mysteries, doubts, without any irritable reaching after fact and reason'[15] – is perhaps an attempt to contrast the active patience of literary reception with the physiology of those automatic reflexes that his medical books called 'irritable'. If so, then Keats was also objecting to the automaticity and reactive simplicity implied by theories of physiologic sympathy. But Shelley, I think, more completely evokes the horror of the 'egotistical sublime', and the struggle involved in actively suspending sensations in the interests of acting ethically. Combating the narcissism of Romantic theories of physiologic sympathy, Shelley invites the reader to a kind of sympathy based not on identification, but on active accommodation of difference.

Notes

1. Mary Wollstonecraft Shelley, *Frankenstein, or the Modern Prometheus: The 1818 Text*, ed. James Rieger (University of Chicago Press, 1982) 13, 22. Subsequent references to this edition will be given in parentheses in the main text.
2. David Hartley, *Observations on Man, His Frame, His Duty, and His Expectations* (1749; Gainesville, FL: Scholar's Facsimiles and Reprints, 1966) 13.
3. George Cheyne, *The Natural Method of Cureing the Diseases of the Body, and the Disorders of the Mind Depending on the Body* (London, 1742) 82–3.
4. David Hume, *A Treatise of Human Nature* (1739), ed. L. A. Selby-Bigge (Oxford: Clarendon Press, 1951) 576.
5. Quoted in John Mullan, *Sentiment and Sociability* (Oxford: Clarendon Press, 1988) 26.
6. Robert Whytt, *Observations on the Nature, Causes, and Cure of Those Disorders Which Have Been Called Nervous, Hypochondriac, or Hysteric* (Edinburgh, 1765) 213–14.
7. William Hazlitt, *Essay on the Principles of Human Action* (1805), reprinted in *English Romantic Writers*, ed. David Perkins (San Diego: Harcourt, 1967) 41.
8. Ibid., 39.
9. Beth Newman, 'Narratives of Seduction and the Seductions of Narrative: The Frame Structure of *Frankenstein*', *English Literary History*, 53 (1986) 141–63.
10. Anne K. Mellor, 'Frankenstein: A Feminist Critique of Science', in *One Culture*, ed. George Levine (Madison: University of Wisconsin Press, 1987).
11. D. M. Knight, 'The Physical Sciences and the Romantic Movement', *History of Science* 9 (1970) 54–75; 59.
12. Thomas Frosch, 'The New Body of English Romanticism', *Soundings*, 54, 4 (1971) 372–87; 380.
13. G. J. Barker-Benfield, *The Culture of Sensibility* (University of Chicago Press, 1992) 21–3.
14. Peter Brooks, *Body Work* (Cambridge, MA: Harvard University Press, 1993) 201.
15. John Keats, *Letters*, ed. Robert Gittings (Oxford University Press, 1970) 43.

Index